THE GRAN TOUR

TRAVELS WITH MY ELDERS

BEN AITKEN

ICON

Published in the UK in 2020
by Icon Books Ltd, Omnibus
Business Centre,
39–41 North Road,
London, N7 9DP
email: info@iconbooks.com
www.iconbooks.com

Sold in the UK, Europe and Asia
by Faber & Faber Ltd,
Bloomsbury House,
74–77 Great Russell Street,
London, WC1B 3DA or their agents

Distributed in the UK,
Europe and Asia
by Grantham Book Services,
Trent Road, Grantham, NG31 7XQ

Distributed in Australia and
New Zealand
by Allen & Unwin Pty Ltd,
PO Box 8500,
83 Alexander Street,
Crows Nest, NSW 2065

Distributed in South Africa
by Jonathan Ball, Office B4,
The District,
41 Sir Lowry Road,
Woodstock, 7925

Distributed in India
by Penguin Books India,
7th Floor, Infinity Tower – C,
DLF Cyber City,
Gurgaon 122002, Haryana

ISBN: 978-178578-648-8

Typeset in Baskerville MT by Marie Doherty

Printed and bound in Great Britain
by Clays Ltd, Elcograf S.p.A.

For my sisters and brothers –
Daisy, Jay, Jo, Lee, Mark, Nicola and Tom.
I hope you get to the end of this one.

Contents

Part 4: Killarney, Ireland

Part 5: Lake Como, Italy

Part 6: Pitlochry, Scotland

About the author

Ben Aitken was born under Thatcher, grew to six foot then stopped, and is an Aquarius. He has four grandparents in working condition, and couldn't be happier about the fact.

Part 1

Scarborough, Yorkshire, England

1

We're hard to spot, aren't we?

'Are you one of the drivers?'

That's the first thing said to me. That's the first impression I've made. I've made it on Pat, who's never seen anyone like me on a Shearings holiday before. She says that on her first holiday she didn't play bingo the first night because she thought it was for old people, but that she played the second night and realised that either it isn't for old people or she's an old person, one of the two. She's been on loads since. All over the country. She says you meet all sorts. She remembers one meal when she was sat with a posh couple that looked stuck-up and not her type of people at all. In the event, they had a blast. 'I didn't think posh people could be funny. Goes to show: you never know who you'll get along with.'

On the M275 eastbound, Pat offers me a cup of coffee from her flask, then tells me she has a flat in Turkey that she bought with the lump sum she got when she retired from the NHS, and that I can use it if I give her enough notice and she's not there. I ask what part of Turkey the flat's in, east or west or whatever, but Pat says she doesn't know, says she doesn't bother with geography. Approaching Havant, she tells me to sit next to her so it's easier to talk.

About half a dozen get on at Havant. They're chirpy, even at this hour, a bunch of larks or nightingales, saying hello and good morning to the coach and all its fittings. I don't think I've been as cheerful my whole life, certainly not before 7.30am. An early indication that whoever said that we're happiest as children and elders, with the bit in between made relatively miserable by responsibility and vanity and anxiety and work, might have been onto something. I used to doubt the idea – that we're least happy in the middle. Youngish adulthood is so routinely associated with pleasure and indulgence and excitement that it's hard to believe that – according to the boffins, according to the stats – it's the stage of life that yields the least satisfaction. Whatever the data, and wherever the peaks and troughs, another elder's just got on and immediately sent round a tin of Quality Street.

My nan could get on here, at this pick-up point I mean. She lives just round the corner. As far as I'm aware she's not been on such a coach holiday. I can't remember the last time she went on holiday, to be frank. She mostly busies herself digging up the family tree. She's dug up two paupers this week already, while a few months ago she hit upon an illicit connection to Henry VIII. She's 81. If this trip goes alright I'll drag her along to Torquay or Windermere or something. Somewhere nice. She showed me a picture once that contained the outlines of two women in one image. A sort of visual puzzle. I only saw the younger one. 'You see,' she said, 'we're hard to spot, aren't we?'

It's hard not to get more interesting as you get older. That's what I've come to think, and that's what's led me here. Some manage it, of course, and manage it well. But as a rule of thumb, one can expect a person over 50 to be more interesting than a person under it, if only by dint of having more grist in the mill. And yet for the most part, I ignore this probably-more-interesting section of society, preferring to robotically and thoughtlessly mingle with my own generation, some of whom, indeed many of whom, are about as interesting as margarine on toast.

So over the past year or so I made an effort to shed my millennial skin. I started spending less time online and more time hanging around bowling greens and bingo halls, hoping for chance encounters. Why? Because it appeared to me that my elders had more to offer. Every time I went near a grandparent, or someone of grandparental vintage, I invariably came away from the encounter with some kind of snack and a new perspective on things.

Then a friend told me that his great aunt had been on a coach holiday to Exmouth with a company called Shearings, whereupon she had enjoyed four nights full-board in a period hotel, return coach travel, entertainment each evening, various excursions, a fair bit of wine, and the uninterrupted company of people of pensionable age, all for a hundred quid. I quickly calculated that I could *live* on such a holiday for less than the cost of renting a room in London, and I just as quickly booked one: four nights in Scarborough, excursions to York and Whitby, twelve courses of dinner, a quartet of cooked breakfasts, plus the outside chance of being mentally extended and winning the bingo. £109. That's how much my sister paid to get into a disco in Ibiza.

My ambition – as you might have deduced – wasn't especially earnest or high-minded. I didn't mean to bridge gaps or get a handle on geriatric issues. I didn't mean to examine myself (or anyone else), or take the temperature of anything. I didn't have a quest, or a resounding or convincing existential motivation – the sort beloved of publishers. I didn't seek wisdom. I didn't seek revelation. I didn't seek vengeance against any baby boomers that might have stolen my future.[1] Simply put, I did it because I thought it might be nice.

On the A3 heading north, Pat says that it's only when she looks in the mirror that she remembers she's 68. She says she's not comfortable with her age, not really. Am I comfortable with my age? With being 32? Not entirely, else I wouldn't routinely tell people I'm 30 or 31 or 29 – whatever I fancy, so long as it's not older than the truth. There's a film, *The Age of Adaline*, which is memorable only for its central conceit: the protagonist doesn't age beyond 29, because she can't stand the idea of being 30. I can relate. I couldn't stand turning 30. I denied it. Deferred it. Kicked it down the road. But why? I don't want to live forever. It's not that. I get bored on Sunday afternoons. What would I do with forever? Perhaps it's a latent fear of non-existence. I might do a good job of pretending otherwise (a bit grumpy, a bit complacent), but the fact is I cherish life, am uncomplicatedly

---

[1] David Willetts wrote a book called *The Pinch: How the Baby Boomers Stole Their Children's Future*, which argues that the boomers (born 1945–65) have pulled up the property ladder and any other ladder they could get their hands on. For the record, I took David's book with a titular pinch of salt. I know plenty of boomers who've barely a rung to stand on, to say nothing of a ladder to pull up.

WE'RE HARD TO SPOT, AREN'T WE?

fond of it, and so I shy away from birthdays, from moving on, from running out. I've no time for death, and so I distance myself from it, however stupidly, however ineffectively. Time to grow up, Ben.[2]

10.00. London Gateway services at the foot of the M1. This is the interchange, where passengers switch to coaches heading to their respective destinations. Shearings has its own lounge. It's like heaven's waiting room – or your average GP surgery. I buy a coffee and take a seat on the edge of things, the better to weigh up the scene. I don't want to put too fine a point on it, but it's fair to say that this lot are probably better at bridge than me. A couple from Reading are off to Bournemouth. Both are retired but busier than ever, don't know how they ever found time to work. She's writing a book about a bear who's made in China and gets up to all sorts. 'For kids, is it?' 'Rather adult, actually,' she confides. Her husband, for his part, is a 'street' photographer. He gives me his card, wishes me a pleasant trip, and then the two of them head off. I stay where I am, wondering what the next pair I chat to will be working on – perhaps a concept album and a pornographic comic. Everyone's got something up their sleeve, I suppose, and I shouldn't be surprised if sleeves get bigger with time.

11.36. Somewhere on the M1. We're eleven in total, but will be collecting another load near Coventry. The driver says: 'We're a small group today, ladies and gents. Average

---

[2] I'm 33.

height, five foot four.' It's not a complicated joke but I didn't see it coming so it does a job on me. I'm in seat 13A. More or less at the back, more or less alone. With nobody to talk to, I give Scarborough some thought. I know Alan Ayckbourn's from Scarborough. I saw a programme about the playwright a few years ago. He was sat in his back garden, which over-looks the town and the beach. I remember thinking: *I wouldn't kick Scarborough out of bed.* It used to be a so-called spa town, put up in the 1800s so well-heeled folk with broken ankles could dip said ankles in medicinal waters and be, well, well healed. It grew to become one of the most popular holi-day spots in the world, before easy aviation got Britons in the mood for Spain and Florida. They used to fish for tuna off Scarborough, and the town's in Yorkshire, God's Own County. That's about all I've got.[3]

13.45. Corley. The East Midlands interchange. A dozen climb on. That's better, they say, 'ere we go then. They look younger, this lot. I suppose they didn't have to get out of bed until mid-morning. Unlike the rest of us, who've bags under our eyes as well as under the coach. Our driver suddenly identifies himself, as if he's just remembered what his job is. 'My name's Roger. This is the service to Blackpool.' A few whispers and doubts. 'Only kidding. We're off to sunny Scarborough. Scarbados they call it – the mad ones anyway.'

---

[3] Not sure why Yorkshire acquired this nickname. Maybe it has to do with the countryside – the dales and the moors. Else it could have to do with Michael Palin, Judi Dench, Alan Bennett, J.B. Priestley, Barbara Hepworth, Sean Bean and the Chuckle Brothers – all of whom are of the county, and a heaven-sent consortium if ever there was one.

That's enough of Scarborough, reasons Roger, let's move on to the essentials. 'You'll get four free alcoholic drinks a night. There'll be no discriminating. Even the oldest will get served. Unclaimed drinks don't carry over to the next night, unfortunately. Given the choice, I'd have sixteen on the Thursday.' Good on you, Roger.

15.00. Yorkshire. England's biggest county, its broad shoulders, its steely, sooty, verdant pectorals. On average, Yorkshire folk are unusually proud of their county. Exhibit A: August 1 every year is Yorkshire Day, whereupon children dress up as Yorkshire puddings and bat stubbornly until September. Exhibit B: Yorkshire County Cricket Club recruited only from Yorkshire until the mid-90s, decades later than any other county. YCCC wanted God's own leg-spinners, and nowt else. If Yorkshire is God's own county, then God knows what Hampshire is. Hampshire folk, to my mind, aren't in the slightest bit proud of their county. They might be proud of their village, or their town, or the size of their mortgage – but not their county. Indeed, most residents of Hampshire, as far as I can tell, are unaware they are residents of Hampshire. They probably all think they live in Surrey.

16.20. The land around the A64 seems ancient, medieval, out of time somehow. The land is *tumbular*, if that were a word, a washing pile of downs and wolds. And when the light goes and a mist comes, it's like we've entered a different genre of book, of story, of land – from old pastoral to neo-Gothic. Out on a limb, is how you feel, and so you might. York's the nearest large settlement to Scarborough and that's 40 miles away.

I like Scarborough's preamble, its build-up. Two colossal hotels headline the scene, while two bridges make light of a valley, with the illuminations of a promenade below. Roger points out what shops we might pop to, where we might break for tea, where we might rent mobility scooters. A longish climb brings us up to the hotel – the Norbreck, a bit of which fell into the North Sea a few years ago, suddenly providing one guest with an unexpected en-suite. We're up on a headland here, a promontory. The next settlement east is a town in the German state of Schleswig-Holstein, while due north, via the Norwegian and Greenland Seas, is the Arctic. And to think this was the spot chosen for Britain's first seaside resort.

I'm in room 312. I've been given my drinks vouchers for the week and told not to photocopy them. A porter, operating on autopilot, insisted on carrying my backpack up the stairs. When I told him not to bother, he said: 'Better safe than sorry, sir.' If he's assuming the incapability of a millennial, I can only wonder what he assumes someone in their 80s can't manage – 'Need some help with that biscuit, madam?' The room is singular: if you had a guest, they'd have to sit on your lap and share your teacup. But it's warm and cosy and done in yellow and green and red, soft shades of each. My curtains bring a fruit salad to mind.

I go down for dinner. I've been allocated table 13, as I was allocated row 13. The table's for four but for now I'm alone. I'm dressed in a new outfit and I'm recently groomed (haircut, shave, etc.) with the result that I look smarter than I have done since my christening. I've made the effort because my nan insisted upon it. She said it wouldn't do to turn up to dinner looking relaxed. She said that her generation 'wouldn't be seen dead dressed casually in a hotel', which is an interesting scenario to consider.

There must be about twenty tables of two, and half a dozen tables of four, tucking into their meals watchfully, each diner as much aware of the strangers around them as what's on their plate. Everyone in the hotel's on the same holiday as me: four nights, excursions to York and Whitby, full-board etc. I read the menu self-consciously. I feel like a menu myself, being read and judged. Anomalies attract attention. That's just how it is. Oddness is intriguing. The odd or anomalous thing needn't have any special qualities or enviable attributes, they need only be odd or anomalous – a potato among plums, for example. I order the fishcakes.

A man sits down opposite me. He doesn't look anomalous.

'I don't know about yours but our driver was full of it. I wanted to chuck him off the coach,' he says.

'That wouldn't have got you far.'

'I only booked yesterday. I fancied exploring. I reckon I've seen enough of Birmingham.'

We talk easily over bread rolls. Alan was married at eighteen, and a father of two at 21. For most of his life he worked in a foundry, pouring liquid metal into a mould, where it adjusted to its cast, filled its boots, and then altered not. Alan tells me he had a couple of heart attacks in 2006 and then retired ten years later. I suggest he might not have waited so long, but he reckons you've to muddle through.

'I used to tell the young lads at work who were moaning about the heat or the tedium – "Don't worry, boys. It's only for a lifetime."'

'I suppose you might have said the same about marriage.'

'I might have indeed. I divorced at 38 – which was twenty years too late, I can tell you.' He orders the chicken, then adds: 'The kids take everything you've got. You've nothing left for each other.'

Alan later remarried, but his second wife has claustrophobia and gets nervous around people. I ask if it's his first time.

'Oh no, I've had chicken before.'

'I meant—'

'I've been to Eastbourne with Shearings. They've got a nice big place down there. I was sat with a young woman for dinner.'

'Oh yeah?'

'Well, she was 60-odd. Flirting, she was. I said, "Stop it, I'm married." She said, "Relax, so am I." We had a nice day out in Hastings.'

Our puddings turn up. Alan looks at his vanilla ice-cream.

'Getting down to Eastbourne opened my eyes a bit. On the way home, I wondered where else I might have liked, if only I'd been. I got settled where I was and didn't know anything else. Everything just sort of got stuck after a while. I thought West Bromwich was the end of the world.'

We sit longer than the rest, talking about the grandkids he doesn't see enough of, and the amount of gel in the waiter's hair. 'He's young,' explains Alan. 'Lad's got bugger all else to do.'

It's three quid to play bingo. The lounge bar is packed – there are more in here than were at dinner. I'm pretty good at bingo. I've only played once, on a ferry from Zeebrugge to Hull, but did alright for myself. There's about a hundred playing tonight, I'd say, but it makes no odds to me – I only go and win again. My triumph doesn't go down well. They don't mean to be rude, I'm sure, but when I go up to collect the cash price, someone tries to trip me up with their cane.

The bingo caller changes his jacket and does a few songs. He's got good range: Roy Orbison, Robbie Williams, The Human League. When he does the latter's 'Electric Dreams', one bloke from Sheffield looks ready to get up on the tables, though he might need a stairlift to do so. '100 per cent Sheffield that is!'

It's not all jolly, mind you. There are a few couples, scattered around the room, who are looking a bit down, a bit left out. After all, not every marriage is a never-ending Fred Astaire routine. When Alan calls it a night, I go and sit with one such couple. They're from Corby, Northamptonshire. Dennis and Clementine, or Clem. The former does most of the talking. He wears the trousers *and* the skirts, I'd say. Nice enough bloke, don't get me wrong, but I wouldn't mind knowing if Clem's got owt to say. When I tell them it's my first time, they've lots of tips for me. I'm to make sure I use all my vouchers; to invest in a travel pillow if I'm going abroad; and to make bacon butties at breakfast and then have them for lunch. And – especially important – I'm not to bother paying extra for a sea view. They did that once and felt like they couldn't leave the room.

Dennis checks his watch. Then he looks at my spare vouchers. He puts two and two together and sends me up to the bar to make use of them. The reason I've got spares is because I've been trying not to drink lately. Edward Albee said everyone's got a certain amount of drink in them, and that while some spread it out over 60 years, others get through it in ten. I fancy I fall into the latter category. When I get back from the bar, Dennis says he's got something to tell me. Oh yeah? He says that he knows my game, that he saw me chatting to your woman at the bar. I hand over one of the two pints (I'm on holiday after all) and tell him, quite sincerely, that I wouldn't dream of it.

2

There's an art to eating happily alone

I slept well. It's not hard when you've bingo winnings under your pillow. And I like single beds. I find the lack of options restful. Boundaries can be good for us – when the world's our oyster, it can give us a dodgy tummy.

I go down for breakfast. We're in the same room as dinner, with the wide, west-facing bay window now full of things it hadn't been – namely, a terrace of Victorian houses and part of the North Sea. I've a boundary down here as well: I'm expected to sit at the same table for the duration of my holiday (says a waitress when I try to sit by the window), so I'd better get used to Alan and 13.

As I investigate the buffet, someone says: 'You did well last night.' Then someone says words to the same effect as I'm waiting on my toast. And then someone says well done as I'm sitting down. At first I'm apologetic – 'It won't happen again. I promise.' Then I change my tune: 'Yeah, I'm good at bingo and I'll be good at it tonight as well.'

I butter my toast nervously. The feeling of oddness is back from last night. I try to look appreciatively over the talking heads and out the window, but I'm kidding myself, I'm posturing. I'm pretending to be at ease, to be nonchalant. There's an art to eating happily alone. I don't have it. Alan arrives and says: 'Aaron Ramsey has gone to Juventus for silly money.' I'm pleased to be wrenched from my own neurotic half-thoughts. I'm pleased to see Alan.

We're off to York this morning.[4] Roger's commentary begins before I've got my seatbelt on. He tells us that Anne Brontë came to Scarborough and liked it so much she never left, which only works as a joke if you know she's buried in the church next to the hotel. He tells us that McCain's (of frozen chips fame) are a big local employer, and that the Eastfield estate on the edge of town is about as troublesome as they come. 'If you want drugs,' says Roger, 'let me know as I can get you a discount.'

When we reach our destination, Roger puts us down in a carpark and tells us to be back in a couple of hours. People head off in separate directions – like a search party splitting to cover the most ground. I pop into a riverside café and ask the barista what's lovable about York, alluding to the fact that the city has repeatedly been elected Britain's best place. 'I like it when the river floods,' he says. I ask him what he thinks other, less peculiar people might love about York, suggesting the ancient walls, the narrow cobbled lanes, the elderly buildings, the city's historic relationship with chocolate, or even the Richard III Experience, which has proved incredibly popular with visitors despite involving being taken to a field and shot at with a bow and arrow. The barista says it's

---

[4] Known as Eboracum under the Romans, and then Jorvik under the Vikings. Then later as Yerke, Yourke and Yarke. Before a true visionary suggested York and they settled on that.

probably the city's beauty. I ask him to elaborate. 'I would, but it's difficult to put your finger on. And to be honest I only notice it when I'm not here.' There's philosophy in that last admission. I bet the lad's not alone in only seeing what's under his nose once it's behind his back, if you'll forgive the impractical construction.

I do a lap of the city's old wall. I join it at its north-ernmost point, round the back of the Minster. Giving the church a once over, I think of the art critic John Ruskin, who reckoned the camera was ruining our ability to notice and appreciate things. And this was back in the 1880s. Instead of photographing things, Ruskin suggested we draw them. I'm not in a position to draw the Minster but I do tarry to look harder, look closer. It's certainly a sizeable item – the second-largest Gothic church in the world, after the cathedral at Cologne – and is much wider than it is tall, with the effect that if you bunch up your eyes you could easily mistake it for a battleship (albeit a battleship with transepts and lancet windows). Of more interest to me than the Minster, however, is the adjoining Deanery, and in particular its back garden. Within the garden, a pair of yellow socks has been left on the grass below the washing line. Perhaps the Dean was in a rush when bringing the washing in, or perhaps he was in a *real* rush when putting it out. In any case, were I to draw the scene before me, I'd be tempted to place more emphasis on the socks, and the small drama they hint at, than the Minster. We each have our own sense of importance, I suppose.

I continue clockwise to Walmgate Bar. During the English Civil War, this bar (or gate) was a key fortification that saw a fair bit of uncivil action. Now it's a wonderful café with an enjoyable roof terrace. During the war, an attempt was made to undermine Walmgate Bar and blow its bricks off, but the plot was discovered and nipped in the bud. Had it not been, whosoever happened to be up on the roof terrace drinking coffee would have been a very flat white indeed. The barista is Australian. When I tell him about Walmgate Bar nearly being blown to smithereens, he says: 'You guys are so lucky to have history.'

I drink my coffee on the roof and survey the scene. Of all its elements – and there are many – it is the non-smoking industrial chimney that holds my attention. Not because it's the most dynamic or curious or aesthetically pleasing element of the landscape, but rather because I recently saw a documentary about a steeplejack called Fred Dibnah, who back in the 70s and 80s, when health and safety regulations were a thing for wimps, would climb such chimneys by a series of conjoined ladders and then knock them down brick by brick, often in the middle of winter, and invariably with a fag in his mouth. Fred said some terrific things in that programme, some moving things, and all in a thick Boltonian accent. On the matter of death, Fred reckoned 'the ideal way out would be, I think, instead of dying in bed of lung cancer or something 'orrible like that, just to drop off a chimney one sunny day.' Turned out to be a pipe dream. Fred died of bladder cancer in 2004.

York is better for its wall. It encourages you to think about its historical function, about who it was meant to repel (Vikings, Normans, Parliamentarians), and what it was meant

THERE'S AN ART TO EATING HAPPILY ALONE

to contain (scandal, cholera, Royalists). To my mind, a walk on the wall has the quality of a ride. It is always a tiny bit exciting to rise above the rooftops, to look down on what is normally above. The change of perspective helps one see more, or see the same things in a different way. So much so that, with a bit of effort, I can just make out, in the garden of the Royal Oak (it's either Royal Oak or Loyal Oat), a crouching figure tying his laces with a fag in his mouth which is unmistakably Alan.[5]

Crossing the River Ouse on my way back to the coach, I remember that book by Graham Swift, *Waterland*, which goes on about this river. I remember a flow of startling pages that made me see the brilliance and magic and circularity of rivers, of history, of time. The book really got the thumbs up from me, which wasn't something that happened often back then. Not because I was a tough critic, but rather because I hadn't really read any books. I was in my second year at university, and was to all intents and purposes, and by all accounts, a dipstick. I'd read only six books right the way through (two of those being diaries of Bridget Jones), and had about as much interest in rivers and history as a poached egg. The best books can do that though, can take you by surprise, can ambush and capture you, no matter what they're on about.

On the way back to Scarborough, Roger tells us about a couple of local news stories. He says an aluminium

---

[5] It wasn't Alan.

rhinoceros was stolen from outside a college a few years ago, and that some penguins at a nearby zoo have been prescribed antidepressants.[6]

Alan thinks the man who smokes cigars might be autistic. I tell Alan that my girlfriend is a teaching assistant at a school for children with autism. I tell him she likes it much more than the school for children without autism that she used to work at, where she routinely opted to wear shin pads, so often did she get booted in the legs for having the cheek to ask what the capital of Kenya was. Alan asks whether my girlfriend takes off the pads when she gets home, implying that I'm in the habit of booting her in the shins as well. I order whitebait to start, then hake, then lemon sponge. Alan says I'm naive to double-fish.

Talk of autism leads to talk of Alzheimer's. Alan's dad had dementia, and Alan was the only one of his five siblings that was prepared to care for him. 'He was strict when we were growing up. He wouldn't let us do our homework. He'd give us chores instead. He wouldn't let Mum listen to the radio. And she wasn't allowed to touch the telly.'

---

[6] I chased up both stories. Regarding the rhino, PC Michelle Neighbour, of North Yorkshire Police, said, rather helpfully, that 'the rhino is not something you could just walk off with by yourself,' before appealing 'to any scrap dealers or anyone who regularly uses scrap yards to get in touch if they remember seeing the rhino being weighed in.' Regarding the penguins, it turns out the reason they were prescribed antidepressants was because they'd grown so thoroughly cheesed off with the easterly wind off the North Sea.

'My dad was the opposite,' I say. 'We'd go to him on the weekend and it was carte blanche or whatever the term is as far as he was concerned. We lived off Pot Noodles and Kit Kats. I don't think we let *him* touch the telly. That or he shared our taste for *Gladiators* and *Baywatch*.'

'Not impossible,' says Alan.

'No, he's a good bloke my dad. Once, I needed a cricket bat but he couldn't afford a smart proper one, so he made one. Me and my brother would play in the concrete garden, three-by-three metres, with a drainpipe for the stumps. I was a decent bowler in my teens and I'm sure it was because I grew up aiming for a drainpipe.'

'Mine didn't make cricket bats,' says Alan. 'Mine was a policeman. He used to come home and play the harmonica and tell us about the scoundrels he'd walloped. Then one day, he just stopped playing. I don't remember him touching a harmonica for 40 years. Then when he got dementia, I bought him one and took it to him. He just stared at it for some time then picked it up and started playing it like it was yesterday.'

I let this sit for a bit. And then a bit more. And then:

'My dad's so cheerful it does my head in,' I say. 'It makes me look awful. There I am, trying to drag myself out of bed, moaning and groaning like I've got swine flu, and in he wanders with a cup of tea for me, whistling a tune, saying he can't wait to finish the wheelbarrow he's been working on, then drawing my curtains like Mary Poppins and looking out at the grim terraces of inner Portsmouth as if they were an orchard of cherry blossom trees. I've told him more than once: "Dad, I'm going to stop you coming in here if you're going to carry on like that. You're making me look like a prick."'

'Fathers, eh?' says Alan.

I go through to the lounge for the bingo. I sit with a couple who live in Rhyl, North Wales.

'You did well last night,' he says. 'The wife's normally very good at bingo but she hasn't won for three years.'

I smile at this idea of normality – that something can still be normal even if it hasn't happened for three years. Then I ask the man why he thinks his wife hasn't won recently. He says he reckons she's got complacent. I ask the wife if she agrees with her husband's point of view, but he says: 'You won't get a word out of her. Not until the bingo's over.'

I buy two bingo coupons from reception. One for me and one for the lady from Rhyl – to save her legs. She tries to give me the three quid but I tell her not to bother. 'Well which one is mine?' she says. I hold out the two coupons. She closes her eyes and takes the one on the left, then puts it back and takes the other.

The lady from Rhyl is off to a flier. She's very focused. Almost possessed. Her feet are tapping away under the table. Her husband says he doesn't like playing but he certainly likes peering over at her card, making sure she doesn't miss a trick. Ten balls have been called and I haven't one of them. It's starting to wind me up to be honest. Then a run of numbers – same both ways, two fat fellas, a pair of crutches – and I'm back in the hunt. Another good run and I only need seventeen. My mind races ahead to the prize ceremony. I'd have to refuse. They'd throw me into the North Sea if I won again.

I don't mind that the lady from Rhyl won the bingo. Not really. I don't even mind that she didn't think, after collecting her 60-odd quid in cash (lots of cheering for her, by the way, which is ageism in action if ever I saw it), to offer me my three quid back, or thank me for presenting her with the winning ticket, or slip me one of her drinks vouchers by way of compensation. Nah, not really. I suppose after a drought of three years, a bingo win is going to cloud your judgement a bit, play a bit of havoc with your manners. She'll probably realise when she's in bed. She'll omit a sigh and put her hand to her forehead, and her husband will turn to her and say, 'What is it, love?' And she'll say, 'That young man. What was his name? Bill, was it? I didn't even *thank* him. I've not won for three years and he goes and hands me the winning ticket and I don't so much as offer him a drinks voucher.' And he says: 'I wouldn't worry, love. I bet he's not given it a second's thought.'

I move to one of the comfy chairs closer to reception. I sit with a bloke called Paul and his two support workers – Doughnut 1 and Doughnut 2, he calls them. One of the doughnuts explains that Paul's got Down's syndrome and that she and her friend take him on holiday twice a year. Paul doesn't think much of her explanation. 'I take you two on holiday, more like,' he says.

Doughnut 1 shows me a picture of her dog and says that she got him after she had a stent put in her leg which enabled her to walk again. 'I was walking everywhere!' she says. 'That dog's done more miles than a Vauxhall Astra. I know it's a cliché but you don't know you've got any legs until you haven't.'

I tell her that my dad had a stent put in his leg to unblock one of the arteries so the blood could get round. The doctor told him that if he doesn't pack up smoking, the other leg's going to block up and they won't give him an operation, because it will be his own sodding fault.

'And has he stopped?' she says.

'Nope,' I say.

'Twat,' she says. 'In a nice way, like.'

I explain that I don't hassle him too much because he gets defensive and worried and ends up smoking more, which isn't really what I'm after. Besides, he's an alcoholic who hasn't had a drink for ten years, which takes some doing, and if he reckons he can't stop, or doesn't want to, then I'm inclined to listen to him, or at least respect his decision.

'How did he give up the drinking?' she says.

'A banjo,' I say.

'You what?'

'One day after umpteen attempts to stop and not managing it, he comes home with a four-hundred pound banjo.'

'That's bloody heavy,' says Paul.

'He'd never played a musical instrument in his life. I guess the thinking – if there was any thinking – was that you can't take something away and just leave a hole. You've got to fill it with something.'

Anyway, now he plays the piano and guitar and drums as well, and is in two bands, and hasn't had a drink since.'

'Fair play,' she says.

'Fair play,' says Paul.

I call it a night. Paul gives me a fist bump. I climb the stairs to the third floor and think: I don't know if I've ever told my dad just how proud I am of him for turning his back on a 40-year addiction, for buying that banjo, for becoming a new man at the age of 57. I'm sure I'll get round to it one day.

3

Why aren't you in bed?

I write a list on my napkin of things I want to do on my birthday. I write down 'lap of town' and 'dinner with Alan'. Then I leave the hotel and head down Castle Road. Some of the houses on this road – tall Victorian or Georgian jobs – would fetch millions elsewhere. Sash windows and columned porches; pediments and porticos: they remind me, at a stretch, of the streets around Victoria in London, or around the seafront in Brighton. Once upon a time, you would've needed a fair bit of money to own a house like this in Scarborough. You would've needed to be flogging a fair amount of donkey rides. Now most of them look vacant, knackered and unwanted. One's for sale for 60 grand.

At the end of Quay Street, I ask a lone fisherman what's being caught around here these days.

'Nothing anymore. Not since the fish went missing.'

'Huh?'

'What comes in nowadays comes from over Norway way.'

'What you doing now then?'

'I'm bringing my pots in.'

'Of course you are.' Of course he is. 'Why are you doing that?'

'To see if there's owt in 'em.'

I leave the man to it and continue along South Bay, still pretty much clueless as to the state of the local fishing scene.

The fish went missing, now they're over Norway way, and yet he's bringing his pots in to see if there's owt in 'em. This is why people Google things.[7]

I enter an entertainment venue called The Spa and ask the girl on the box-office what she reckons of Scarborough. She says she used to live in Manchester and Leeds but is happier here. She says that, rightly or wrongly, here's where she's from. She says that some people can't put their finger on where they're from but she can. She says that the people she loves and the people that love her are concentrated in this town, by this sea, among these streets and below those moors, and that's just the way it is. I ask what she'd do if she had one day in Scarborough, hoping for some inspiration. 'I'd walk my dog,' she says.

Having no dog to walk, I climb through the Italian Gardens and up to Esplanade Crescent. The latter is some street. The stone tenements are five stories high. They put

---

[7] Back in the day, tuna was the prize catch locally. Or tunny, as they called it. In 1930 Lorenzo Mitchell-Henry landed a tunny weighing 250 kilograms. The fish was a tourist attraction. It was exhibited and people paid to take a peep. The tunnies gradually realised that they were better off snacking elsewhere, and not a single one was caught in British or Irish waters for 50 years. Then Alan Glanville, 76 and Irish and retired, bought a rod on a whim and slung his hook, hoping for a nibble at worst or a perch at best. With his first cast, he hauled in a whopping bluefin tuna, which he swapped for about £30,000. It's considered one of the great angling stories of all time. After making his catch, Alan had this to say: 'I think it's all downhill from here.' In my book, Alan is a positive role model for elders around the world. Any septuagenarians not catching fish bigger than cupboards might want to take a look at themselves.

me in mind of Edinburgh and the old (sorry, older) residential streets south of the centre, around the Dalkeith Road, where the likes of Hume and Hobbs and Walter Scott did their thinking and scribbling, their pipe-smoking and pipe-dreaming, and were aided in their efforts by fifth floor servants, whose liberty to think and scribble was reliably compromised by their obligation to serve, but so it goes. I sit on a bench facing the sea, my back to the emphatic Victorian terrace, and think: *I could live here, with or without love.* Then I get a text from my mum. Parents remember first. 'Happy birthday darling xx hope your balls drop.' Presumably an awkward bingo reference.

I return to the town centre and then head north-west on Dean Road. As I do, my girlfriend calls to tell me she's going to stop being a teaching assistant and start being an artist. I tell her to think seriously about what that would do to our finances. 'We'll be the poorest couple in England, Meg. Think about it. Somebody has to put the sourdough on the table.' But she's resolved. She's going to be a painter first, and something else second, rather than the other way around. At the end of the call, I don't tell her I love her, because she knows I do. By the same logic, she doesn't mention my birthday, because she knows I know it's my birthday. That or she's forgotten.

'Oh, by the way,' I say.
'What?'
'It's half-term next week, right?'
'Yeah.'

WHY AREN'T YOU IN BED?

'Do you want to go on holiday to St Ives?'

'Would it just be the two of us?'

'No, it would be a Shearings holiday.'

'In which case, okay then.'

I find North Bay. It's twilight now. There's a golf course up on the cliff. A pair of gentlemen, presumably unmarried and insane, are persisting with illuminous balls. The promenade stretches south for a mile, then turns left toward the castle and my hotel, which for now is a vague smudge in the distance. The tide is out, and on the flat, hard sand, owners exercise what's theirs – balls are flung and kicked for children and pets. There are a range of colourful beach huts – orange and green and yellow, somehow still glowing in the dusk. Inside one such hut, a couple sit entwined under rugs, a pair of low dogs peeping out from between their feet. I think of Larkin's couple at Arundel. *What survives of us is love.*

An upward path takes me to the North Cloisters, a lofty run of stone enclosures, a place to come and sit and contemplate the view, half-sheltered from the weather. Writing is on the wall. Support is pledged in dark pen – to the nation, the region, the town, this or that cause. Someone has written: 'Every piece of meat begins with an animal begging for its life.' Beneath this, someone else (at least, I presume it was someone else) has written: 'Bacon – yum!' The stone surface is a veritable message board, a forum of competing leanings, a chatroom of public pledges – evidence of the various directions in which emotion can travel, the various ways passion can take. To my mind, much of what's written isn't meant, not really, not fully. Were you to bring any pair of on-paper adversaries up here and sit them down in front of the sea, perhaps under a rug with a flask of tea, like that pair in the hut, I'd be surprised if they so much as raised their voices. Sure, they might not get on like French and Saunders, but they wouldn't be unkind to each other. I don't think so. From a distance it's hard to see what connects us, but up close it's easy.

Call me easily pleased, but to my mind there's nothing like walking in a new town, with no plan other than to run an eye over the place. For others, there are plenty of things like walking in a new town, plenty of humdrum unremarkable things, like ironing shirts or cutting the grass, because for them there's nothing in it, no promise, no prospect, no dividend, but for me it can afford a pleasure like – if not like nothing else, then like few other things. Going about a new town, I am both restful and engaged; at once at ease and on edge – on the edge of novelty, drama, distress, beauty, history. I lose my sense of self (which is mostly a boring and bothersome sense, unduly predominant, reliably dull) and gain, in its stead, a sense of place, of place and people, of other and else, of here and hereafter, of besides and instead. I am lightened by the weight of it all, for the more novelty, the less me. And if the town's by the sea, all the better, for then a salty wind will whip me further, and offer a timeless prospect to mull over and chew on. *Towns.* Bloody wonderful things really.

Alan used to get hit by a slipper. I shouldn't have asked. He was trying to eat a chicken wing to start and I just came out and asked what he remembers about being a boy. 'I used to get hit by a slipper. That's what I remember. Other than that, not a great deal. I was the youngest. Not expected to amount to much. Not relied upon. It can weigh you down not being bothered with. You start to drag your heels. And once you've dragged your heels for 30 years, believe me, you know about it.'

He excuses himself. I'd say he's gone to wash his hands, given the chicken wings, but I can't be sure. I order the cod and the espresso Martini cheesecake. Alan returns with two pints of lager.

'It's Valentine's Day tomorrow,' he says.

'Yeah, and you'll be having dinner with me, Alan.'

'Would you remind me? In the morning. In case I forget.'

'Have you got her something?'

'There was a lovely cake in York I saw. In a bakery. It was heart shaped.'

'I'm sure she'll like that.'

'No I didn't buy it. I took a photo of it. I'll send it tomorrow.'

'I expect she'll be delighted with that.'

'Why, have you got your Megan something?'

'I haven't actually.'

'So stop telling me how to suck eggs.'

Not having a clue what Alan means by this, I ask him how he met his second wife. 'I met her in the pub. We were both working there. This was after the iron foundry closed – early 90s. She was a chef, you see, at the pub, a cook. It just sort of happened.'

'How do you mean?'

'As I say, it just sort of happened.'

I don't reckon it did just sort of happen, I reckon there was more to it than that, but I also reckon I'm not going to get any more out of Alan on the subject. I reckon he'd rather talk about anything under the sun – cookbooks, soap operas, the menstrual cycle – than how he fell in love. Then, to my surprise, he says:

'I used to go in with the orders. At first I'd just say what it was, haddock and chips, pie and mash, and clear off. Then I started taking longer to tell her. That's how it happened.'

I go out to see what Scarborough gets up to of an evening. My first port of call is The Sun Inn on St Thomas Street. I drink a pint at the bar, where I get talking to two lads. You'd call them geezers where I'm from – in their twenties, athletically dressed, forthcoming. I tell them I'm on holiday. They're fine with this – tolerant. I tell them I'm on holiday with people much older than me – they're fine with this also, encouraging even. I tell them I think Scarborough's nice – they're not fine with this. 'Nice and shit, you mean,' they say in unison.

Because it's my birthday, and I'm feeling buoyant and risqué, I buy a packet of cigarettes from the One Stop on Newborough. I light up outside the shop. There's a group of boys hanging around the entrance, in the way that boys of a certain age and inclination will. They're not lads or geezers, or oiks or yobs, just boys on bikes that think it's their civic duty to offer a remark to anyone entering or leaving the shop.

As a way of killing time, I can see its appeal. I hate to say it, but the boy nominated to remark on my exit from the shop won't be getting the Nobel Prize for Originality. 'Gis a fag,' he says. Because I'm feeling a bit like Ebenezer Scrooge on Christmas morning, when he orders the biggest turkey and gives Bob Cratchit a pay rise, I hold out the pack and tell him to help himself. The boy takes four or five – one for each of his girlfriends, he says – then asks if I'm a policeman. I assure the boy – let's call him Tim – that I am no such man. He doesn't believe me. I tell him I write books, which he seems to believe even less than I'm not a policeman.

'Write books?' he says, 'What's man saying?'

But then his friend says, 'Nah mate, people do do that.'

Tiny Tim wants my name, says he's gonna Google me, and if there ain't no books to my name he's gonna … gonna not finish his sentence, presumably. I tell him my name. He Googles me.

'Man writes books,' he says, and I think I'm off the hook, but then he adds, 'Don't mean you can't be a policeman, though.'

The good sense one demonstrates and articulates when sober – 'just a couple', 'I know my limit' – is no longer operational when not. There's a crucial line, a trip wire, two and a half pints thick. You think the line's a long way off and then, bang, you're straddling the damn thing. A drunk person has little respect for – and often little recollection of – their sober self. Alcohol is a retardant, it slows you down, distorts your operating system, trips the circuitry that you depend on to live a civilised and law-abiding life. All this is to say: I know where I am, I know I've crossed the line, I know I'm in The Lord Rosebery ordering my fifth pint of the evening.

My night peaked outside One Stop. I can see that now. I liked those boys – rascals though they were. I should have pinched their cheeks and polished their faces with spittle and a hanky, then turned on my heel and gone back to the hotel, where I might have had a cheeky nightcap with Alan, or Paul and his doughnuts, or some other kindly person, and with that nightcap some cheerful chit-chat until the barman called last orders at 11, which he does because he knows that 11 is enough, that 11 is good for us, that the best way to liberate someone is to subject them to limits. That's what I should have done. Instead I headed up Westborough to The Lord Rosebery, whose clients must rank as some of the most spirited in Yorkshire, especially one lady, a committed apostle of Malbec, who, when I mention it's my birthday, buys me an Archers and lemonade, calls me a policeman, then tells me to go to Bacchus. I do what I'm told, but when I get to Bacchus it's closed, so I follow a man called Archibald (who is just as thirsty for the extending caress of alcohol and the company of anyone) to a place called Marley's off the Albion Road, where I buy him a large Chardonnay and he reads my palm, and then to a nightclub called L'amour, which is inexcusably awful, and then to a casino on St Thomas Street, where it takes me two hours and several more pints to lose five quid. When I get back to the hotel, I can't get in. The door's locked. The night porter's asleep in the lounge. I knock on the window. We talk through the glass.

'What do you want?'
'To come in.'
'Do you have a room here?'
'No, I just thought I'd pop over to say hi.'
'What number?'
'312.'
'Why aren't you in bed?'
'It's my birthday.'
'For f*ck's sake.'

4

I'm the right side of 80, she says – 81

I wake up at 12.15pm. I was meant to be in reception by 9.15am for the excursion to Whitby, which is said to be one of the finest small harbour towns in the solar system, and also where Dracula came from. He used to fish herring. With his teeth. His false teeth. He'd stick them on the end of his line. Instead of bait. That's what I dreamt.

Of course I feel bad. Doubly. Bad as in 'Oh my goodness, it hurts when I blink'. And bad as in 'For heaven's sake, what am I like?' The first type of badness is the easiest to address. The second type doesn't respond to paracetamol, and in the long run is arguably more damaging. The first is a feeling, an ouch. The second is a solidifying truth – that I'm a liability, a loose cannon, a sad clown.

I walk down Castle Road then take a left on Queen Street, taking deep meaningful breaths to reboot my hippocampus. I buy painkillers on St Nicholas Street then return to Westborough – the main pedestrianised drag – in order to visit the local Waterstones, where I hope to find something soothing and palliative to take away. The first thing that grabs my attention is a book called *How it Works: The Grandparent*. After flicking through the book's 50-odd pages, I can say with some confidence that it wasn't written by a grandparent. The various characters featured in the book don't understand basic medical science, only eat pills and tablets, can't operate a television set, have nothing better to do than redecorate the house each year, have spent their children's inheritance redecorating the house each year, moan a lot, drink a lot and are only good for one thing – babysitting. I turn my nose up.[8]

In the middle of the shop two dozen bestsellers have been squashed together to form an overachieving book ghetto. Stephen Fry is here, with his guide to the Greek myths. I expect the story of Tithonus is in there somewhere. Tithonus was the bloke who was granted immortality but who forgot to specify that he wanted to be sexually resplendent forever, not older and older and older forever. That Tithonus pays for his life extension with personal decay might serve as a warning. You don't need me to tell you that people are generally living longer these days, and you also don't need me to tell you that if the pensionable chunk of a society continues to increase relative to the working-age chunk of a society, with the result that there's less money to pay bigger bills, then you've got something that might loosely be described as an issue on your hands. The solution isn't obvious. Ask ten people how they would resolve the dilemma and you'll probably get ten different responses. Anthony Trollope, in *The Fixed Period*, a short story of 1860-something, satirically suggested that the answer was to kill off all men at 67 with chloroform, while Kurt Vonnegut fictionally suggested that the answer was one in, two out. For my part, I think all retirement should be

---

[8] I later showed the book to my grandad and told him to brace himself because what he was about to see was 50 pages of the most outrageous ageism imaginable. He zipped through it and laughed his head off.

part-time. Monday to Thursday, retirees can do whatever the hell they like, while Friday through Sunday they should be out fishing for tuna. Either way, I walk out of the shop not with Stephen's myths or that enlightened yarn about the pill-popping serial decorators, but, instead, *The Unexpected Joy of Being Sober* by Catherine Gray.

I go into a bakery a few doors down – Cooplands – and ask the girl what's peculiar to the area. She points to her colleague and says, 'She is.' I take away a curd tart, which I enjoy walking Friargate, Market Way, Eastborough – all excellent streets. Then I walk The Bolts, Leading Post Street, Dog and Duck Lane, and decide I'd have those three in Portsmouth as well. I climb the latter now, dogless and duck-less, up towards the church and the castle, turning often to watch the sun call it a day. Scarborough, I've come to see, or come to *feel*, is a pain in the neck – every few steps it gives a fresh scene to turn for, stoop for, put one's neck out for.

I walk to Marine Drive to buy cigarettes at the One Stop. There's a dry cleaners next door. I'd be better off in there of course, for a spin and rinse, but so it goes. I smoke outside and admire the wide, softly curving, partly sloping street, lined on both sides with the kind of house a Jane Austen heroine might fetch up at. I want to call it gracious, and proclaim it up there in my book with Gray Street in Newcastle, and Regent Street in London, and any number of half-moons in Bath. When I thought I couldn't be more smitten, Marine Drive lays its ace – a cricket ground, half-way down, wedged between houses, behind back gardens.

I look through the gap of its main gate, and smile at the bright untouched grass, the hidden wicket, the empty stands, each waiting on spring. To think that from a third-floor back bedroom I could watch the mighty Yorkshire pad away overs of Somerset turn, or hook at will a Kentish attack, or block a spell of Glamorgan yorkers – all while ironing my underpants. I shouldn't mind coming back up in the summer when Yorkshire play Hampshire here. Indeed, I shouldn't mind living in Scarborough full stop. I could rent a flat on Esplanade Crescent. I could go to the cricket in season. Pop to the hotel for bingo. Play the odd round of golf at midnight. Do some bar work at L'amour. And maybe get a dog, so I could walk it and want nothing more.

Alan says he was about to send out a search party. He says people were getting worried, especially that man over there. 'Dennis?' 'Yeah, him. He reckoned you'd been taken advantage of.' I order the mushrooms and lasagne. 'So go on then,' he says, 'what happened?' I keep my confession brief – too long in town, too short in bed. He indulges me, pretends to be disappointed, enjoys hearing me paraphrase the conversation I had through the window at 4am.

'Did you enjoy yourself at least?' he says.

It's a good question. 'You know what, I can't be sure, Alan.'

'Well, we've all done it. When I was 21 I drank a bottle and a half of whisky. I was late for work the next morning. I worked in a butcher's. My boss said I looked less human than the turkey mince. I threw up on the giblets.'

Alan goes to the toilet and comes back with two pints. I groan. 'Give me a break, Alan.'

'Have a couple tonight, then come off it tomorrow.' He looks down at my book – the unexpected book. 'Joy's not something to rush into.'

There's no bingo tonight. It's the first time I've felt let down by Shearings. But there is a singer – Marie Sinclair. She's currently warming up (at the bar, by necking a shot). She's seen a few Easter Sundays this one, and she's the better for it: when she does her opening number – 'Private Dancer' – you can tell she really *means* what she's singing. After her opening number she says that if it's too loud then we're welcome to turn our hearing aids down. I seem to be the only one to find this offensive. 'I'm the right side of 80,' she says – '81. And if you don't believe me, gents, I'll blimming well show yer.' She does another number – 'Nessun Dorma' – then another shot at the bar. She takes the mic with her, leans on the bar and asks if any ladies got anything nice for Valentine's Day. Half a lager, says one. Did I heck, says another. A car, says someone else.

'A car?'

'A card!'

'Well you know where you can put that, don't you?' says Marie. 'And it's not on the bedside table.'

I move forward towards the stage and join a table of four women. There's Lorraine and Donna, and their mums, Jacquie and Daisy. The daughters are in their 50s. They're used to being the youngest ones on a Shearings. Apparently

I'm stealing their thunder. Donna says: 'Do you know what? We thought you were French. Jacquie was convinced of it. She said you looked like someone who'd go on strike a lot. We thought you might be going through a divorce. We thought she might have kicked you out. No, we didn't think your wife was French. We thought she might be local – a Yorkshire lass. We had it all figured out. We're good at sussing people.'

When the daughters get up to dance, their mothers are like a pair of paparazzi, up on their feet taking endless pictures and videos. It's nice to watch. It would seem a mother never stops collecting things for the scrap book, never stops feeling proud. There's something reassuring about Jacquie and Daisy's desire to capture their children dancing. And there's also something reassuring about their children's adult craving to be caught by their parents – to make them smile, to make them feel proud.

When the children return to the table, Jacquie starts going on about her grandson, Ted, and within ten minutes I know more about Ted then I know about my girlfriend. He could be my specialist subject on Mastermind.

'In April 2003, Ted was born. In which hospital?'

'St Mary's.'

'Correct. By all accounts, Ted is a what?'

'Very nice boy.'

'Correct. At the age of fourteen, when Ted saw a lady struggling with her shopping on the high street in Southport, he went straight over to her. To do what?'

'Nick her shopping.'

'Incorrect. To help the lady. Ted's nickname growing up was—'

'Super Ted.'

'Correct.'

And so on.

Donna points to a man on the dance floor and says, 'Bloody hell. He's breakdancing.' She's not wrong. Or not entirely wrong. It might not be breakdancing, but it's certainly something.

'There's life in that old dog yet,' says Donna.

'Too much I'd say,' says Daisy.

'That dog needs to be put to sleep,' says Jacquie.

'He must have new hips,' says Lorraine.

Then Marie Sinclair goes around the tables with her microphone. For a bit of small talk. She comes up to me, sits on my knee.

'A little birdie told me …' – she tilts her head and does something with her eyelashes – '… that it was your birthday yesterday.'

'That's right.'

'How old were you?'

'Sixteen.'

'Then you shouldn't be drinking that,' she says, taking my double whisky and coke and knocking it back. 'Now tell me the truth or I'll be cross.'

'I was 32.'

'Thirty-two ladies and gentlemen. I'll tell you something about 32. It's a wonderful age for a woman. Especially if she happens to be 81.'

Then Marie Sinclair looks at me, growls, says 'You wouldn't touch the sides,' and grabs my jaw and plants a smacker on my lips.

'How was that?' she says.

'Probably illegal,' I say.

'One of your five a day more like.'

She returns to the stage and does a Patsy Kline number. Jacquie gives me a voucher and tells me to get a brandy for my nerves. When I get back with the brandy, Jacquie raises her glass and says, 'To absent friends.' She's got one in mind – her late husband. She says that since she lost him, she likes to get away, sometimes with Donna, sometimes alone. She says it's her brandy. Lorraine agrees that it's good to keep busy but adds that it's not without its dangers. She tells us about a couple she was speaking to yesterday. He's 90 and until last year was going out for a five-mile jog each day. Then he had a couple of falls and got lost a couple of times so his wife got him a treadmill and put it in the bathroom so he could get straight in the shower. Since then he's had a fall but hasn't yet got lost. Anyway, Lorraine's forgotten the point of the story. I know the feeling.

I go outside for a cigarette. Alan's out here as well. After his second heart attack, the doctor told him his heart was so weak that one a day would kill him. Which is why he has two.

'The wife would kill me,' he says.

'Did she like the cake?'

'Sod off.'

'No, serious.'

'She did actually. She sent a picture back.'

'Of what?'

'I'm not telling.'

I tell him I'm off to bed and that I won't see him in the morning as my coach is leaving at 6am. I tell him it was nice talking to him. He acknowledges this with a single slow nod, as if unsure, as if doubtful, and then says, 'Just watch what you're doing.'

Part 2

St Ives, Cornwall, England

5

Any student discount?

Megan and I met on Halloween, 2016. She was living on a barge at the time – a rite of passage for History of Art graduates – and was hosting a Halloween party alongside her barge-mate Flora, a mutual friend. I went along and was sufficiently disguised – I had a pumpkin on my head – as to be attractive. When push came to shove, Megan got one of my seeds stuck between her teeth.

In the days after the party, Flora told Megan to avoid me because I was unreliable. But Megan wasn't deterred; she spied the outlines of a kindred spirit; now we're unreliable together. We currently conduct the relationship (which is, I suppose, akin to an electrical charge, albeit an erratic one) over ten days a month between London and Portsmouth. Very occasionally, Megan will complain she doesn't get enough of me. The rest of the time she won't. Whenever she cooks, it all happens in one pot, and whenever she picks up the phone (which is seldom), her tone is doubtful, as if she's never done it before – 'Hello?' That's all you need to know really. I love her very often.[9]

---

[9] Alain de Botton wrote that it is rare to be uncomplicatedly happy for longer than fifteen minutes. I reckon it's similar with love. Outside of my family, who are sort of different, I love Megan more often than anyone else. In second place is Benedict Cumberbatch, which tells you just how well Megan is doing.

It might be claimed without upsetting the apple cart that people of different generations tend to prefer different things – clothes, music, food. Without putting too fine a point on it, Megan's taste is roughly in line with that of someone born between the wars – and I'm not talking about the Gulf Wars. Her idea of a good night is a radio adaptation of a Virginia Woolf novel and a suet pudding. So I'm not surprised that she has assimilated quickly to her new surroundings – the waiting lounge at the foot of the M1. She's already in conversation with her neighbours regarding the three times they've circumnavigated the world – one for each of their sons.

'What, you mean on each occasion you went with a different son?' asks Megan.

'Oh no,' she says. 'We do it *for* them, not with them.'

Our driver is Michelle. Youngish. Londoner. As we reverse out of our bay, I spot Roger taking a fresh load up to Scarborough. Judging by the laughing faces of the passengers, he's just made that joke about today's being a small group. Michelle doesn't start with a joke. She starts with a confession – it's only her third trip, and her first to St Ives, so buckle up. When we hit the M25, and with Cilla Black on the radio, I make a start on the crossword. I'm soon stuck on 'egg white seven letters'. I turn to the chap behind for help. 'Dunno, mate,' he says. 'Stopped doing 'em years ago. I'm not up to date anymore.'

We slip between Slough and Windsor and hit the M4, which runs all the way to south Wales, via the Prince of

Wales Bridge that spans the Severn. I know this not because I've used the M4 much but because of *Gavin and Stacey*. The M4 is one of the show's main characters. It is a crucial artery connecting the two titular hearts. I think the Prince of Wales Bridge should be called the *Gavin and Stacey* Bridge if I'm honest. I mean, what's Charles got to do with it? He's probably never been on the thing. I might get a petition going: civic works named after popular culture favourites. *Call the Midwife* Viaduct. *One Foot in the Grave* Suspension Bridge. People have been elected on worse platforms than an *Only Fools and Horses* Tunnel.

I've been to Cornwall before. There was a holiday when I was young to Polperro, and then there was a short stop in Looe (a Looe stop if you will) in 2009, during a tour of the UK I undertook in a campervan called Roger. As well as a campervan, Roger was an early example of a food truck. I sold avant-garde omelettes through a side window, because I studied English literature and it was the only career path available to me. The business was called Eggonomics. My first gig was at a campsite in Dorset. I got tipped a fish. That fish was the equivalent of Alan Glanville's tuna. Things went downhill from there.

So yeah, I've been to Cornwall. And yet I remain all but ignorant of the place. Which is how I like it, to be honest. Prior to a holiday or trip, I try to accrue a decent amount of ignorance in relation to wherever I'm going so that I stand to gain more by going there. I'm pretty good at it. The accruing, I mean. It comes naturally. But even so, dodging knowledge is like dodging oxygen – you'll avoid most of it, but not all. For example, I know that etymologically, the 'corn' bit means peninsula and the 'wall' bit means foreign. So Cornwall is the unusual knob, or the unknown extension, or the odd extra bit. I also know that the Romans didn't really bother with the place, because the sitting tenants (the Celts) weren't in the mood for straight roads,[10] and that the region is officially 'undeveloped' according to the EU, which is why it's had more funding than any other part of England over the last twenty years, and presumably *not* why Cornwall overwhelmingly voted to leave the EU in the 2016 referendum. I ask Megan why she thinks Cornwall voted to leave. 'So the pasties can be irregular,' she says, then goes back to sleep. It is on such characterful interventions that love rests.

At the Menbury services we gain a passenger – Chris, who needs a lift home. He introduces himself over the public address system. 'Hello everybody. I'm Chris. I'm a driver for the company, but I'm on holiday. Just need a lift home. I'll be pointing out things of interest, so you might not hear from me again!'

But we do hear from Chris again. Plenty. Which I don't mind at all because there's a nice West Country lilt to his speech. His delivery is also accidentally or oddly poetic. Here's an example: 'Bristol imported slaves and has two

---

[10] Cornwall is one of the 'Celtic nations'. The others are Scotland, Wales, Ireland, the Isle of Man, and Brittany in France. The Celts used to occupy most of Europe, but they were gradually pushed west, to the fringe of the continent.

modern shopping centres. The M32 is shorter than a chante-nay carrot if you know the sort, and said carrot will connect us to the M5, which binds Exeter to Birmingham and is heavy going in summer. To your left are the Mendip Hills, whence the stone of Bath was quarried. Behold Somerset – the land of cider and willow. Note yonder Willow Man. A 40-foot sculpture that was reduced in size by 20 per cent in 2012, in accordance with the government's austerity programme.'

The trouble with being a youngish couple is that people think you're into each other. I mean, they think you're self-sufficient in terms of entertainment, and therefore not keen for mixing or chit-chat. So far, no one has said a word to us – apart from that guy who hasn't heard of egg white. We're not being left out of the banter deliberately or unkindly. People are just sticking to what they know, and what they know is each other, is their generation. I was thinking about this over the weekend – about intergenerational relations, to put it grandly. It's not much of a survey, but I asked a load of friends if they had a mate over 50 who they weren't related to. The answer was no across the board. Evidently we are inclined to our own age group. Sayings such as 'don't match May with December' aren't exactly helpful in countering this inclination. I guess the logic behind that particular idea is that a common age promises a common disposition and common interests. That may well be true – or true to an extent – but it doesn't mean that May–December matchings are without value. In my opinion, having less in common is an attractive deficiency, because it means there's more ground to cover, more learning to be done. May can speak of flowers, and December of snowflakes. And the pair can unite in their distrust of August. Sounds good to me.

For my part, I've had two significant May–December friendships. I say had, because both of my mates are dead now. Richard Flynn I met in Adelaide in 2010. I'd just finished studying and went out to South Australia to spend some time with my family (my dad's first two children moved to Australia with their mother before I was even an idea), and generally vacillate in good weather. I got a job in a café and started reviewing plays for a local website. Richard was the editor. He was about 80 when I met him. He could spot a dangler from a hundred yards, sloppy thinking from a mile, a weak turn of phrase from— you get the picture. Because of his keen editorial sense, and my generally messy writing, we gave each other a lot to think about. When he had a plus one for a play I'd sometimes go with him, and when I had a plus one he'd sometimes come with me. We'd go to a Chinese restaurant on Gouger Street after the play and debrief. Richard liked me well enough but could see I needed reforming. Over the next five years or so, he'd send me occasional emails dispensing what I suppose you'd call encouragement. He reckoned I needed to pull my socks up; that the road to hell is paved with good intentions; and that I really must start responding to his emails more promptly. I wrote back to his last email three weeks after receiving it, by which point he was dead.

I still write to him sometimes, just a line or two. They don't bounce back, which is nice.

I met Julian Edwards at Liphook Golf Club in the year 2000. A few times a year, the golf club pitted the juniors against the seniors, and it so happened that Dr Edwards and I were drawn against each other several competitions on the spin. On each occasion, I'd show him how to get up and down, or play a bunker shot, or where his ball was, and in return, he'd tell me, quite like Richard Flynn, the various ways I needed to transform my character, starting with a subscription to the *Telegraph*. When I reached eighteen, the fees ballooned and I could no longer afford to be a member. Julian and I kept in touch and would meet once a year or so, either for a game of golf (until his ankle went AWOL), or lunch at the Hawkley Inn, where he'd dust off his preferred theme – that I really ought to have serious job by now – and present it to me anew. I remember one time moaning to Julian about how boring working at Café Rouge was proving to be. He heard me out and then said: 'I'll tell you what is boring. Cancer.' At his memorial service, someone asked how I knew Julian. I said we played golf together, albeit terribly. She said, without pausing for thought, as if it were a given, 'What matters is that you played.'

Finally, I've got a sort of older mate called Terry. First time I met him was in the sauna at the gym. We had a little chat about something inconsequential, and then when we got out to shower and dress etc., it turned out our lockers were next door but one. As if emboldened by the coincidence, Terry said: 'You won't believe this, but my wife accused me of being a transvestite this morning.' I didn't really know what to say to this, so continued drying my feet. Then Terry said: 'I wasn't going to put up with that, obviously. So I packed all her things and left.' I saw Terry most Mondays after that, around 10.30am, either in the sauna or elsewhere in the gym. He was well liked by everyone it seemed – by all the staff, and all the boys that had been going to the gym for decades. Anyway, last winter, the winter just gone, I didn't see Terry at the gym for months. Eventually I asked someone if he was alright.

'He's gone to another place,' they said.

Ah. Bugger. That's … 'I'm sorry to hear that,' I said.

'Yeah the old bastard's joined Virgin Active. He reckons they've got a better jacuzzi.'

When we enter Devon, Chris taps the microphone to get our attention. The lady in front of Meg struggles to wake up the man in front of me.

'Kieran. He's got something to say.' A small, London accent.

'I don't care about no willow man.' A large, Irish one.

The news isn't willow-based. It's to do with the planned excursions. Chris tells us that some are included in the holiday, but that others carry a £10 supplement. I ask if there's a student discount.

'I'm deaf as a post – would you say that again?'

'Any student discount?'

'Any student— No. What do you think— twenty years I've been on these coaches, folks, and I've never heard anything quite like that. Tell you what young man, even if you were pregnant with students, you'd still not get a discount. How's that?'

By the time we get to St Ives, I'm pretty keen to get off the coach and stretch my legs, but have to wait on the large Irish fella in front, who has misplaced something. He's on his knees in the aisle. It's his phone.

'Oh, Kieran. When did you last use it?'

'It was before Christmas.'

'Oh, you know what I mean. You're always doing this.'

'Don't be giving out on me, Imelda – it's not my fault. If they're going to make them small, then what do they expect?'

Despite his backchat, it's clear that before me – or beneath me rather – is a sweet, soft man, albeit one built to scare the bejaysus out of people. He finds the phone. It was in his other pocket. He can't believe it. 'I swear to God, Imelda, I've never put a thing in that pocket my whole life.'

We've been allocated a table for two near the fire exit. Someone has to be, I suppose, and it makes sense to stitch up the youngsters – after all, they've more time to get over it. I've got my back to the wall and can see the other diners, but Megan only has a view of me, bless her. Halfway through the fishcake it dawns on me that we've only ourselves to talk to. I miss Alan.

'What did you say?'

'Nothing.'

'Did you say, "I miss Alan"?'

Other couples have been paired up and put on tables of four. They're currently enjoying the first movement of an eight-meal, four-day symphony. Whoever did the seating plan evidently thought it best not to mix May with December. Anyway, I'd better say something to Megan. She's currently squinting. I think she's trying to watch the action of the dining room via its reflection on the wall behind me. I ask about her great grandparents, what she knows of them.

'My nan's mum was Nanny Lil. She lived in Clacton with Grandad Bob. It was a cottage. It had a pretty garden. I remember there was a jar of 2p coins in the living room, which we'd take to the arcades on the pier. Bob would drive us on his mobility scooter. He'd let us pretend to direct him. Bob was a real softie, but Nanny Lil wasn't. She was a hard woman. I don't remember ever cuddling her. After Bob died she went downhill. She went into a home. She wouldn't eat the dinners. She wasn't used to being cooked for – she rejected the emancipation. She would make herself ham sandwiches. She was tiny at the end. I painted a portrait of her for my A-level coursework. I was working from a photo – she was dead by this time – but it brought me closer to her. I gave the painting to my mum because she loved her Nanny Lil. It's in the spare room.'

There's another couple sat on their own. He's got her name inked all over his arms (at least one hopes it's her name), and she's taking a picture of him finishing his soup the way he always does. He's laughing, pretending to lick the bowl. I think of that John Betjeman poem about the couple in a teashop.[11]

We go through to the entertainment zone. The set-up is much like the set-up in Scarborough – a bar, a small dance floor, a little stage, tables and chairs, a few sofas. We get a small table, next to Bryan and Yvonne, former teachers from Birmingham.

'You two are a bit young for this,' says Yvonne.

'I thought it was an 18–30 sort of thing,' I say. 'Turns out it's an 1830s sort of thing.'

'Ah, you're rotten. I've got a mate who's 66 but he won't come because he says he's not old enough. He's two years younger than me.'

While the compère sets up his random number generator for the bingo, the four of us talk about education, about teaching. There's talk of grammars, comprehensives, privates – the pros and cons of each. Bryan says that one thing he's noticed over the years is that the parents of the children struggling the most in class were the least likely to come to parents' evening. He says that's telling. He says that shows that education starts and finishes at home. 'School's the cheese, the pickle, the peanut butter, but parents are the bread. If you take away the bread, you've no chance of a sandwich, to say nothing of a picnic.'

---

[11] '"Let us not speak, for the love we bear one another— / Let us hold hands and look." / She such a very ordinary little woman; / He such a thumping crook; / But both, for a moment, little lower than the angels / In the teashop's ingle-nook.'

I attempt to make a mental note of this analogy.

'That said,' says Bryan, 'there's always exceptions. I know a kid whose parents tried very hard with him. But he got in with the wrong crowd and he hasn't looked back since. So I suppose you could say that even with bread and filling you might not end up with a sandwich.'

'One thing's sure,' says Yvonne, 'kids are less engaged and less respectful these days.'

'You know Socrates said the same thing,' I say.

'Meaning?'

'Meaning it might not be children that change, but our perspective of them, our relation to them.'

'Well,' says Yvonne, 'Socrates clearly didn't teach at Solihull Park.'[12]

Yvonne met Bryan at a disco in Birmingham. They were both about sixteen. Yvonne and two of her mates went up

---

[12] Is this generation gap different to the gaps that came before it? It's possible. For a start, this gap has digital immigrants on the one side and digital natives on the other. Then, there's the simple fact that new technology has altered how people relate, how they converse, how they mix. Search engines have threatened the role of elders as repositories of information, anecdotes, advice. Practical acumen is no longer handed down manually or verbally as it once was. Instead, people Google. Technology has also changed the way we entertain ourselves. We are now masters of our own entertainment in a way that was unthinkable only ten years ago. When I was a kid and went to visit elder relatives or family friends, I had to hang out with the adults. Although unbearable at the time, I can now see the dividend that such encounters paid. Now, kids and teens and young adults can whip out their phones and be on another planet. You can't tell me that hasn't had an effect on intergenerational relations. You can't tell me that hasn't widened the gap.

to Bryan and two of his mates and asked if they wanted to play Postman's Knock in the hallway.[13] A consequence of the game was that Yvonne had to kiss Bryan – and more than once. At first she didn't think much of the experience, but after the fourth time – Bryan was obviously a keen postman, with a lot of mail in his pouch – she'd somehow acquired a taste for it. As Yvonne grew accustomed to kissing Bryan, so the other two girls grew accustomed to kissing the other two boys. Between them, the three couples have now been married for 130 years. 'And you know what?' says Yvonne. 'To this day, whenever the postman calls, we have a little smooch.' 'Yeah,' says Bryan, 'which is why I've started telling my bank to email instead.'

Since Scarborough, I've learnt a few things about bingo. Here are the highlights: 1) Bingo Airways was a Polish airline which ceased operations in 2014, probably because the airline was explicitly associated with a game of chance. 2) Bingo is a town in the Bingo Department of Boulkiemdé Province in central western Burkina Faso. 3) In 2003, Butlins holiday camps modernised their bingo calls in an attempt to

---

[13] A kind of kissing game, like spin the bottle, wherein you get a mixed group (or not) and send one person away to be the Post(wo)man. The Post(wo)man then closes their eyes and knocks on a door. In return for the letter they deliver, they get a kiss. This kiss could be from the person they fancy, or it could be from their mate Tony. For the record, I played spin the bottle once. Every time the bottle was pointing at me, which meant Lucy or Sandy or Wilma had to kiss me, they'd say it was pointing at someone else, even if it was irrefutably pointing at me. I learnt that day that people believe what they want to be true, not what's blindingly obvious.

bring fresh interest to the game. One addition was Stroppy Teen for fifteen, which is ageism of the most blatant sort.[14] 4) Carolyn Downs of the University of Lancaster published a social history of bingo in 2005. Much of the work explores links between bingo and criminality. Listed among the bingo-related acts of criminality is what happened to me in Scarborough last week, when that lady from Rhyl shafted me after I gave her the winning ticket.

Megan is in most ways my superior – morally, practically, intellectually. She knows how to make red pepper hummus, paints like Vanessa Bell, runs like Hermes, and cares about anemones and arachnids. In spite of her wide-ranging superiority, she can sometimes be bone stupid. For example, when I present her with a book of bingo coupons, she studies them for a short while then asks, 'Am I meant to fill in the gaps?'

During the first game, I have to keep an eye on her. It seems to be taking a long time for the information (the ball number) to travel from the caller's mouth, into Megan's ear, into her brain, and then onwards to her hand. I've never seen her look so flustered or anguished. It's like she's never heard the numbers before, it's like they're being called in Yiddish, and have been represented on her coupon in Roman numerals. I knew she was easily confused, but this is taking the piss. I win the first game – just a line – and get a tenner for

---

[14] I got in touch with Charlie Blake, Professor of Popular Culture at the University of Northampton, who was responsible for the modernisation of the bingo calls. I asked about the apparent ageism of Stroppy Teen for fifteen. He was unrepentant: 'Look. I had a fifteen year old at the time and he was a stroppy $%£&.'

my efforts. I don't even celebrate. I'm just glad it's over for Megan's sake. Between games one and two, Megan pops to the loo. I hope she pulls herself together in there, because she's embarrassing our generation the way she's carrying on. When she returns, her face is damp and she's tied her hair back.

'Alright?' I say.

'Yeah,' she says.

'Ready?'

'I think so.'

She wins the next game twice. This is how she did it. She needed one more number and it came up so she shouted 'bingo!' and the caller stopped the game, at which point Megan realised that, in fact, it wasn't bingo and that she still had one more number to get. She communicated this to the room by saying, 'Nope. Sorry, nope. I haven't won. I didn't see. I missed. I need. Sorry.' The next ball called was the one she needed. You'd expect her second call of 'bingo!' to sound somewhat apologetic, muted, humble even. None of it. She cried 'bingo!' so loud you'd be forgiven for think- ing she was trying to get the attention of someone in Bingo, Burkina Faso.

'You seemed to enjoy that,' I say, when she's back with her 50-quid winnings.

'I did. I really did. When I won, my vision went blurry. Something physical happened. It was amazing.'

After the third game, in which neither of us prosper, Bryan gets another bottle of red in and our caller becomes our crooner and the dancing starts. Within a couple of minutes, there's a dozen or so on the dance floor, and Megan's among them. Imelda's up there as well, swinging her arms around, and so is her fella Kieran, who's doing some kind of crouching move. Perhaps he's looking for his phone again. Megan invites me to join her, but I'm unresponsive. It's not self-consciousness that holds me back, but a straightforward, well-thought-through dislike of dancing. I'm not a big fan of random limb movements in any context, and even less of one in front of others to Billy Joel. My friend Charlie's the same. He can't see the point. But he deals with the pressure and expectation to dance in a very different way to me. He gets up and does it as absurdly as he can for as long as he can. He wants everyone to look at him and think, 'What the f*ck is he doing?', and thereby be prompted to ask themselves, 'Hang on, what the f*ck am *I* doing?' He's been undermining dance floors for years.

Megan skips towards me, still that bingo-grin on her face. I fear she's going to try and pull me up.

'You can't make me do it,' I say.

'Sorry?'

'I'm not going to dance, Megan. I know you think I'm boring but I can't do it very well and I'd—'

'Ben. It's alright. I just wanted to ask if you've got any spare vouchers.'

6

Well, pardon me, Mrs Robinson

Brushing my teeth, I watch Megan out of the corner of my eye sat up in bed, frowning at her phone. She's prone to worry and anxiety, and I wonder how much that has to do with her age, and how much to do with her phone. Children and elders, from what I've seen, are generally less fussed about things. You only have to watch a toddler draw or bake, or an elder share a political opinion, to see they've little concern for precision or correctness – they're just after making a splash, giving it a whirl, slapping it on, getting it out. Megan has none of that flippancy. Watching her scroll and thumb and swipe, it occurs to me that, on top of her age, Megan's anxious disposition can't be helped by comparison websites like Facebook and Instagram. She's not materialistic. She's not vain. But she's human, and humans turn to each other in search of meaning, direction, to see how they rank, how they differ, how they compare.

Today's millennials might be in their prime, but they also feel the pinch. The stage of the life course they currently occupy has been so relentlessly glamorised and airbrushed and hyped-up that it is rarely associated with struggle or pain or sadness or difficulty or imperfection or failure; instead, it is readily associated with beauty, energy, success, indulgence, perfection, gaiety, enterprise and adventure. The life template millennials are shown (and propagate) is often wildly at odds with the reality of the millennial experience. A lot of millennials expect *a lot* of themselves. They expect to earn, produce, climb, compete, seize the day, live the dream, have a kid, set up sticks, pay off debt, splash the cash, love like they do in the films and songs and poems, stay in touch, stay young, stay hip, keep fit, keep up, earn more, grow more, win more, chill more, give a TED talk, juice, stretch, blend, be happy, be open, be careful, be woke, be liked, be followed, be shared, be seen, be real, be *un*real. That's a lot of expectation. Some won't expect all that of themselves, but a lot will, and some will expect even more. All I'm getting at is this: it can be a tricky phase of life. It lacks both the frivolous obliviousness of youth, and the perspective and philosophy that come with age. And it's a phase of life that's been made that little bit trickier, I feel, as a result of much of it being played out online. When I finish brushing my teeth, I ask Megan what she's up to. She says: 'Vicky got promoted and had a boob job on the same day.'

We go to Falmouth for a river cruise (£10, no student discount). The steps from the pier down to the boat are very slippery. I have to hold on to Michelle, who has to hold on to Megan. Kieran almost falls in. 'Watch yerself, Imelda. It's feckin' deadly.'

Once aboard, I get myself and Megan a cup of tea, while she nabs a couple of seats up on deck. It feels good to take to the water. Here's a description of the scene using all five senses: I can smell the sweetness of Megan's tea but not the sweetness of my own – odd; I can hear the bobbing and lolloping of buoys and small sailing boats; I can see a sky that is grey and teal and mint and green, and Megan's windswept hair as she sketches; I can feel the heat of my tea, my beard when I touch it, the wood of my seat; and I can taste nothing because I burnt my tongue five minutes ago.

The boat's commentator – up in the crow's nest with a megaphone – is a droll fellow. All these guides and escorts must come out of the same finishing schools, because their humour is of a kind. This one directs our attention to a castle put up by Henry VIII, the Penryn Job Centre, and then a distant baroque mansion, which, according to him, 'is where all the Shearings drivers live'. There is no sign of Bryan and Yvonne. And I didn't see them at breakfast either. Perhaps that red wine last night did them in. Perhaps they're recuperating in bed, watching *Escape to the Country*.

I fetch a coffee for Marie (glasses, hair up in a bun, red anorak). We got chatting up on deck, going past the oyster dredgers and mussel farms. She's from near Bradford. She used to be part of a travelling theatre company. They'd go all over the world, adapting the classics for younger audiences, bringing theatre to the people. Russia, Mexico, Colombia, even Burkina Faso. ('Bingo?' 'Never heard of it.') A truly itinerant theatre company.

'And was that fun, Marie?'

'Fun? It was more than fun. It was food for the soul.'

'In which case you must miss it?'

'I do. I'd still be out there on the road if I hadn't mucked up my spine coming down a mountain. I'm not full of regret though. I mean, I got up the damn thing, didn't I?'

As we approach the end of the Fal Estuary, our audio guide points out another mansion. This one's owned by a local Viscount. It's certainly a nice-looking house – and the land attached to it is considerable, about 4 per cent of Cornwall. 'I wonder how they got all that?' I say to Marie. 'Piracy,' she says, without irony. 'Pure and simple piracy.' I suppose you don't spend 30 years travelling the world with a troupe of actors and not acquire any opinions. 'They should be forced to relinquish the land,' she continues, dusting off an old record and dropping it on the turntable. 'It's ill-gotten. You know, I used to be a revolutionary, but I had to give it up because of my blood pressure.'

Another significant landowner locally is Prince Charles. As well as Prince of Wales, he is Duke of Cornwall, and custodian and beneficiary of The Duchy of Cornwall, which is a part of the Crown's estate. The Duchy was created with the purpose of providing income to the heir apparent to the throne. The Duke of Cornwall nets around £20 million annually. This has been going on since the 1300s, when Edward III set the whole thing up. In total, the Duchy owns 0.2 per cent of UK land, and hundreds of holiday cottages. Apparently, the holiday cottages are managed directly by the Duchy. I like the idea of Charles manning the phones. 'Now then, let's get to the bottom of this, you're saying your egg came with insufficient soldiers?'

Megan's not spoken to me for an hour. She's sketching a group of three sat gossiping at the back of the boat. I eavesdrop on the group a while. The talk is pretty bawdy. The biggest culprit is a tall man not unlike Prince Philip.

He must be at least 90. He's sat cross-legged, and taps his crutch on the deck gently as he talks, unless he wants to make a point, in which case the crutch comes up and is poked meaningfully into the air. He's currently letting the other two in on a secret. Namely, that since his wife died, he's started watching pornography. 'I can't say it's been entirely effective,' he says.

The couple Prince Philip is sat with – perhaps twenty years his junior – are lapping up his sauciness. After one of Philip's *bon mots*, one of the couple says: 'I love old people. They're ever so interesting.' Prince Philip allows himself a rueful laugh, then says, 'Then my dear, you clearly haven't met enough of them.' She asks if Philip wants a tea. 'No, no,' he says, 'I've had quite enough of that. My wife was an incessant tea-maker. Whenever she doubted whether she'd done the right thing in marrying me, she'd make a pot of tea. I'd drink it for her sake, though I never liked the stuff. It must be the most overrated thing in the annals of man.' To this the younger woman replies, in an affected accent, 'Well I'm pleased to say I know bugger all about the annals of man.' They all laugh at that, and then Philip says: 'Oh go on then. Get me a tea.' I hope Megan's sketch includes speech bubbles.

I go below deck. Everyone's pressed against the starboard window – there's been a dolphin sighting. There's one lady not making a fuss. She couldn't give a monkey's about dolphins. She's dressed formally, *properly*, nicely, and is looking out the window on the other side of the boat. In effect, she's got her back to the stage, and such postures attract me, so

I go over and say hello. Her name's Chris, and she'd been wondering when I was going to introduce myself. Well, pardon me, Mrs Robinson. She reminds me of Angela Merkel and Ziggy Stardust. She's somehow between the two. She's in a cream, cashmere trench coat and heels. (And other things besides, but those are the highlights.) She must have struggled down those slippery steps. She probably found the captain's arm for support. She says she used to be in politics but now she wants to write.

'Write what?' I say.

'Only my demons,' she says, 'Won't you sit down?' I will sit down. 'Now,' she says, 'let me tell you something: there's no civilisation, only animals.'

Megan and Marie (glasses, hair up in a bun, anorak) join us. Marie and Chris are familiar with one another. They both came on this trip alone, and have been taking their meals at the same table. Marie wonders what we were discussing, and Chris says, 'Oh, I was just telling Benjamin how awful the world is.' Marie sighs knowingly, and then counters that as far as being a woman is concerned, things have never been better. She remembers her mother and what she had to contend with. 'It was a double shift that never ended. From one workplace to another. And what did she get for thanks? A clip round the ear.' Then Chris asks Megan if she feels free. Megan says she knows enough about how things were for women in this country before (and how things continue to be for women elsewhere) to know that she's well placed now. Indeed, Megan can't remember ever experiencing an explicit disadvantage because of her sex. 'Perhaps it's unfashionable to say so,' she says, 'but I've never met a cruel man in my life, just stupid ones.'

15.00. I wake up from a nap, splash my face, drink an instant coffee sat on the windowsill. I enjoy the view. There's a palm tree, part of a beach, a piece of the Celtic Sea. I'm overlooking the foreground of course – a row of parked cars. One's getting a ticket. The owner appears in a panic. 'I'm delivering something,' she says. 'Yeah, and so am I,' says the warden.

Megan's nowhere to be seen, so I go through to the lounge with my book. A woman is sat on her own in a bay window, her fingers laced, her expression serious. I sit down next to her, and look where she's looking.

'That's the lighthouse Virginia Woolf wrote about,' she says.

'Is that right?'

'Well it was the last time I was here.'

'What happens in that story again?'

'*To the Lighthouse*? Gosh, now you're asking. I ought to know, we did it for O-level. Doesn't she get murdered by a fisherman?'

'I wouldn't like to say.'[15]

---

[15] She doesn't get murdered by a fisherman, and the titular lighthouse is actually on the Isle of Skye, although it was this one (Godrevy) that gave Woolf the idea for the novel, whose dramatic highpoint is when a professor snaps at a poet for requesting a second helping of soup, or so Megan tells me.

Debra is from Newark, which is Lincolnshire way. She reminds me of Victoria Wood, the actor and writer and comedian and dinner lady. There's something effortlessly maternal about her, something conspiratorial, something endearing. She makes me feel like the two of us have been sat here gossiping for years. It's the way she screws her nose up sometimes, and turns to me and says, 'Here, have you …' She moved to Cornwall twenty years ago and it was the best thing she ever did. But then she went back to Newark, to help out with the grandkids. The grandkids have since flown the nest, meaning she's stuck in Newark more or less on her own. 'I work in Asda. But only as a cleaner. When I told my colleague I was coming to St Ives on holiday, she said, "Make sure you come back!" She's put an idea in my head, I don't mind telling you.' At the end of our conversation, when I get up to resume my search for Megan, she says, quietly, 'Have a nice day, love,' as if I was going off to school.

I'm at the bar getting a couple of drinks to take through to dinner. Kieran's at my side. By way of a greeting, he says it's been lovely seeing me. I take this on the chin, though I can't say his use of the past tense isn't slightly unsettling. It's like Kieran knows something I don't. It's like he's arranged for my demise later this evening.

We swap positions at the table, so Megan has a view of something that isn't me. She has the soup and the hake, while I have the whitebait and the special. I tell Megan she looks nice, because she does, and then add: 'Nicer than the whitebait anyway.'

'You always do that,' she says.

'Always do what?'

'Almost be nice.'

'Sure.'

'It's okay to adore me, you know. You are allowed.'

I give this some thought, because it bears thinking about, then ask if she's having a good time.

'Yeah. It's nice sitting on this side.'

'No, I mean overall.'

'I love it. I feel like I'm actually on holiday. I like not making decisions. And I've enjoyed sketching. That man on the boat was funny. And Imelda is sweet. What time's bingo again?'

Kieran says we're to sit with them for the evening. He fetches some chairs especially. During the bingo, Kieran amuses himself by heckling as the balls come out. Forty-nine – 'My age.' Ninety – 'Imelda's age.' Fifty-three – 'When I lost my virginity.' None of us win, and none of us mind.

After the bingo, Kieran leans into a Joycean, Woolfish, highly-carbonated stream of consciousness. 'I was 27 and in London. I went along to an Irish dance in Kilburn there – do you know the place? – and who did I find? This one, looking lovely. It was Halloween and I was half-cut so I asked this girl for a dance. When she said yes I swear to God I couldn't believe my luck. I did some Hail Marys right there on the spot, twenty of the feckers. "Hail Mary, full of grace, the Lord is with you. Hail Mary, full of grace—" She said, "I didn't say I'd marry you. I only said I'd dance with you," but she didn't understand, she couldn't see what I could see – which was her. I asked for a second dance and she said: "You should go off and find someone who isn't a widow with two children." I said I don't want to find any eejit else, and we got married six months later. Will you have another lager, Megan?'

Kieran returns with three pints of lager and something soft for Imelda. Then Kieran asks where he was, where he got to. We say you just met Imelda at the dance in Kilburn. He resumes: 'Her mother didn't make it easy, mind. She was a hard woman. She'd knock your head off and think nothing of it. She was wary of me. She didn't want me adopting the kids, didn't want them taking my name and so on. But after about 25 years she came round, did she not, Imelda? It took her that long to warm to me. Same can't be said of Imelda here. She'd warmed to me by the time we'd got to Willesden Junction. I've loved her every minute since I met her. Not so much as a tea break.'

The singer is from Southend. She's good, sassy. Between songs, she tells a few jokes. I've got Kieran in my ear so don't catch them all, just the punch lines really. 'You'd better dig a big hole because I'm sat on a donkey.' 'There's a man sat outside with no trousers on – it was his wife's idea.' 'I nibbled on her ear and she farted and flew out of the window.' It's not easy to work backwards from these, to trace the setup, not least because there's no let-up in her material, no time to think. She'll deliver a punchline – 'And so I hit him with a shovel!' – and then go straight into 'A Teenager in Love' by Dion and the Belmonts, after which she'll say, 'Come on then

– who's in love? Put your hand up if you're in love.' Oddly, nobody puts their hand up. In the end I put mine up, if only to break the silence. Miss Southend spots me and says, 'At least someone can be bothered. Who you in love with, pet?' I point to Kieran and she says, 'Well better luck next time.' Then she's straight into a joke about Viagra, then there's an announcement she'll be selling chutney after the show, and then it's 'Single Ladies' by Beyoncé. When she calls for all the single ladies to get up on the floor, just one or two creep forward. When she calls for all the ladies that want to be single, a dozen are on their feet, Megan and Imelda among them. Kieran looks at me. 'It's been lovely seeing you, Ben.'

With the ladies on the tiles, Kieran leans in for a man-to-man. He gets his index finger out for the occasion, then gets it somewhere up near my nose. It's like a Cumberland sausage. 'It's been lovely seeing you, Ben, sure it has, but you're to let Megan do what she wants, do you hear? You're to feed off each other, not stifle each other. I've loved Imelda every minute since I met her. Not so much as a tea break. But believe me, some minutes were longer than others. It's imperative that you open the content of your minds – the two of you. And if you really want my advice? Sure you're better off without it.'

Imelda and Megan return. He gives Imelda a kiss and says he loves her. Then he looks at me as if I'm meant to do the same. He tells Megan to sit down for a minute because he wants to talk to her about her painting career, what's going to happen, what she has to do. He says she's never to sleep with the brush under her pillow, and that she's to do what she wants, even if that's going off for six months somewhere to paint and leaving me to fend for myself. Then he turns to me and asks if I play football, because when Megan goes off for six months I'll be wanting to get myself out of the house, sure I will, and he manages a team, St Augustine's, down in Kilburn there, so do I play football or not? I say I'd be happy to play if he was short, but he's already having second thoughts. He wants to see the size of me. I stand up and he says, 'And where's the rest of you then? You're a folk singer if you're anything. I'd sooner have St Augustine himself on the pitch than a wee fella like you.' No, he says, he couldn't do it to me, I'd go and hurt a finger on my debut and that would be my folk career finished, sure it would. 'Now have you seen *Mama Mia*?' he says. 'Now that's a good film. It looks lovely in Greece there, and Meryl Streep is grand. Sure the second one's not as good, when the baby comes along, not by a long shot. *Ghost* is another one. That's a deadly film. Your man comes back from the dead to look out for Demi Moore there. I cried my eyes out. Bejesus, Imelda, it's just occurred to me – we've not checked on the dog.'

It's past midnight. We're the last ones to leave the lounge. Kieran's not finished his pint, so he's taking it up to bed with him. I ask Imelda if she ever drinks. Before she can answer, Kieran says, 'No she doesn't. We can't afford for the both of us.'

7

Older people should be exploited

I'm standing on the front steps, waiting for Megan. Debra (Newark, Victoria Wood) and another lady (Dawn, I think) are coming up the hill. When Dawn spots me standing on the steps she says, 'Flipping 'eck it's Poldark!' I know he's not, but I ask if Poldark is in *EastEnders*. Dawn says, 'He'd be in my bedroom if he knew what was good for him.'[16]

Megan appears. She's been chatting to someone.

'Old people are therapeutic,' she says.

'That sounds patronising.'

'They say things and they have weight.'

'I think that's just historic phlegm.'

'You know what I mean. They've more substance. More words. They shouldn't be allowed to retire.'

'Sorry?'

'They should keep going.'

'Yeah, but they might be knackered.'

---

[16] Dawn might have had Ross Poldark in mind because he's a local boy. At least, the Poldark stories are set mostly in Cornwall. They were a series of books initially, authored by Winston Graham. There was a telly adaptation in the 70s, and there's another that's ongoing. There was also an attempted adaptation by HTV in the 90s. HTV produced a pilot episode that didn't go down well. Fifty members of the Poldark Appreciation Society picketed HTV's headquarters in period costumes. No further episodes were made. I think it's fair to say there can't have been a lot going on in 1996.

'It's just a shame.'

'For who?'

'I don't know. For me. For them. Wouldn't it be nice if everyone was 80? If the barmaid was 80? If the pilot was 80?'

'The pilot?'

'Or if the person collecting tickets on the train was 90? Why is there never anyone really old on *Top of the Pops*?'

'Because *Top of the Pops* doesn't exist anymore.'

'Older people should be exploited. They've got all that wisdom. All that skill. All that grist in the mill. Think of the all the flour they'd come out with if you started winding them up.'

'Can I write this down?'

'They should be put in a room – a nice room – and told to come up with ideas, make things, figure things out.'

'It's called the House of Lords.'

'It just seems like a waste.'

'Have you run these ideas by anyone?'

'No.'

'Do so tonight, okay?'

We go down to Porthminster Beach – the one beneath our hotel window. There's a fair bit going on. Dogs are chasing balls, spades are filling buckets, adults are going in goal, while some are out in kayaks and others are surfing. A few fishing boats, laid up like ducks out of water, look proud and dumb on the sand. We walk across that sand, and around a corner, to what they call Harbour Beach, where two piers enwrap the water like arms. We enter a harbourside restaurant and get a window table that offers a view of the beach and all its mellow drama. I have monkfish and it doesn't taste of much. I say so to Megan.

'It's delicate,' she says.

'Which is another way of saying it doesn't taste of much.'

'You're never happy.'

'I'm often thinking this about white fish. It's overrated.'

'You shouldn't generalise.'

'There's nothing to them. Cod, haddock, plaice, sea bass.'

'You're a philistine.'

'Meg, it's a fish. Not an opera.'

'You lack sensitivity.'

'Look. It's Imelda.'

'No it's not. You just want to steal a chip.'

'Megan it's effing Imelda.'

'Oh yeah. Where's Kieran?'

'She looks lost.'

'She looks happy.'

We go to the Tate gallery and join a free tour of the permanent exhibition with Andrew Jackson – a local retiree. AJ doesn't hang around. Just about the first thing he says is: 'The industrial revolution, coupled with the advent of photography, occasioned a splitting of painting. Its job of carefully representing this-and-that broke into a number of isms or styles. Consider this, for example ...' He shows us a Matisse, *Notre-Dame*, and says we're to understand it as an example of Impressionism, which is to say the painting carries the 'emotional investment' of the artist. It's what the artist saw, and how they felt, all in one, all mixed up. I like the sound of it. 'The church is bathed in light,' says Jackson, 'but note the plume of smoke cutting across its bottom half. A warning, perhaps.'

We move along to Picasso's *Bowl of Fruit, Violin and Bottle*. 'Picasso was a maverick,' says Jackson. 'He felt that the efforts made by painters to make things appear real and lifelike were tricks. Instead, Picasso shows that the canvas is flat, that paintings aren't real. Here he has taken a conventional still life and broken it up and reassembled it madly. By breaking up the fruit bowl, he breaks convention, he breaks the fourth wall, and he brings the whole endeavour and practice of painting into question. He – and this painting – ask no less a question than: *what is painting for?*'

Andrew looks at us. We look back at him. Then he says that his last question wasn't rhetorical, so does anyone have an answer? I look at Megan. She did History of Art for heaven's sake. Surely she knows. They must have taught her what painting was for. Still, no one says anything. Andrew looks disappointed. He knew the 2008 recession had had some unfortunate effects but this, I think he feels, is taking the Michelangelo. He's about to move on to the next room when a young girl, no more than seven, says, 'Painting is for looking at.' Andrew is quite taken by this remark. 'Out of the mouths of babes,' he says.

It isn't the only thing the young girl has to say about art. She can't believe Henry Moore got paid for doing 'Two Forms', and says she did something very similar to Mondrian's *Composition with Yellow, Blue and Red* for her art

OLDER PEOPLE SHOULD BE EXPLOITED

homework and got an F. She did like Bryan Pearce and Alfred Wallis though, and so did I. Both Wallis and Pearce were so-called 'naïve' artists, meaning they hadn't been trained, and didn't bother with such bothersome things as scale and perspective. Jackson tells us that Wallis was 'discovered' by Ben Nicholson and Kit Wood when the two young Londoners popped down to Cornwall in the 1920s to check out the scene. They found Wallis buried under four tons of crabmeat round the back of a restaurant. 'Gosh, blimey, Kit, look what we've discovered here. It's a jolly old man. I wonder if he can paint.'

The two lads asked Wallis what he thought he was up to undiscovered beneath so much crab. Wallis, unsurprisingly, gave a somewhat crabby response. He said he was a retired mariner, thank you very much, and a widower to boot. He said he started painting when he was 67 after the death of his adoptive mother who he also had séx with. He said his conversion to painting wasn't a bad redirection of purpose, all things considered, and a strong argument against what Anthony Trollope had in mind for anyone reaching the age of 67. He said he didn't paint bowls of fruit or members of the nobility; nor did he paint pretty pastoral scenes or self-portraits; instead he painted what he remembered, and he did it without giving a second's thought to technique, or precision, or verisimilitude, because he knew intuitively that it's not *how* you paint that matters, but rather *what* you paint. Finally, he said that if he must be considered naïve, then it should be allowed that naivety can produce much better results than any amount of instruction or training.

There's a danger of sounding patronising when praising the work of Wallis and Pearce – 'Oh didn't they do well given they had to use their toothbrush' and so on. None of that. I loved *Blue Ship* (Wallis) and *Monday* (Pearce) for their honesty, their wit, their pathos, their warmth, and their defiance – witting or unwitting – of the status quo. *Monday*, for Pearce, is a humble domestic scene, is washing hanging out on the line, with the back door open and, I imagine, the radio on. I like that. I like that Monday. It might not have scale in the traditional sense, but it has scale in a worldly sense, for it reduces the world – or one seventh of it – to a simple, normal thing. It says: 'This is what Monday is for me, and I make no bones about it.' And his *Three Pears* is better than Picasso's corrupted still life in my book. It shows three pears on a plate on a striped tablecloth. The brilliance and secret and genius of the painting (*for me*) is that one pear has fallen over, is on its side, has ignored the artist's demand to 'sit upright you silly pear!' and has opted instead to lie down. The prone pear is a small act of subversion, and it makes the painting come alive.

Before we leave the gallery and head upstairs to the café for refreshment, a final word on Andrew Jackson. It's not easy to bring paintings to life; to make sense of the abstract; to captivate children by somehow transforming Mondrian's defection from realism into a dramatic act of treacherous brilliance. Because it's not easy to do such things, it's my feeling that Jackson should have his retirement interrupted and be despatched to Grimsby and Falkirk and Wrexham and Derry to whip up enthusiasm for Bacon

OLDER PEOPLE SHOULD BE EXPLOITED

and Wallis and Hepworth and Pearce; for painting, for art, for the creative act. Jackson is fluent and animated and inclusive. He's a credit to the gallery, and to Cornwall. He should be framed and hung up. I'd certainly like to hear what he'd have to say about that.

We wander down to Porthmeor Beach and then up to what the locals call the 'island' – the green mound that sticks out into the sea. St Nicholas Chapel sits at the top. A sign says it's possible to marry here. I've seen worse spots. Megan looks lovely next to the cold stone of the church. I choose my words carefully, then ask, 'Would you like to get married here?' A pause, and then: 'Nah.'

Heading back to the hotel, we stop at the Sloop Inn for a quick drink. I have a half of Rattler cider, while Megan enjoys a pint of Sea Fury. It's a pub with character. That's what you'd say. Low ceilings, dark wood beams. All you need is a shoal of fishermen to burst in and promptly burst out in song – a shanty about all them pilchards that got away. Despite it being February, lots of people are sitting outside. They're drawn to the sea. They're watching the tide come in, watching it recover the bay. The sea is hitting the harbour walls, jumping up and rinsing children, who dance beneath the salty shrapnel.

I have another half and Megan another pint. She means business. If this carries on, by the end of the night Kieran will be saying to me, 'Do you never drink, Ben?', and Megan will be saying back, 'We can't afford for the two of us.' So be it. If she's going the way of Kieran, that's fine by me. What isn't fine by me is that she's becoming a broken record. She keeps saying stuff like: 'Such a good holiday, so therapeutic, can't wait for tonight, love bingo, such a good holiday, not sure about pasties.' When Megan says she wants a pint of Cornish Knocker (7.8 per cent abv) and she doesn't care who knows it, I decide it's time we made tracks to the hotel, and got some dinner in us.

We both start with chicken wings. Megan's not saying much. I think she's already hungover. She's trying to construct something from the remains of her wings.

'Are you alright?' I say.

'Who?'

'You.'

'Yeah, yeah. Need more wings.'

'Hm. What are you working on there?'

'Kieran and Imelda dancing.'

After a main of cassoulet and a pudding of panna cotta, we go through to the lounge. It's second nature by now. Las Vegas could be outside and we wouldn't give it a moment's thought. We get a table between a fella called Michael Jackson (who won the bingo last night) and a fella in shorts. The fella in shorts hasn't been out of them all week, as far as I know. He's dressed for a game of tennis, or to varnish the garden fence in summer. I've seen him about. You can't miss him, really. Every evening he sits with his partner, they have a pint or two, and then she disappears. In her absence, he'll have a few more pints and sit quietly on his own, tapping his foot to the music. Megan goes in for the bingo but I don't bother. In the event, Michael Jackson wins the jackpot again. He tries to do a little moonwalk when he goes up for his prize.

Tonight's entertainer is Gary K. He's got his own portable signage. Megan's in the loo. She's been in there a while. When the dancing starts – 'There Goes My First Love' – Debra and Dawn appear out of nowhere and try and pull me up onto the dance floor. Dawn lets go of my arm when I say I'm not keen, but Debra – who's had a bit of Sea Fury, I fancy – won't take no for an answer. She's got hold of my arm and is trying to yank me to my feet. It must make an odd scene for a neutral. In the end I've no choice but to yield. By now it's 'Locomotion' and Gary K's doing a good job of it. I've always loved the song, so make an effort to convey this with my body, but struggle to find a rhythm. Debra says I've got to behave like nobody was watching, which isn't the most effective inducement because if nobody was watching I sure as hell wouldn't be doing this. Debra's nothing if not persistent. She's grabbing my fingers now and shaking my arms around, as if I was an old car on a cold morning and this was how you got me going. I wish Meg was here. I could hide behind her. I try and copy Imelda. Do what she's doing. Imelda says I should just shake it. I try to just shake it but something's missing. I'm like a Hepworth sculpture – suggestive of life, but that's about it. For some reason, Imelda and Debra and Dawn and Chris and Marie and some other ladies have put their handbags in a pile on the dance floor and are dancing around them and finding it hilarious. Chris is looking brilliant and feline in a black onesie. She's turning heads all over the place, turning them all the way round in some cases. I get through 'Locomotion' and 'Da Doo Ron Ron' and then someone comes up and says, 'I think your girlfriend's been sick in the toilets.'

I put Megan to bed then return to the lounge and sit down next to the man in shorts – Mick. He says his wife goes up early because she gets tired and that he's from Leicester, as if the one explained the other. He says he left school at twelve, got into construction, practically rebuilt post-war Leicester and then retired at 42, which was about 35 years ago. He's one of thirteen children, but isn't close to his siblings. 'We were four in the same bed growing up. I reckon after that we just wanted the space. Having said that, the old man didn't set the best example – in terms of closeness. I don't remember him saying a single thing to me all my life. I used to do some rotten things just to get him to say something. I remember we were all on the bus and I pushed my brother off when it was going down Church Gate. All my father did was push me off 'n' all.'

Mick's 70-odd but hasn't got a single grey hair. In fact it's jet black, and clashes proudly with his chunky gold necklace. I ask if Mick lost his front teeth in a construction accident, or maybe when he got pushed off the bus that time, but it turns out he lost them in Skegness, when he was hit by a motorbike. He's going back to Skeggy next week in his caravan, then Lowestoft the week after. He more or less lives in his caravan these days. Says you've got to keep moving, lest you get second thoughts. Before I get second thoughts, I ask him about the shorts. He admits he's worn nothing else since he was 28. I ask him why. He gives it some thought, as if no one's ever asked him before, then says, 'I just find them easier to put on.'

There's philosophy in that response. What kind of philosophy I can't be sure, but there's definitely philosophy.

8

Although owls appear zen and wise, they're actually thick as sh*t

'They've put you in a cage,' says Megan, pointing to a cocka-too from Indonesia called Ben. (We're at Paradise Park, a wildlife sanctuary six miles from St Ives.) Turns out that Ben the cockatoo is prone to self-harming: once he starts pluck-ing his feathers, he just can't get enough of it and will keep going until he's practically starkers. Megan says that Ben is a message.

'A message?'

'A message to you.'

'He's not a message to me, Megan.'

'Look Ben in the eyes and tell him he's not a message.'

I look Ben in the eyes and tell him he's not a message. Ben replies by starting to pluck his feathers. 'See,' says Megan.

The great grey owls are exceptionally mindful. They haven't even a clue I'm here, gawping at them. They're too busy focusing on their breathing, their feathers, their wings. I read that although owls appear zen and wise, and although they're reputed to be sage and smart and so on, they're actually thick as sh*t. And not as peaceful as they seem either. Great grey owls like nothing better than hunt-ing small little lambs. They swoop and snatch them with their talons. Imagine the poor lamb, one second innocently nibbling grass, the next flying high above the Shropshire

Levels, wondering what on God's earth they'd done to deserve such a turn of events. I briefly imagine being similarly snatched by a swooping Kieran. 'Now I've got yeh, yeh feckin' wee eejit!'

The donkeys aren't getting much attention. Nor are they getting much work these days. A sign explains that they've been unemployed since the EU imposed an eight-stone weight limit on their cargo. It is said the ass community can't wait to take back control from Brussels so they can get some punters back in the saddle. Beyond the donkeys is a field of cauliflower. It's lit by the sun, and in the distance across the River Hayle, over towards Lelant, I can see the train returning to St Ives. It's a pleasant scene.

'Why are you smiling?' says Megan.

'Hm?'

'You're smiling at the cauliflower.'

'Am I?'

'You didn't smile at anything at the Tate.'

Mention of the Tate makes me wish Andrew Jackson was here to introduce me to all the birds and animals. I'd like to know his thoughts on the scarlet ibises. They're lovely. Bright red plumage, long curved beak, and apparently they've a co-operative nature. A sign says that 'juveniles start off a greyish colour and become scarlet as the birds mature.' That'll be right, I think, the gaining of colour with age; I've seen enough of that recently to believe in the idea. It's when the sign goes on to say that 'the birds nest in large breeding colonies' that their symbolic appeal breaks down. Kieran appears at my shoulder. I say to him, 'They don't need cutlery with beaks like that,' and he replies, 'True, though I should like to see how they get on with a bowl of soup.' Then Megan squeezes between us and says they're pinky-red because they eat prawns. Kieran tells her not to be fecking ridiculous, but she insists it's true. She says she once drank so much Ribena she turned purple, and I say, 'And that's why you think these birds are pinky-red, is it?'

The penguins are being fed. The spectacle is one of the park's main attractions. Among the penguins is a solitary duck. Perhaps it identifies as a penguin. In any case, all eyes are on the penguins and the duck, which means that all eyes are not on the two seagulls perched above the action, on the summit of the rockery within the penguin enclosure. Their presence is hilarious. They're desperate to pinch some of the penguins' lunch but they also remember what happened last time. They keep turning to one another, just for a second, as if to say, 'Shall we?' Despite being objectively far more diverting than the spectacle of twenty penguins eating sweetcorn, the seagulls are an unseen sideshow, seagulls being too common to summon our attention, unless, that is, they're making off with our lunch. I think of Philip Larkin again. 'Sun destroys the interest of what's happening in the shade.' A pair of shady seagulls indeed.

The best is saved to last – the chough. (Pronounced, I think, chuff.) It's black apart from its beak and feet, which are red. It's generally underwhelming, but with flashes of colour. More so than Ben the self-harming cockatoo, I can relate to the chough. Megan comes up to me and asks what's wrong.

'Nothing,' I say.

'But you've been staring at that bird for ages.'

'Have I?'

'It's horrible, isn't it?'

'If you say so.'

'What's it called?'

'A chough.'

'Must eat a lot of Marmite.'

When we get back to the hotel, Megan goes to Barbara Hepworth's studio and I go out for a longish walk, in order to get a sense of St Ives beyond its postcard streets down by the harbour. To risk stating the obvious, to know a thing requires familiarity with the whole of that thing. A sliver can give the wrong impression. If you only saw me for the first hour after waking, you'd conclude I was good for nothing but medical trials. So it is with places. We need to give them more room, more space, so they might make a fuller impression. A place is the sum of its parts, not some of its parts.

I cross the road and go down the steps to the beach. Because it's half-term there's a bucket-load of kids about. Freed of their education, the kids are currently behaving in ways that suggest they've never had any. The adults are little better, mind you. Here, a father has dug himself into a hole up to his neck. This undertaking was presumably done for the sake of his children, but they are nowhere to be seen, which is precisely where the father will be if he keeps this up. I'm not sure why, but I'd hazard the man's an accountant.

I want to head inland but pause for a moment outside the Sloop Inn to watch the action on the beach. A boy in blue is sat atop a large pile of sand – purportedly a castle, but I'm not convinced. His friends, who are in yellow and green, are caught in the castle's moat. Blue isn't sympathetic about the plight of Green and Yellow, that much is obvious. Indeed, when Blue tells Green and Yellow that he is the cherry on the cake and they are the crumbs, and flings some sand down at them as if to illustrate his point, you'd be forgiven for thinking Blue was taking pleasure from the suffering of his peers. It would appear that Blue will soon get his comeuppance, however. He's presently attempting to increase the height of his castle by transferring the sand between his legs onto the summit (berk), allowing his foes to approach from behind undetected. It would seem that those with the tenacity to achieve power aren't always blessed with the wit to retain it.

The names of the properties behind the Sloop Inn give you a clue as to their purpose. You're not called Serendipity Cottage if you mean to accommodate students or deckhands. What's more, a lot of the properties advertise websites in their front windows. I don't know what percentage of the properties around the harbour in St Ives are second homes or holiday rentals and the like, but I shouldn't be surprised if it was all of them, which is okay if you're a landlord or a holiday maker or a QC in London or Oxford who fancies a pad by the sea, but pretty rotten if you're a local and need somewhere to live that doesn't cost a million quid.

I cut through a cemetery and then walk the length of Clodgy View West to Alexandra Road, where things start to get a bit normal; there are signs of residency like washing lines and pebbledash, garages and recycling. None of the houses have sweet names with Dove or Honey or Eden in them. None are named after virtues or gods. These are first homes, full-time homes. Here, the bins go out on a Tuesday, and the washing on a Monday.

The best piece of evidence that this is a down-to-earth part of town is a handwritten notice attached to a garden fence. It asks that people 'stop putting their <u>full</u> poo bags in my hedge'. The underlining of 'full' hints that if the bags weren't full then there wouldn't be a problem. The notice goes on to say that both the police and the council have been informed about what's going on, before making clear that whosoever happens to be reading the notice is being watched. I'd be surprised if this intervention hasn't knocked the problem on the head.

I continue west towards the sun, across training pitches, empty fields, hoping there might be a way through the thicket and foliage to an edge, the coast, a cliff. It would be good, I presume, to see the sun come down on the sea and reflect on the passage of time. But in the event, there's no way through, or not from here anyway, and so I reverse and pick up a narrow footpath round the back of the rugby club. It runs behind gardens. In one, an older person is saying to a younger person, 'If you don't like it then you can do it yourself.' It would have been nice if the sentiment had been different, but there you have it.

I cross a main road and then continue eastward until I reach an industrial park. A menu at the entrance lists its contents. The St Ives MOT Test Centre is here, along with Celtic Fish & Game, and the office of a local accountant

– perhaps that bloke up to his neck on the beach. I don't know why I find all this ordinariness pleasing. Surely, the discovery of an industrial park shouldn't be satisfying unless you require one. I guess I was craving a break from the coach holiday's pleasant structure, its softly hedonistic agenda, its sweet reliability. I needed a few doses – a few hours – of unknowing and chance. When I go away I'm used to tramping about where I'm not wanted, having a nose, turning stones. I'm not used to bingo and penguins, followed by tea and trifle. Don't get me wrong, I like it, and it's doing me some favours. But if I'm in any way an adventurer, then it's of the urban, pedestrian kind, who seeks out normal things that are momentarily lit or framed or tainted so as to seem abnormal. I find the ordinariness of roads and shops and parks somehow reassuring. I find a back garden vignette – 'If you don't like it then you can do it yourself' – as pleasing and moving and provoking as any pack of lions, any range of mountains, any amount of bingo and penguins. So yeah, I guess I just wanted an adventure.

At the end of St Ives I turn down a side lane and chance upon a man and his dog. He is Bill, and he doesn't mind telling me how to proceed, not at all. After taking his direction, I ask if it's a shame how the natives have been pushed to the top of town. Surprisingly for someone of his advanced age, he's not in two minds about it. 'Oh yes! Great shame! It's like the suburbs of Disney World up here, where all the workers live, all those who dress up as mice so the emmets [visitors] can have a nice time of it. It should be the other way round.

That would be the correct order of things. Then I wouldn't have to walk so far to the pub.'

I walk between a pair of fields to a large car park, which offers a panoramic view of the town, the terraced homes like teeth, leaning seaward. They look strictly grey from here, but I know there's more to them than that because I've seen them up close. The sun is only catching the top of the parish church and the chapel on the island.

The car park pertains to a leisure centre, whose swimmers shriek and squawk like gulls. I hear less of them as I pass through the car park towards a flight of stone steps that will lower me, by turns, to the town centre. At the top of those steps a young girl is having her laces tied by her mother. The young girl hasn't been very successful at getting something across, because her mother is saying, 'I'm afraid you are going to have to explain yourself better, darling.' To this, the girl replies, 'Or maybe you are going to have to understand myself better, mummy.'

When I get back to the hotel, I sit on the wall opposite and watch awhile. Through the basement windows, I can see the waiting staff warming up for dinner, bracing themselves for service, savouring their final moments of freedom before going over the top to face the droves of elderly emmets who want cheese but no biscuits, curry but no rice, steak but well done, cake but no custard. Victor's there, and Nikolett, and Gemma Aitken (no relation as far as we know) grabbing some extra bottles for the bar. Above them, in the lounge, I can see Debra with a glass of wine and a faraway look, and

Kieran at the bar making Gemma Aitken laugh, with Imelda pulling on his sleeve, telling him not to forget her orange juice. Tonight's entertainment is erecting his address system. Michelle the driver is enjoying a pint. Mick's in his shorts with a bag of nuts and the paper. And here comes Megan. She's got her sketchbook under her arm and some pencils. It looks like she's washed her hair, or brushed it, or done something to it. Or perhaps it's the same but you just see things differently from a distance. It looks nice anyway. She's put herself in a corner, at one remove, the better to weigh up the lounge, to get it down on paper. She might draw herself into the scene, and me as well. She likes to do that, I've noticed. And if she's in a playful mood she'll give me Prince Philip's cane and Kieran's belly; and she'll have herself on the dance floor in Chris's shoes and one of Imelda's tops, dancing around the handbags while the others make a start on their soup. She turns and looks out the window. It seems she's looking right at me, but she can't be, because I'm waving and she's not waving back.

Part 3

Llandudno, Wales

9

Just eat your bread roll and don't touch me

The evening before I was due to go on a coach holiday with my nan to Wales, I spent eleven hours in the company of an Argentinian friend with a broken heart, who was adamant the best way to deal with said heart was a combination of lager, whisky and Chesterfield cigarettes. I regret to say we displayed zero originality in the face of an emotional crisis.

I took the last train from London Waterloo to Portsmouth. I got into bed about 2.30am, still thoroughly poached. I was on all fours groaning into my pillow until about 4am, cursing Argentina, cursing love, cursing the brokenness of all things. I was woken up two hours later by my nan, yodelling through the letterbox. I thought it was a nightmare.

'Hello! Yoo-hoo!'

Oh Jesus flipping fishing hell.

'Benjamin! Yoo-hoo!'

Flipping fat sugar pants.

I move downstairs without grace. I open the door.

'You'd better get dressed, darling. Grandad's waiting.'

I get dressed. I pack a bag. I brush my teeth subconsciously. I ask Nan if I can make a coffee and bring it with me in a mug. She says I can't. We get in the car.

'Hello Ben,' says Grandad.

'Hello Grandad,' I say.

'Everything alright?'

'Yeah. Peachy.'

Then silence. Well, Radio 3. All the way to the pick-up point in Queen Street by the dockyard. They both know what's gone on. My nan would have phoned my dad last night asking if I was in yet. She's not daft. You don't teach her to suck eggs. Oh well. What can I do? She's a bit cross with me but it will pass. Over my lifetime, I've probably spent about two months in my nan's bad books, made up of roughly 30 two-day sentences. You might think from this that my nan's bad books are relatively easy to get out of, but believe me, it doesn't always feel that way. She's not a hard woman, or a strict one, but she has a set of lines and if you cross one, she'll be sure to let you know about it. It's effective governance, in my book. A sort of benign dictatorship. If it weren't for my nan's lines, and my mum's for that matter, I'd probably be in a correction facility right now, instead of this car.

Grandad struggles to park. He always struggles to park. He has to weigh up every option before committing to one. In the end he parks in a bus stop.

'Alright, see you on Friday,' he says.

'Alright, see you on Friday,' she says.

We watch him drive off. Nan looks happy. 'Do you think he'll be alright?' I say.

'No,' she says, smiling and waving.

The steps onto the coach are a bit of a nuisance for Nan. They're quite steep. I turn my back and force her in as if she were a fridge freezer. She's not a big woman, nor is she unwieldy; but now and again, she's partial to a bit of anti-gravitational force. I hadn't noticed the steepness of these steps before. So it goes.

Nan's one of those. Cheerful. She says hello to the driver, to those sat at the front, in the middle, at the back. Morning, morning, morning! Ordinarily this would warm my heart, but today my heart is dumb to cheer, to warmth, to goodness. Were I to witness the most astounding act of kindness, altruism, bravery, wit or sacrifice, it would stir me not. Such is the diminishing, degrading, disheartening impact of a hangover.

'I'm sorry I'm hungover, Nan.'

'Yes, well. Your dad said he spoke to you last night, and couldn't figure out what you were trying to say. Something about Argentina.'

At Petersfield, she says that my uncle lives in a flat behind the school we just went past. I ask what Uncle Matthew was like as a boy. 'Oh, he was naughty,' she says. 'He once invited the local vicar round for dinner without me knowing. When the vicar turned up he said Matthew had invited him for dinner, but I told him we'd already had the dinner and there wasn't anything that could be done to bring it back, not even by a vicar.' I tell her I've not heard the story before. 'Well, we've not been this way together before,' she says.

When we step into the waiting lounge at the interchange, which is packed as usual, Nan says, 'So this is where they all are.' She finds us a spot where she can keep an eye on everything, and I go and buy a pair of coffees, several bananas and a litre of water. On my return, I ask Nan what she knows about Wales.

'Not very much. Harry Secombe was Welsh. So was Tommy Cooper. And there's laverbread of course.'

'I've never heard of such bread,' I say.

'Oh no it's not a bread. It's seaweed.'

'What?'

'It's seaweed.'

'What are you talking about, woman?'

'It's true.'

'So why do they call it bread?'

'I don't know. Do you want me to Google it?'[17]

I know a few things about Wales, but not many. I know that Dylan Thomas line, the one about not going gently into the night, which I take to mean we're to make a fuss about dropping off. I know the Welsh have a thing for leeks, and that Edward I of England built lots of castles in Wales to keep the locals in check. And I know the England and Wales Cricket Board pick a team made up of players from England and Wales and yet the team is called England. That's about it really. Again, I've packed light.

I ask Nan if she can remember where she went for her first holiday. 'It was Somerset,' she says. 'I was three and a half. I went there as an evacuee because our house got bombed. We were lucky, really. We went up the shops and

---

[17] Laverbread is an edible seaweed rich in iodine. The Welsh often serve it with cockles for breakfast. I suppose the thinking is that with a breakfast like that, things can only get better.

when we got back our house wasn't there anymore. My sister started crying, but apparently I thought it was funny.'

When we drive past the Amazon warehouse in Bedfordshire, Nan points to it and says, 'They'll have my book in there one day.' She's working on a history of her life and her family. It will be called *The Daisy Chain*. She's been working on it for years. She's writing it all out by hand. I said years ago that I would transcribe her pages onto a computer as she went. I did a few hours one evening, and haven't done anymore since. God knows what I've been doing that I consider to be more important. Anyway, one thing I remember transcribing was the story of Nan's great-grandmother, who spent her final days in a workhouse with her four children. Nan has a copy of the parish records. The family were registered – in no uncertain terms – as paupers. One of the children, George Pitt Pidsley, became an insurance agent and settled in Portsmouth, where he met Nellie Eliza Tharle and got down to business. This was in 1874, which is where I got up to with my transcribing. Perhaps I felt I didn't have another 150 years in me.

I never met my nan's dad, Wilfred Parsons, but I did meet my nan's mum, Olive Parsons. She died when I was about eight. I didn't think much of her to be honest. I mean that literally. I didn't give her much thought. I wish I'd had the maturity and curiosity to pay Olive more attention, to show her more love, to wonder about her life, but I was eight at the time and my world revolved around Sonic the Hedgehog and firing foam bullets at my brother. The only thing I can do to atone for my indifference to Olive, perhaps, is to make sure that any eight year olds I come to acquire know everything there is to know about their great-grandparents, whether they like it or not.

I ask about Wilfred Parsons, my great-grandfather. Nan says that he wasn't called up to fight at the start of the Second World War because his present employment – the building of undercarriages – was vital to the war effort, but then his luck changed and he was sent out to Africa to lay roads. 'And it was during his time in Africa,' says Nan, 'that Olive took up with an old flame. The old flame was a Catholic, and Olive was a Protestant, but that didn't appear to bother them. The Catholic came around to the house a few times, but my sister and I didn't like it so it didn't happen anymore. I dare say they found somewhere else to meet though. She knew what she enjoyed, my mother.'

It's funny when people talk about the past. How they move from one thing to another, how they leap across decades, at odd angles. Because now Nan says, 'When Olive was dying, when she was right at the end, I went to the nursing home with your mum, and we sat on either side of the bed, talking to her, saying that we loved her, things like that. She obviously didn't think much of what we were saying because she did that thing with her hand [the gesture that approximates a mouth opening and closing, to indicate that someone's going on and on …]. We had to laugh. All she wanted was a fizzy drink. That was her dying wish. I read her favourite psalm. "The Lord is my Shepherd". And then I told her it's okay, she can go now. And she did. Mr Kelly, the director of the nursing home, brought a bottle of red wine in. He raised a toast. "To Olive. Who now knows what we don't." And then she suddenly shot up! It was all the gases in her body. All that fizzy drink. Apparently it happens. Your mum spilt her wine.'

It's also funny what people ask, what they want to know. Having been told of my deceased great-grandmother shooting up in bed, my question is: 'Did you like Olive?' My nan doesn't remember being asked that before. She says, 'I loved her. But I didn't always like her.' I ask why that was. 'She didn't seem to care. I was five years old and it was two miles to school. "Off you go," she said. And then when I was a bit older, eight or nine, I'd go off with my friend Molly into the fields. We'd pack jam sandwiches and be gone for hours. When I'd get home she wouldn't say a word. She wouldn't have even noticed. I can't say I didn't enjoy the freedom, but I wish she hadn't been so *hard*. Her mother – my grandmother – was very different. She was a real softie. I remember one time she swallowed her own teeth.'[18]

After each stop at a service station, Nan returns to the coach with new gossip. She seems to be a very effective gatherer of the stuff. So-and-so has twenty grandchildren. So-and-so will

---

[18] That was only half the story, it turned out. My nan's nan, Nellie Eliza, fell down the stairs, broke her neck, and died. Her teeth were never discovered, so it was assumed she'd swallowed them. She was put out to rest in the kitchen, with her mouth strapped shut with a tea towel. Then someone came round to plug all my great-great-grandmother's openings. Of all the elements of this tragic occasion, my nan chose only to mention that a pair of teeth were swallowed.

only drink loose leaf tea because she reckons she can taste the bag. So-and-so has the same Kindle as me but doesn't appear to know how to operate it. On each occasion – at each services – she is only out of my sight a couple of minutes, and according to her, only spending a penny, and yet her gossip haul is reliably large. Had she not trained as a nurse before getting into cleaning big houses, she might have served her country well as a stool pigeon or double agent or whatever. I dare say she'd still be an effective spy now. Indeed, she might even be a *more* effective spy now, seeing as she's unlikely to attract much attention by straining to hear.

At Corley services, two familiar faces join us. It's Dennis and Clem, who I met in Scarborough. It was Dennis who told me not to bother paying for a sea view. I give it ten minutes then go and say hello.

'Clem thought it was you,' says Dennis. 'Didn't you, love? You thought it was Ben. I said don't be daft, he wouldn't do it twice. Who's that with you?'

'That's my girlfriend.'

'Well you're punching above your weight, let me tell you.'

'It's my nan.'

'Is that right? You know, the only other person we've seen twice on a Shearings is Mrs Greggs. To be fair, you couldn't miss her. We called her Mrs Greggs because the coach hadn't finished parking before she was in Greggs buying a couple of pies and a Chelsea bun. Anyway, you'd better sit down before your nan thinks you're organising a foursome.'

17.00. Flintshire, north-east Wales. We're on the A55, which connects Chester in the east to Holyhead in the west.

Our driver, Tim, says the road was funded by the EU, and wonders whether we should tell it to pack its bags and sling its hook. And then, as we approach the town of Llandudno, and people start to shuffle happily at the prospect of arrival and dinner and maybe a glass of wine, Tim says that it should be borne in mind that free bus travel doesn't apply in Wales. This announcement is met with boos and tuts, and the odd four-letter word. Had Tim announced that all grandchildren were to be sacrificed by a group of Welsh druids next weekend, it's hard to imagine this lot being any more distraught.

The County Hotel is on the seafront. When we pull up outside, a hotel employee called Eva gets on. She sounds at once Polish and Scouse. She promises to keep it short and sweet and then goes on at some length about what's for dinner (laverbread and cockles), what's planned for this evening (bingo and singing), and what time our medication will be administered. I find this last joke offensive, but nobody else seems to – it goes down very well in fact. I've said it before but it's worth repeating: these old numpties don't know when they're being victimised.

Nan's in 318 and I'm in 317. The lift takes two at a time. It's explained to us that the two-person limit was introduced last summer, after a gentleman in a mobility scooter inexplicably attempted to drive into the lift when several people were already in it. I unpack and have a short doze, then go next door to check on Nan. She's happy with the room but is a tad worried about the bath. She reckons the last time she had a bath she couldn't get out. I tell her to stop underestimating her abilities. 'I promise you, darling. I couldn't get out. I had to yell for Grandad. But he was watching the golf with the volume right up. I was in there for two hours.' I ask what happened two hours later. 'Tiger Woods won,' she says.

The waitress explains that, as we booked late, our table's a bit out of the way. I don't mind, and nor does Nan. She can see more from here, and if she cranks her hearing aids up, she can still deduce the thrust of just about every conversation going on in the room. And there's a fair few. The dining room is packed – there are three coach loads in this week. We've got a table for four to ourselves, so we sit next to each other rather than opposite, so we can see the same thing. Nan thinks everyone is looking at her.

'Why are they all being so nosey?' she says.

'Because a bowl of soup and a partner of 50 years are only so interesting, Nan.'

'Yes, well.'

'They're probably not looking anyway.'

'They are. You'd think they'd never seen a …'

'Seen a what?

'Oh dear.'

'What?'

'They must think you're my toy boy.'

'Oh sod off, Nan.'

'I'm not joking. It's what I would think.'

'Would you?'

'They probably think I'm being exploited.'

'What?'

JUST EAT YOUR BREAD ROLL AND DON'T TOUCH ME

'They think you're after my money.'

'Oh steady on, Nan. You're making me uncomfortable.'

'Just eat your bread roll and don't touch me.'

It's the taste and smell of dried oregano I most associate with Nan. When it comes to cooking, I mean. She used to put loads of it in her bolognaise. It was one part mince to two parts oregano, as far as I can remember. For her 80th birthday I got her eight grandchildren to each remember ten things about their nan – small things that have stayed with them over the years. I put all the memories into a block of text, colour-coded them, and then made it look nice and printed it out and framed it and so on. It amused me how many of the memories were food-based. My cousin Beth, who is 24, remembers most of all that Nan would always make her a bowl of plain pasta with cheese because she was fussy. My brother remembers the homemade carbonated drinks. I remember all the oregano I could possibly hope for. I enjoyed putting the thing together. It was nice just to sit down and remember.

Not all my food memories relating to Nan are positive, mind you. When I was a student, she would send me off at the beginning of each university term with a box of stuff from the back of her cupboard. Trouble is, she had quite a deep cupboard at the time, and quite a relaxed attitude to expiration dates. I recall half a jar of Maxwell House coffee which passed its best in 1993 – a good fifteen years before it wound up in my philanthropy box. When I mentioned this to my nan years later, she said it was to build up my immune system.

I ask what food Nan remembers from the 40s and 50s. She says there was lots of stew, and lots of soup, and bread and dripping, and—

'Bread and dripping?'

'Yeah.'

'Is that a pudding? Like bread and butter pudding?'

'No, darling, it's not a pudding. It's the soft fat that forms when the juices from a piece of meat have cooled and solidified.'

'Then what do you with that?'

'Eat it.'

'Are you winding me up?'

'No.'

'Did you lot have a death wish?'

'It wasn't that unhealthy. We had bread with it.'

'And did you eat out much?'

'What do you mean? Picnics and such?'

'No, restaurants.'

'Restaurants? There weren't any. I wish I could take you to the 1940s, Ben – I think you'd learn a thing or two.'

'There goes two gays,' says Nan during her plum and apple sponge.

'Sorry?'

She nods towards two women, who have just got up from their table and left the dining room. 'I should like to talk to them,' she says.

'Would you?'

'They're bound to be interesting.'

'What makes you think that?'

'Well, all gay people are interesting.'

As I'm wondering if it's offensive to suggest that all gay people are interesting, Nan continues:

'There's a lovely gay man at the hairdressers I go to,' she says. 'Lovely as anything. Though I'm not sure about them adopting.'

This has to stop. 'Aren't the curtains nice, Nan?'

'I'm sure they would be wonderful parents, but the child would surely be teased.'

'This melon is excellent.'

'I'm all for them getting married though. In a church or wherever they want. After all, a woman who is twice divorced can hardly go on about the sanctity of marriage.'

It's nice to talk to Nan like this. Not necessarily *about* this – the hypothetical bullying of children with gay parents – but like this, at this pace, in this way, somewhat off the cuff, somewhat ad hoc, just chewing the fat, just riffing off our shared perspective. It's unhurried and meandering. Not that talking with Nan is normally hurried or monotonous. I'm not saying that. It's just that normally when I see Nan it's at her house, an environment we're both quite familiar with. There are no potentially gay couples in Nan's living room. So the conversation, although nearly always pleasant and enjoyable and what have you, tends not to go off in unlikely directions – towards homosexuality, say, or bread and dripping. What's more, when I visit Nan, the spotlight is usually on me, the visiting grandchild. Same goes for my cousins, I'm sure. She wants to know how school is, how university is, where I got those trousers from, what I think my sister is playing at, and so on. To my shame, I don't often redirect the spotlight in her direction. But sat here like this, next to each other in the dining room of a Welsh hotel, looking out above the heads and across the tables, out towards the Irish Sea, our minds wandering, independently but somehow aligned, until one of those minds catches something and turns to the other and says, 'There goes two gays,' well, I kind of like it. Anyway, she's back with her coffee.

'No skimmed milk,' she says. 'Perhaps they don't have the technology in Wales.'

Downstairs is a 'ballroom'. In effect, it is a bar and lounge with a small stage and dance floor, but in name it is a ball-room, and for that reason alone we resolve to pop down for a quick one. At first, Nan suggests that we sit separately to avoid stoking the rumours, but then comes to her senses. We're just in time for the bingo, which will be called by the resident entertainer, Jim, who doesn't waste much time before sharing his life story. To be fair, his CV is rather succinct: I used to be a Marine, now I call bingo. He doesn't give any more detail, just leaves it there. Which is fair enough, I suppose.

Not long into the first game, I realise that whenever I get a number Nan doesn't, and vice versa. I think that's how they print the tickets. If you buy two, all 90 numbers will be split between them. It's a shame because it means we can never both be happy. Or maybe that's not right, because Nan seems pretty pleased no matter what number comes up. In fact, she even gets visibly excited when I go on a roll, even though this means she's doing totally rubbish. This doesn't surprise me. Not really. I know for a fact that Nan would rather I won the bingo than her. And perhaps that's just her, her personality, though I wouldn't be surprised if it has something to do with her age, for it seems to me that the longer we live, the less self-important we become, the less competitive. Or maybe not. Maybe I'm jumping the gun a touch regarding Nan's age-related altruism, because I can see now – just after the end of the second game – that her selflessness only extends up to a point. With me out of the running early in that second game, Nan very nearly went on to get the win. She was one short. When the winner got up to collect his cash prize, Nan turned to me and said, quite seriously, 'I don't like him.'

We call it a night after the bingo. I'm sure Jim sings like an angel, but that will have to wait for another night. I walk Nan to her room – I'm a gentleman like that – then watch something in Welsh while I do my teeth. I can hear Nan next door on the phone, chatting away to someone. Within a minute of her finishing the call, I get a text message from my mum. 'Hi was just on phone to Nan. She thinks they all think you're her toy boy. Have fun and tell them she's your nan! xx'.

10

Ask your mother while you can

When I enter Nan's bedroom at 8.45am she's nowhere to be seen and the window's open. Just when I'm thinking I must have said something wrong and she's gone and absconded on me, she emerges from the bathroom and says, 'I can't find my teeth – have you seen my glasses?' If our holiday were to end here and now, I would go home satisfied it was a good and momentous one, if only for that single question.

I didn't go into Nan's room to see if she was there, but for toothpaste. I get the toothpaste then return to my room and brush my teeth watching BBC Breakfast. Dan Walker, the show's co-anchor, is in the midst of an announcement: 'So that's the lesson for today, folks. Ask someone if they're okay.'

Religion is the morning's topic of conversation. It started when I asked Nan if she believed in God. She asked why I was asking, and I said I'd seen a man cross himself before starting on his porridge. Nan says that she used to be religious, even going so far as to arrange her own baptism at the age of seventeen. She remained quite devoted to her church until she was kicked out for getting pregnant outside of wedlock. Turns out, Reverend Sparks grew concerned when my Uncle Michael arrived six months after Sparks had married my nan (to my grandad, that is), and it's fair to say

Michael hadn't come by plane. Sparks cornered my nan after a Sunday service and asked if the baby had been premature. Nan didn't much like what he was getting at, so replied, 'No, he was two weeks late actually.' Sparks responded by saying that he would have to discuss Nan's membership of the church with the congregation. When he did so, it was decided that Nan was no longer fit for purpose. 'So I washed my hands of the church,' she says, 'and haven't been in one since.' Go, sister.

We're gathered in reception, waiting for the minibus that's going to zip us around town. A man is asking the receptionist if she could arrange for someone to help him with something, but the receptionist says she's not in a position to do so, and encourages the man to visit the hospital, perhaps by taxi. It doesn't look to me that the man's in the mood for doing what he's been told, not least because he's joined the group waiting for the minibus, and is whistling a little tune and tapping his walking stick.

'Are you okay?' I say.

'Hm?'

'I heard you at reception asking for help with something.'

'Oh!'

It transpires that Patrick needs help with his eyedrops each evening. He can't manage easily on his own because he's blind in one eye and can't raise either arm above the shoulder. And nor, I presume, can he get his eyes below the shoulder and facing upwards.

'So you just need someone to put the eyedrops in?'

'Yes, that's it. My wife used to do it, but recently my neighbour's been dropping in, if you'll excuse the pun. And I don't need to explain that my neighbour isn't so obliging that she's prepared to move to Llandudno to continue doing so.'

'I can do it.'

'Can you?'

'I reckon so.'

'Well that's settled then.'

During our little tour of town, driver Owen fills us in. He starts with a word about the conception of Llandudno. It's pleasingly put. 'Purpose-built Victorian resort. The arrival of the railway useful to this end. The promenade's two kilometres long and if you're caught dropping a fag it's a twenty quid fine.' At the western end of that promenade, Owen asks us to consider the Grand Hotel, which is 'positioned, as you can see, at the foot of the Great Orme, so-called because the Great and Little Ormes plus the land in between resemble a worm in Old Norse.' While we try to decode this, Owen continues up and round to Happy Valley, a popular little park, of which he has this to say: 'Unlike the Grand Hotel, Happy Valley is a misnomer in my book – I broke up with my girlfriend here and had a fight with my cousin the same afternoon. The two weren't related.'

Happy Valley is decorated with characters from *Alice in Wonderland*. The couple that Nan has earmarked as homosexual (which is a sentence I never thought I'd have to write) nip out to pose with the Cheshire Cat. Nan certainly likes the look of the place. She didn't realise Llandudno had a connection with Alice, while I didn't realise Nan was such an

Alice fan. 'Oh yes,' she says. 'I read them as a girl, and then again recently. Your Auntie Jo is having an Alice-themed party for her 50th. I'm going as a playing card.'

Owen points out where Lewis Carroll would sit at the top of the park. 'He sat there in order to come up with his books,' says Owen. 'Then this Alice girl turned up and started larking about on her own. Mr Carroll obviously saw some potential in the girl, because he just sat there watching her for three days. He was lucky to be living in more tolerant times, because if I did something similar today I'd be put on the rack until I agreed I ought to use a different park.'[19]

Above Happy Valley is a dry ski slope, one of two in the region. Owen recommends the slope to anyone who's 'still got their original joints'. He says the same applies for the toboggan run, which at 750 metres, must surely be one of the 'longest superfluities' in the country. Nan's bold enough to ask what a superfluity is. 'A waste of time,' says Owen.

Next to the ski slope is the base of the cable car conveyance. From here you can ride up to the summit of the Great Orme. It was built in 1969. There's been one tragedy of note. In 2007, a 33-year-old Polish woman jumped out and fell a fatal distance onto the rocks below. The last thing she

---

[19] I read *Alice in Wonderland* for the first time not long ago. Delicious nonsense. Although a trifle ageist. This is Alice contemplating the prospect of getting stuck at the age of seven: 'That'll be a comfort, one way – never to be an old woman – but then – always to have lessons to learn! Oh, I shouldn't like *that!*' Alice sees that the price of youth is ignorance, and the reward of maturity is knowledge.

said to her mother was that she was going out for milk. Of all the things I might think of given this information, I think of Dan Walker.

We don't take the cable car to the summit. Instead, we are driven there. When we get out it's somewhat disappointing to see that there's not much to see. The mist has seen to that. It's an absolute pea-souper. Owen had whetted our appetite irresponsibly by saying that 'on a clear day, you can see as far as Bolton, and with it Fred Dibnah up a chimney'. Someone remarks, unfairly I feel, that they never believed it would come as a blow not to be able to see Bolton.

The first time I saw this grassy summit was on telly. It was a rerun of a *Two Fat Ladies* episode, which was filmed in the town. The titular ladies were Jennifer Paterson and Clarissa Dickson Wright, a pair of chefs. As well as chefs, they were sizeable, posh, garrulous, far from spring chickens and not in the habit of counting calories. They were prone to topping cake with cake, and stuffing birds with caramel and bonbons. I remember finding the ladies exceptionally entertaining. They seemed to me to have more charisma and wit and personality in their bunions than today's TV chefs have between them. In the Llandudno episode, they are tasked with producing a picnic for a local male voice choir. They do a Welsh lamb pie, a leek and potato soup, and baguettes filled with peppers, olives, tomatoes and anchovies. Jennifer considers the latter to be a delicious addition to the picnic, 'despite its vegetarian overtones'. The two fat ladies wouldn't survive on television today, I dare say; they'd be hauled off for offense to vegetarians, or for fat shaming, regardless of the fact that any questionable quips or cheeky slips of the tongue were atoned for tenfold with genuine *joie de vivre* and skill and charm and warmth; and no matter that between the pair of them they clearly had about as much malice as a bowl of custard – no, forget all that, off with them, the impolite, incorrect devils, may they be banished to Mantua, or BBC 3.

Clarissa and Jennifer would have done something nice with the wild goats roundabout I'm sure. They're scattered all over the summit, precariously tip-toeing among the rocks, a mile above the sea, thinking nothing of it. Goat numbers are controlled by use of contraception, says Owen, 'which doesn't bear – or baa – thinking about.' While I'm bearing thinking about goat contraception, Owen says that we should also watch out for shags. This gets a few knowing laughs, but not from me. Owen lets me stew in my own thoughts for a bit then explains that the Orme and its cliffs are home to lots of seabirds including cormorants, guillemots, razorbills, puffins, kittiwakes, fulmars and, yes, shags. Owen asks what I had in mind, which gets a laugh from the rest of the group. I'm glad Nan headed straight for the toilet, and didn't have to witness any of this.[20]

There's a visitor centre at the summit. I find Nan in the giftshop. As she peruses, I flick through a joke book. There's

---

[20] As if it wasn't enough that these goats are forced to use contraception, I discovered another rum fact about them. Each year, The Royal Welsh, a large regiment in the British Army, is obligated to choose an animal from the herd and make it an honorary Lance Corporal. I'm just going to leave that there.

one about a Welshman stranded on an island who builds two churches from banana leaves. When the Welshman is finally rescued, he is asked about the churches. The Welshman says: 'That's the one I go to, and that's the one I don't.' I wish there wasn't some truth in this daft illustration of how identity is as much about what we aren't as what we are, but there you go.

At the bottom of the Great Orme, on the south side, the Bishops of Bangor used to live in a fancy palace. As far as Owen can remember, the bishops were put in place by the King of England, which can't have made it easy for them to get on with the locals, who were Celts, and not in the habit of receiving visitors lying down (just ask the Romans). In 1400, one local in particular decided he'd had enough of the English in Wales, and so set about ruffling some feathers. His name was Owain Glyndŵr, and his backlash chiefly involved declaring himself Prince of Wales and pinching a few castles. Owain's rebellion lasted for another ten years or so, at which point he fled to the mountains and hid in a cave, which is where he remains. 'But you might want to check up on some of those details,' says Owen. 'If not all of them.'[21]

---

[21] I watched a BBC documentary fronted by a young Huw Edwards. It told the story of Owain Glyndŵr. It was a wholly engaging programme, made comic at times by the automated subtitles, which struggled to render Owain's name each time Huw mentioned it. I made a list of how Owain Glyndŵr was represented in text at the bottom of the screen, because I clearly had nothing better to do. Here it is: oh inland duel, glynn doon, a wine glyn dude, Glinda, Linder, our England or Wales, Noah and Linda were, ginn do, endure, hinder, blender, and

Within an hour of Owen's tour finishing, we're back on the coach with Tim and heading west to the island of Anglesey, which sits off the country's north-west coast. I don't know anything about the place other than Prince William used to live there and it can be reached by two bridges. We cross via the younger of the two, the Britannia. At its far end, Tim encourages us to get off for a picture. It's undeniably an attractive vista, with the older suspension bridge in the near distance, and the verdant banks on either side, and the tricky water of the Menai Strait beneath. But what I like – and what I photograph – is the others looking, taking, capturing. Most of the present paparazzi were born under an Edward or a George, and here they are snapping a bridge put up under a Victoria (if that's not too awkward a construction), as well as the dashing river below, that was put down by no man or monarch, but rather given by the grace of geological chance. Patrick has a nifty digital camera. You'd think he was a millennial the amount of time he spends checking the images, fiddling with his haul, doctoring his shots – something of a perfectionist. When he returns to the coach, I ask if he got something nice. 'Fifteen self-portraits by the look of it, so I'd say yes!'

We drive for fifteen minutes or so then pull up at RAF Valley – where jet and helicopter pilots are trained. This is where Prince William lived for a few years, and Kate Middleton also. They were occasionally spotted in the local

---

my personal favourite, given that Owain was a Welsh freedom fighter, oh England dude.

Waitrose considering kiwis. This information causes a few intakes of breath, as if shopping in Waitrose were beneath a prince. Then someone asks, quite sincerely, whether it's possible to stop at the Waitrose on the way home.

Tim says Waitrose is out of the question because our next and final stop is Llanfairpwllgwyngyllgogerychwyrnd robwllllantysiliogogogoch, a small town (ironically) near the Britannia Bridge. There's a train station, a small department store, and a chip shop. Nan's quite at home in the department store, sashaying between sections like a dancer around a ballroom, toying with this, fingering that, flirting with the other. She buys a bar of chocolate whose wrapper says BEST GRANDSON.

'You didn't have to do that, Nan.'

'I didn't do that, it's for Oliver.'

I take a picture of Nan on the train station platform, under the sign with the longest place name in the UK on it. Everyone's doing it. Tim said we might want to do it, and it turns out we did. Tim also said that Llanfairpwllgwyngyll gogerychwyrndrobwllllantysiliogogogoch is only the second longest place name in the world, which invites the question as to which is the longest.[22]

---

[22] Taumatawhakatangihangakoauauotamateaturipukakapikimaunga horonukupokaiwhenuakitanatahu is the longest place name in the world. Translated literally from Maori, it means The-Summit-Where-Tamatea-The-Man-With-The-Big-Knees, The-Climber-Of-Mountains, The-Land-Swallower-Who-Travelled-About, Played-His-Nose-Flute-To-His-Loved-One. Fancy typing that into your satnav.

With ten minutes to kill, I nip across to the local chippy. The lady inside is dealing with everyone in Welsh, which is lovely to hear. When she gets to me, I reply to her jolly and mysterious icebreaker by hesitating for some time and then pointing in the direction of the chips. '*Siaradwch, chi fabi gwirion Saesneg,*' she says, which I assume has to do with salt and vinegar. I nod twice, one for each. But nothing happens. All the other punters are enjoying the standoff. In the end she bags me up some chips with an amused huff and then refuses payment, saying '*Peidiwch â bod yn dod yn ôl i mewn ar gyfer eich cinio,*' which, given the name of this town, might well mean goodbye. Leaving the chip shop, I'm sure I pass in the doorway the lad who played Elton John in *Rocketman*.[23]

Nan takes a phone call from my Auntie Jo after her main course. Turns out Jo was after some advice regarding the *Alice in Wonderland* party, something to do with painting white roses red. I ask Nan if she and Jo have always got along. She says that they have for the most part, and adds that one or two traumatic episodes strengthened their relationship when Jo was quite young, namely when she suffered two ectopic pregnancies in her late teens. While I eat my turnover and cream, Nan describes how Jo went to the hospital complaining of abdominal pain but was sent home and told it was constipation. Apparently my mum kept an eye on Jo that night and saw that her arms wouldn't stop shaking, and insisted Nan took her back to the hospital. Jo was kept in overnight,

---

[23] Could be true. Taron Egerton went to school in the town.

during which time her temperature rocketed and her heart rate plummeted – and you know it's an emergency when things are rocketing and plummeting. Fortunately – in fact, thank f*ck – a nurse noticed that Jo was rocketing and plummeting and got the surgeon out of bed. Had she not done so, says Nan, Jo might well have died. This happened twice, and it left my auntie feeling a bit rubbish, and not wanting kids anymore. I think two ectopic pregnancies is enough to put you off the idea. But the desire for children never really left her, and after several attempts she gave birth to the first set of twins conceived through in vitro fertilisation (IVF). The doctor that assisted my auntie was Robert Winston, who got famous after he did a telly program on the BBC. Those twins – who knew nothing of all this at the time; embryos are nothing if not navel-gazing – are Beth and William, a gorgeous bubbly pair that are easy to tell apart. William's in construction and Beth's a nurse. I hope she keeps an eye out for any rocketing or plummeting when she's doing her rounds, and isn't scared to wake the surgeon up. My mum was also a nurse, and so was Nan at one point. Either our genes are inclined to caring, or lack imagination.

The theme of childbirth somehow survives through pudding and into coffee. Nan says that her mum lost her first baby during its delivery. She remembers that her father built a little white coffin for the child, but that she has no idea where her brother was buried. 'I wish I'd asked my mother,' she says. 'In fact, I cannot forgive myself for not asking her.' Then she points at me with her spoon and says, 'Ask your mother while you can. No matter the question.'

Listening to Nan talk about these things, something becomes clear to me: the extent to which this woman has lived for, and in the service of, her family. To do so, for her, I can see, has been instinctive and unquestionable. Her family is her instinct – her hope, her fear, her happy, her sad. It's the chocolate bar for Oliver. It's the present in the post for her great-granddaughter Annabelle. It's the white roses she'll order so Jo can paint them red. It is a good luck message for Daisy, my sister. It is – I regret to say – my survival boxes when I was at university. It is her never failing to phone and sing on a birthday. It's her lines, her bad books, her disappointed looks – they all exist because she cares. I'm seeing all this clearly now because I'm seeing her clearly now. The waiter asks Nan what she made of the cake. 'Lovely,' she says. 'My mother did a good roly-poly. Thank you.'

Patrick's room is under the stairs – like Harry Potter's. He has left the door ajar. We knock and enter. He's sat at the end of his bed, the better to see the television. He's pleased to see us – or pretends to be at least.

'You're looking well,' says Nan.

'Oh don't say that, Janet. When Ibsen was on his deathbed his nurse said he was looking well and he promptly died.'

'Oh,' says Nan.

Patrick passes me the drops and then looks at the ceiling. Standing over him, it occurs to me that I hadn't expected to be doing this at the start of the week. I squeeze the little bottle; it's more resistant than you might think. I miss Patrick's right eye but it's okay because some of it goes in the left.

Patrick calls jokingly for Janet to take over, but I tell him I have to learn and one only learns by missing the target now and then. At the next attempt, I get a decent drop in each eye, and a bit on his nose and chin, which encourages Patrick to ask of Janet whether it has miraculously started to rain indoors. Then he has a laugh at my expense by pretending to dry his face with the hairdryer.

'No, seriously though, did enough go in?' I say.

'Oh yes, plenty. Good as new.'

Then Nan asks, impertinently I feel, what Patrick does for a living.

'Oh, Janet!' he says. 'It's kind of you to imply otherwise, but it's been many years since I did anything for a living. When I *was* doing something for a living, I mostly did it in the suburbs of Cheltenham.'

I'm happy to leave it there, to make my own mind up as to what Patrick got up to in the suburbs of Cheltenham, but Nan presses for more detail.

'I worked at GCHQ [Government Communications HQ],' says Patrick, 'and I'm afraid if I told you much more than that, Janet, I'd have to kill you.'

I ask Patrick if he fancies joining us for bingo, down in the ballroom.

'Oh I couldn't possibly.'

'You'll be alright. It's easy.'

'No, I mean I couldn't possibly get down those stairs!'

We share a table with Barbara and Keith from Cumbria for the bingo, which proves fruitless. Less fruitless is the company of said Cumbrians. I'm interested to learn that Keith was employed in an iron works all his life, and that Barbara's a big Tom Jones fan. She remembers a concert in the 70s when all the girls were throwing their knickers on the stage.

'I wasn't, of course,' says Barbara.

'No,' says Keith, 'because you didn't have any on.'

Then Barbara gets a message from her daughter saying she's got no nappies left. I ask whether Barbara's daughter shouldn't be out of them by now, but either I can't be heard over the music or my remark isn't considered appropriate, for nobody responds. Anyway, Nan and Barbara start talking about nappies and don't stop for about half an hour. They talk about methods of washing them back in the day, how they wouldn't dare hang up a stained one, and how modern mothers would go on strike if they had to do it like Nan and Barbara had to do it. Having grown somewhat comfortable with each other, Barbara confesses to Nan that she thought I was her toy boy. 'I was watching you at the bar,' she says to me. 'I thought, "I wonder if they're in a twin or a double."'

Just as I'm worrying that our chat might have run its course, Keith comes out with something that breathes new life into our double date. He says he races pigeons.

'What?'

'I race pigeons.'

'How?'

'How do you enter?'

'How do they race for heaven's sake? *What* do they race?'

'Other pigeons, of course.'

'And where do they race? Not on a track?'

'Yeah, on a track. They do the 400 metre hurdles.'

'So not on a track?'

'Not on a track.'

'So where?'

'Well, the last one started in Barcelona.'

'Barcelona? So you took your pigeon to Barcelona so it could—'

'I didn't go to Barcelona.'

'So it went by itself?'

'No, it went with the other pigeons.'

'Are you pulling my leg?'

'Why should I be?'

'So did they fly or catch the train?'

'They go by road.'

'They drive?'

'They're transported.'

'And then your pigeon races some other pigeons?'

'Thousands of pigeons.'

'And each pigeon has a different … coach?'

'No, they go in the same vehicle.'

'No coach as in trainer.'

'Yeah, yeah. Different trainer.'

'And each coach …'

'Trains their pigeon to fly home.'

'Now just how the f*ck do you train a pigeon to fly home?'

'You've got to put the hours in.'

'Yeah, but doing what?'

'Good question,' says Barbara.

'First you have to locate where their home is.'

'Cumbria, right?'

'Yeah but the pigeon's home might be elsewhere.'

'What?'

'It's called one-loft racing. The organisers choose a location, and then the pigeons share a loft.'

'Share a loft?'

'Yeah.'

'They sound like hipsters. And then?'

'And then the pigeons learn to return to that particular home, to that loft, to that finish line.'

'How?'

'You take them out a bit further each day. And then when the pigeons have developed a strong sense of home, they're taken to the start line.'

'Barcelona?'

'In this case, yeah. The pigeons are taken to Barcelona and then released and the winning pigeon is the one that gets home the quickest.'

'And do you go to Barcelona?'

'No. I wait at the finish line, with all the other racers.'

'For how long?'

'Until the pigeons arrive.'

'And how long can that take?'

'A few days.'

'Do you have an understanding wife?'

'No.'

'And what's the prize?'

'I won 40 quid once.'

'Keith. Please tell me you're joking.'

Keith sighs. Then he leans in and looks me square in the eye. 'There's no better feeling,' he says, 'than seeing your pigeon on the horizon.'

And at that moment, and with that declaration, I decide there really is no accounting for taste.

11

Alexa, find Facebook, says Nan

Our first port of call for the day is Betws-y-coed, a pictur-esque town that sits in the Conwy Valley, beneath the hills and mountains of Snowdonia. After being put down outside the post office, Nan and I wander over to the visitor centre to watch a film about the local area. I don't mean to be dis-respectful to its creators, but the best part of the film is when Nan turns to me and says: 'I saw the pigeon racer at break-fast. To look at him, you wouldn't think he did something like that.' After the film, we take a quick look at the River Llugwy and the modest waterfall there, before returning to the coach via the village green, where a puppy called Bilbo is currently being chased by its elderly owner. When Nan pops to the ladies, Patrick approaches out of nowhere.

'Same time tonight?' he says, looking away from me.

'Sure.'

'You remember the number?'

'Under the stairs, right?'

He nods and then walks away, and I'm left feeling like something illicit just happened.

Approaching the old slate town of Blaenau Ffestiniog, the scenery changes planet. Instead of fields and woodland, there's a landscape of slate – hills of it, dunes of it, a very sea of the stuff. The local slate industry boomed after the Great Fire of London in 1666, because all of a sudden, everyone needed a roof. Oakley's quarry was the biggest in the area, employing 6,000 men. 'I say men but there were lads as young as twelve working in the mines and quarries,' says Tim. 'They'd do 60-hour weeks and be expected to die at 38, which is certainly something to think about the next time you moan about the demise of British industry.'

We pass through Blaenau and continue to Porthmadog, a small coastal town which grew up to serve the local slate industry. It was from here that the slate would be sent by boat to wherever it was wanted. It was big business while it lasted, but nowadays the town relies on the likes of us to tick over. It won't be getting much off the man Nan's talking to however. He's refusing to look around anymore shops or have another coffee. He's rejected his wife's claim that all shops are different, and that every coffee is unique, and is standing his ground in the car park. He says his wife likes to say that a hot drink is like a river, in that you can't step into the same one twice. He says that he wishes coffee was a river because at least then he could fish in it. He also says he wishes they had some grandchildren with them, like Nan does. He says he's not short of grandchildren, nor is he short of great-grandchildren, though you'd be forgiven for think-ing otherwise, so rarely do they pop over. He sums up his great-grandchildren thus: the boys are boys and the girls are angels. To my mind, the man's summary is a bit reductive, but I suppose it's not for me to tell great-grandparents how to advertise their descendants.

I take Nan to the Royal Sportsman Hotel for lunch. Upon our arrival, I unnecessarily inform the barman that I stayed at the hotel when I was retracing the journey taken by Bill Bryson in *Notes from a Small Island*. While Nan looks on proudly as I regale these details, the barman gets the wrong end of the stick and phones the owner, who is at Tesco, and tells him that Mr Bryson is at the hotel. The owner rushes back in time to see Nan and I making a start on our lunch. I watch a look of disappointment unfold on the owner's face as he realises that neither Nan nor I are Bill Bryson. To his credit, he is magnanimous enough to come over and ask how the rarebit is. In the loo of the Sportsman about five minutes later, I find myself facing the wall alongside a lad called Ron who's also on the Llandudno holiday. As we do our business, I say I'm thinking of Eastbourne next. Ron says, 'Don't mention Eastbourne, or you'll get me excited.'

Heading back to the carpark, we run into Patrick. He and Nan link up for a stretch, while I walk behind. It's a nice prospect, the pair of them ambling along, enjoying a bit of back and forth about Cheltenham or the fine weather or how good it is to be alive or the circular nature of all things or how nice it is to be able to put one foot in front of another and so on until one has got somewhere. That's how I imagine their chat. In the event, when I overtake the pair, on the lovely stone bridge that crosses Porthmadog harbour, I hear Patrick say, 'So in conclusion, Janet, I won't be buying *those* crisps again.'

We take a ride on a steam train, from Porthmadog to Blaenau, where Tim will meet us with the coach. This stretch of railway was laid 150 years ago so slate could be carted down from the quarries at Blaenau. Now it carts a different load – often as dense – back and forth for a laugh. It's a terrific course: a steady, turning climb north-east, through forests and hills, by villages and meadows, through that lovely sweet countryside caught so well by the paintings of Rob Piercy. And what's more, there's no commentary. As much as I'm a fan of Tim and just about everything that exits (and indeed enters) his mouth, it's nice to just sit and watch and not listen. It's nice to just gander the flat sands of Cardigan Bay; a glistening cemetery; a gardener in Penrhyn who stops what they're doing to stand up straight and wave happily at the passing coincidence. I wave back at the gardener enthusiastically, and compare my cheerful reaction to how I behaved when I last rode this railway, just a few years ago.[24] Just beyond Minffordd, we come to a halt beside a run of back gardens. The back walls are made of slate tiles, piles of them like black-grey books. Along the top of one wall are a few old boots, sprouting flowers. 'Nice to see flowers in odd places,' says Nan.

When the refreshment trolley comes by, the ladies next to us, Val and Deborah (Madonna and child), inform the trolley that if they were any more refreshed they'd get gout. Nan takes confidence from this remark and leans across the aisle to say, 'Aren't the noises nice?' Val and Deborah both agree that they are, despite probably not knowing what noises Nan is on about. I reckon she has the train's warning hoots in mind; and its old-fashioned respiratory system, the in-out

---

[24] I put my middle finger up at a young boy.

of its combustive lungs; and the slow scrape of our upward progress, as we climb a metre for every 40 metres of track. Val points to the little spring lambs falling over each other in a neighbouring field, and remarks how giddy they are to be alive, how pleased with it all. 'Mint sauce,' says Nan. I can only guess she heard a question that hadn't been asked, or was kicking-off a sort of word association game, without warning anyone else.

I eavesdrop awhile. Bits and pieces from the conversations around me – senseless when taken out of context, but pleasing and intriguing nonetheless. 'I had a terrific birthday, thank you. It lasted a month.' 'Well, you know Trevor.' 'She's nice but just not at that time of year.' And then from Val: 'Manchester United have signed another Frenchman, Deborah.' It occurs to me that the sum of these bits, these scraps, these chance soundbites, better reflect a people, a generation, a species, a carriage, an afternoon, than any canon of literature. Literature is too *thoughtful*, too affected. I should like an anthology of one-liners overheard on the train. I'd have that as my desert island item. You could spend years guessing at their stories, their contexts, their before and after. It would be called *Mint Sauce*.

Tan-y-Bwlch is not a Wi-Fi password but a station, a place. We pause here a while, so the engine can catch its breath. The platform is lively with children, who must be off school or skipping it. They are running amok, tripping each other up, sitting in the barrels meant for flowers. They're like the lambs, this lot, giddy on life, thinking it's all a great game – and I suppose it is, really. Watching the children, I half expect to hear Nan say mint sauce again, such is their likeness to the lambs. In the event, she holds her tongue, knowing that children need nothing on the side. As the train takes a corner, its locomotive comes into view. Heads swerve to get a glimpse of the old carthorse.

The climb keeps giving. Wild gorse, a nuclear power station, trees thinking of spring (or remembering winter), rusty shrubs and dark rock, a reservoir, a football pitch. The scene grows as we climb, gains weight as we go. And with that going comes perspective – it's easier to see from up here, to sense the bigger picture. Not that many are looking back. They're too busy finishing ice creams and stacking the tubs on shared tables, or taking pictures of dogs with their tongues out. As we approach Blaenau, more people wave as we pass, and Nan or Val says how friendly people are. Deborah counters that people only wave at things there's no chance of them actually having to interact with. Nan sees Deborah's point, and says it's a shame that we restrict our waving to passing trains and boats, but then, after briefly imagining the alternative, corrects herself and decides it's best as it is. 'Why, you wouldn't stop waving,' she says.

Tim meets us at the terminus. He's had an hour alone. I like to think he spent the time telling himself about the local area. I ask him about his job and he says he used to go to Europe, to Italy and Holland, but then came to the opinion that Europe isn't somewhere you want to drive to once a week for the rest of your life. Besides, he says, when you do a Europe trip you're obliged to travel with a co-driver (i.e. co-historian, co-comedian), which, in Tim's opinion, isn't ideal for Tim. When I get on the coach and sit down next to Nan, she says, 'Did Tim mention a wife?' No, Nan, he didn't. 'And is it true he lives in Peckham?' I admire Nan's curiosity. It's up there with Alice's. If there was a rabbit hole, I don't reckon Nan would look twice. She'd fall to the bottom, dust herself off, and then ask the White Rabbit, 'Does the Mad Hatter have a wife?' Nan says she used the toilet at Blaenau and that toilet is *toiled* in Welsh, which sounds about right to her. Then she notices that Deborah's back on the bus, but Val isn't.

'Do you think Deborah's realised?' says Nan.

'She'd have to be pretty absentminded not to, Nan.'

'Well they are these days, I'm afraid.'

'Nan, Deborah's over 50.'

'Oh, here's Val. She must have been on the *toiled*.'

Tim puts the radio on. It's The Hollies, 'He Ain't Heavy, He's My Brother'. People sing quietly, privately – and yet somehow together. I've heard the song dozens of times, but I've not heard it like this. On this occasion, its claims sound more real – 'the road is long', 'no burden is he' – and its questions less rhetorical – 'that leads us to who knows where?' Just as I'm thinking that Nan's brother was buried in a little white coffin, Nan says:

'Grandad's off to West Ham on Saturday.'

'I'm sorry to hear that.'

'He'll do these things now and again. Go off on his own. It's good practice.'

'What's he been up to, did he say?'

'Oh, the usual. *Bargain Hunt* mostly. Walking the dog. Plus they've got the scaffolding up now. They're painting the shutters. I told him about all the people I've had little chats with and he says I should let people have some peace and quiet.'

'It does seem that you know everyone in the hotel by now.'

'Well, you've got to, haven't you? We're only here for four nights.'

'Alexa, find Facebook,' says Nan.

We're sitting in the upstairs lounge, our backs to the sea. Alexa does what Alexa is told, and then Nan shows me a video of two of my young cousins – Erin and Anya – climbing all over me a few years ago. 'I've got them all stored,' she says.

Dinner is paté followed by korma, and not bad at all. During the latter, I bring up The Hollies, and in particular their winding road that leads to who knows where.

'What about it?' says Nan.

'Well, where does it lead?'

'Basingstoke, probably.'

'I'm being serious, Nan.'

'I'm not worried either way.'

'Are you not?'

'I've had a good stint. Can't complain.'

'And you don't worry about …'

'Not really. I was dead for millions of years and I didn't mind it one bit.'

'Fair enough.'

'And anyway. Say there was an afterlife. Well, when does that end?'

'Good point.'

'And can you imagine the conditions?'

'How do you mean?'

'The overcrowding.'

'I suppose.'

'A hundred billion have died before me. Now, what's for afters?'

'Well, that's the thing Nan, nobody knows.'

'Well *you* might not know, but I'm having the Bakewell tart with custard.'

Patrick's door is ajar. I'm better with the drops. I manage first time, with very little spillage, causing Patrick to say, 'Well that wasn't very exciting.' And my bedside manner is better, I like to think. I was a bit anxious yesterday, and the whole thing became more about me than him. This time I know roughly what I'm doing, so I'm more relaxed. I'm even able to chat with Patrick as I do the business, as a hairdresser might. He says the best part of his day was having his packed lunch in the sun – apart from the crisps. I tell him I'm heading out to watch the football.

'I thought I'd give Nan a break from me,' I say.

'Well she's welcome to chat with me in here.'

'Your best bet is to find her in the lounge, by the reception.'

'I'm not sure if I could make it that far if I'm honest.'

'Tired?'

'Very. I'll probably call it a day soon. How old is Janet out of interest?'

'Eighty-two.'

'Eighty-two?!'

'Yep.'

'Far too young for me then.'

'I'll tell her you said that.'

'Not if I tell her first.'

I go to a place called 147. It's dark and cavernous. The only light is coming from the twenty or so screens showing football. Nineteen of those screens are showing Liverpool, with just one showing Manchester City. This imbalance makes sense because most people in North Wales are Liverpool fans, but what doesn't make sense is that the majority of the people in the bar are watching the Man City match. I raise this with the barman and he shrugs and suggests that maybe it's more important that Manchester lose than Liverpool win. I think of the Welshman who built two churches so he didn't have to go to one of them.

I call it a day at half-time. Walking back along the promenade, with the sea on one side and hotels on the other, I can't decide which way to look. The obvious choice is the sea, but my instinct is to look into the front windows of the hotels. I'm drawn to their small stories, their short scenes, their panes of life. On the front steps of the Imperial, a concierge is juggling grapes.

When I get back to the hotel, Nan's still in the lounge, telling Alexa to do things.

'Oh hello, darling,' she says.

'Alright?'

'Did you have fun?'

'Not really.'

'That's good.' She's still fiddling with her device.

'I decided that windows are better.'

'That sounds nice.'

'Have you seen Patrick?'

'Sorry?'

'Have you seen Patrick?'

'Yes, I did actually. He was carried downstairs for the bingo.'

'Are you joking?'

'No. It was quite entertaining.'

'Cheeky git told me he was having an early night.'

12

It sounds to me like you could do with some grief

We have a little breakfast as per usual. Val and Deborah give us a wave, and Dennis gives us a wink. No sign of Patrick. 'He's probably still downstairs,' says Nan.

There are no planned excursions today, so Nan and I go out for a walk. She's a mind to get up to Happy Valley and have a better look at the Alice sculptures. It's a fair trek from the hotel, so we make a meal of it, stopping in bookshops and bakeries, and at the odd bench. By the time we get there, I'm ready for a prolonged sit down. Nan, on the other hand, is already doing a lap of the park, nosing the March Hare, prodding the Mad Hatter, stroking a caterpillar. She even goes over to inspect the ski slope, for the hell of it. When she returns with two coffees, I ask:

'Nan. Remind me. Alice went down a rabbit hole, right?'

'That's right.'

'And then what?'

'Then she met the Queen of Hearts and had a tea party and became a giant and played croquet using a flamingo as a mallet.'

'And what does it mean, to go down the rabbit hole?'

'It means to go down the rabbit hole.'

'Yeah but not actually, right?'

'Well, no.'

'Then what?'

'I suppose it means to be curious.'

'Even if your knees get dirty.'

'*Especially* if your knees get dirty.'

As we wait for our coffees to cool down, I can't help but think that I've never enjoyed waiting for anything more. I guess what I mean is I'm happy, now, here, briefly on this bench. It's been said – and I'm inclined to go along with this – that it's rare to be uncomplicatedly happy for longer than ten minutes. Well, I manage twenty minutes, just sat next to Nan, listening to her go on about Alice, watching the seagulls terrorise a couple of kids with chips, waiting for our coffees to cool down.

The kitchen finishes on a high: pea and ham soup, beef stew, black cherry trifle. A man I saw streaming the football last night has balloons tied to his chair, so either it's just a thing he likes to do now and again or it's his birthday. Clearing our plates, the waitress asks Nan if she's had a good holiday, but Nan must mishear because she answers, 'Could have done with a bit more spice.' Then she says there's something on her mind.

'What is it?'

'I'm a bit worried about you getting off at London and me continuing down to Portsmouth alone.'

'I thought you said you'd be fine doing that?'

'Oh it's not that I wouldn't be fine.'

'Then what is it?'

'I'm just worried they'll all think you're clearing off before I get back to my husband.'

'But that's exactly what I will be doing.'

'Yes, but you know what I mean.'

After dinner I sit in the lounge for a bit, in one of the two armchairs in the bay window. Deborah – daughter of Val – is in the other.

'So what are you, 40?' she says.

'That's the end of the conversation, Deborah.'

'What, 30?'

'I'm 28 plus VAT.'

'So you're in your prime.'

'Good of you to notice.'

'On paper at least. I was shit at 30.'

'Really? Why?'

'I was a kid with adult issues, with one of those issues being kids.'

'I see.'

'I didn't feel at ease. I didn't feel settled. Do you feel settled?'

'Not really.'

'No?'

'If I'm honest, I feel a bit all over the place.'

'Is that so?'

'Not majorly but yeah.'

'What grounds you?'

'You mean ...'

'What's your anchor?'

'I don't know. My mum?'

'I hope you're joking, Ben.'

'What's wrong with my mum?'

'Your mum's fine until you're eleven. Mortgage?'

'Nope.'

'Career?'

'Not really.'

'Kids?'

'No.'

'Well that explains something.'

'Does it?'

'Yeah.'

'What?'

'Why you're on a coach holiday with your nan. You need more weight, Ben.'

'You think so? If anything, I thought I could do with—'

'I mean weight as in ballast.'

'I know.'

'Weight as in responsibility.'

'I got it.'

'It sounds to me like you could do with some grief.'

'What have you got in mind?'

'I could push your nan down the stairs?'

'We take the lift.'

'No, but seriously. I got better at being happy after some truly, truly rubbish things happened.'

'Like?'

'Dad dying, divorce, cancer. Janet's great by the way.'

'Bollocks.'

'Sorry?'

'What time is it?'

Patrick's door is less ajar and more open. One explanation is that he'd given up on me and was planning to shout at the next person he heard passing – or just bellow 'Janet!' until she got the message. Fifty years at GCHQ ought to have taught him how to communicate. When I enter, he's counting his liver spots. 'Either I'm losing my marbles or I've less than the last time I checked,' he says. I can barely hear because Handel's blaring out the radio.

'I hear you went down for the bingo last night?'

'What?'

'Look, can I turn this down a bit?'

'Oh. Sure.'

'I hear you were carried down for the bingo last night?'

'Something like that.'

'I bet that was fun.'

'It was. I felt rather like a Roman emperor. That or a sofa.'

As well as Classic FM he's got the History Channel on. It's a war documentary. He points to it now and asks if I know what a doodlebug is. Turns out I don't, so Patrick explains that it's like a very explosive drone. When you heard one you were meant to stop what you were doing and put your hands on your head. Patrick remembers one occasion when he was swimming in the sea and heard a doodlebug and stopped what he was doing and put his hands on his head. He hopes his memory's playing tricks on him, however, for he likes to think he can't have been as daft as that.

'How old were you then?'

'About fourteen or so.'

'So you avoided service, did you? During the war?'

'Not quite. I was sent to Bletchley Park towards the end of the war – which was cracking, of course.'

'You've used that line before.'

'Guilty.'

'And did you run into Alan Turing?'

'You know, everyone asks that. You've got to remember he hadn't been in any films back then. There were probably a dozen Alans just in my department.'

I do the drops quickly.

'Good job!'

'I'm getting better.'

'The first night was a baptism.'

'Yeah, sorry about that.'

'I shall have to promote you at this rate.'

'To what?'

'Oh, I don't know. I'm sure I could find you some odd jobs.'

Nan pops in.

'Yoo-hoo,' she says.

'Hello, Janet!'

'How are you, Patrick?'

'Extremely tired.'

'Well, it's been a busy week.'

'No, it isn't that.'

'Then what is it?'

'It was waiting for young Ben to turn up.'

'Oh dear. Was he late?'

'Late? He was almost early for tomorrow.'

At the bar downstairs, I bump into the daughter of the man who had balloons tied to his chair.

'That your dad?'

'Yeah.'

'Birthday?'

'Yeah. Ninety-five.'

'He seems a lively sort.'

'Aye, he's a card.'

'He doesn't sit still for a second. He's like a 95 year old with ADHD.'

'He's got spirit all right.'

'You can say that again.'

And before she can say that again, Jim has got a recital of 'Happy Birthday' going and 95-year-old Arthur is on his feet with his arms aloft. He's wearing a bow tie and has got more hair than I have. He reminds me of my mate's son William, who's five.

'What would you say you've learnt from him?'

'Dad?'

'Yeah.'

'I don't know. You don't think about it.'

'I guess not.'

'He's a good advert for later life, that's for sure.'

'A poster boy for the 90s.'

'Yeah.'

The highlight of the evening is 'Jim's Irish Raffle', which is basically a backwards raffle, and for that reason, about as politically correct as saying all gay people are interesting. 'Anyway,' says Jim, 'it works like this. Everyone gets a ticket and if your number is called you have to say "Oh no, Jim!" and you're out. So the winner is the person whose number isn't called. Get it?'

It's hard to explain exactly how Jim's raffle manages to keep everyone amused and laughing (sometimes to the point of tears) for the next half an hour, but what I can say is that its appeal has something to do with not knowing how the next person is going to say 'Oh no, Jim!' At any rate, the winner of the raffle is a lad called Rodney. The prize is an Easter egg. When Jim informs Rodney that convention dictates that the egg be shared with the evening's entertainer, Rodney says, 'Fair enough. Just let me know when he turns up.'

When Nan moves to the upstairs lounge to make some calls, I nip outside to bum a cigarette. I get one off a lady from Folkestone, who says her highlight of the week was seeing a Punch and Judy performance. She thought the marital disquiet was hilarious. She understands why it's not everyone's cup of tea, however, and wonders if it would be more politically correct if it was a same-sex couple. As I'm giving this some thought, and finishing the cigarette, Nan spots me out the window. She's on the phone. I bet she's telling my mum right now. Bloody windows.

Turns out it wasn't Mum on the phone but Granddad.

'He's mown the communal lawn,' says Nan.

'Oh yeah?'

'Well, not all of it.'

'What do you mean not all of it?'

'He left a bit.'

'Why?'

'Next door's grandchildren have been over.'

'So?'

'And they left some toys on the lawn, which is against the rules, so Grandad mowed round them.'

'Jesus bloody hell, Nan.'

'I didn't think you'd approve.'

'Have you heard of William James?'

'No.'

'Well he said that wisdom is knowing what to overlook.'

'Well William James didn't have my neighbours.'

'No, he didn't. But if he did, he would have mown all the lawn *and* invited his neighbours for tea.'

'Bullshit.'

I've never heard Nan say the word. 'Pardon?'

'I'm sorry, but he just wouldn't.'

Nan goes to bed and I get another pint. Or I try to get another pint rather, because Jim insists on getting it for me. He's sat in the upstairs bar with a few others. It's nice to chat to him. He says he was in the Marines for twenty-odd years and reckons the alternative to telling jokes and calling bingo was post-traumatic stress disorder. Not that his life's entirely stress-free these days, mind you. He's in a new relationship, you see – 'a May–December one,' he says with a wink, as if I know *exactly* what he's talking about.

When Jim calls it a night it's just me and Gary from Leeds. A big, burly, stoic-seeming fella. He used to drive a lorry all over Europe. He says his wife worked at a university and would get in the cab for six weeks each summer. Those were the best times, he says, though they did have a run-in with the German police once because they thought she was a prostitute. His wife used to joke, 'We've been married 40 years but I've only seen him for 25.' Gary reckons that might be the secret to a happy marriage – fifteen years off.

'You say "used to joke", Gary.'

'She died in 2012. Cancer. She was 65. Got it at 47. It came and went. She couldn't take the chemotherapy anymore. Said she'd had enough. So I said alright, and we stopped it. I held her hand at the end.'

I look at Gary apologetically.

'I've still got her though.'

'That's the spirit.'

'She's in t'boot.'

'Sorry?'

'She's in t'boot.'

Turns out Gary keeps his wife's ashes in the boot of his car, and whenever he finds a place he thinks she'd like, he scatters some of her there. I raise my glass to the man. He raises his and says, 'T'boot.'

When I get back to my room, I text Megan to tell her about this oddly romantic gesture, and that I'd like to do the same with her one day. Of all the things she might have said in response, Megan writes back: 'But you don't have a car.'

⌲

At breakfast, I tell Nan about Gary and his wife in the boot, which prompts her to remember a friend who buried her husband in the garden, but when it came to winter couldn't bear the thought of him out there in the cold so dug him up and brought him inside. Now each year she buries him in spring and exhumes him in autumn. 'Seems like a lot of work to me,' I say. 'Lugging a body in and out like that.' 'No, you brush. He's in a small tin.'

We've ten minutes before departure, so I go through to the lounge. Val's here, sat in the window. We instinctively account for our better halves. She says Deborah's having a final walk, and I say Nan's making bacon sandwiches for the road. Then she asks if I've learnt much this week. I mention Lewis Carroll and the slate industry and she says, 'Yes, but anything bigger?' I say it's hard to put your finger on such things, because they tend to creep up on one after the fact, or register via a side entrance. I'm sure something's incubating – whether to do with Patrick or Nan or Dan Walker or Gary – but for the time being, it's all just grist for the mill.

'But you've enjoyed yourselves, haven't you?'

'Yeah, we have.'

'And that's it really, isn't it? That's all you can ask for. I know Janet's enjoyed it. She said she'd stay longer if it wasn't for seeing the podiatrist on Monday.'

'And what about you, Val? Good week?'

'Very. I met a man who races pigeons. That was interesting. And when I sprained my ankle was funny.'

'Was it?'

'I did it the first evening and it got rather swollen so I came in here and put my foot up. One of the staff – a young man – came in and asked if I was alright. I asked if he had a bag of frozen peas I could put on it. He went off and came back shaking his head. He said he was very sorry, but they've only got mixed veg. Of course I thought he was joking, but then when I realised he wasn't – well, it was even more funny.'

When she asks what I've enjoyed the most this week, I start to give a silly answer, about baptising Patrick or whatever, but then check myself and say: 'It's been my nan, really. Getting her take on things, hearing about her life. It sounds silly, but I might start calling her Janet. After all, she was Janet before she was my nan. Janet's sort of the whole thing, if you know what I mean.'

Val chuckles to herself. She can't help it.

'What?' I say.

'Nothing.'

'Is that too cheesy?'

'No, it's not that. It's just. I asked the same question of your nan.'

'And?'

'She said the jam roly-poly.'

Somewhere on the M6, Tim's asked what he'll do this week-end. 'I'll probably get the wife out the cupboard for starters, then I might cut the grass, then it's back to Wales on Monday with the next round of you lot.' Deborah snorts at this, and then turns to give me her paper so I can do the crossword. With Nan's help, I get all but one of the answers. None of the answers resonate or connect with the themes of the week – there's no heaven or grandmother or rabbit or boot. Instead, there's crossbow and caravan and Calcutta and cheese. I pass the crossword to Patrick and point to what I'm struggling with. He chews the end of my pen (cheers, mate), looks out the window, invisibly rifles through the words of his life, and then, after a few minutes, and wearing an expression at once doubtful and cheerful, says, 'I'm afraid this is all I've got', and fills in the gap.[25]

At the interchange on the edge of London, I set Nan up in the lounge next to Patrick and Val and Deborah. They're all going different directions from here, but can sit together for now. Nan's presently telling everyone that her next holi-day will be in France for her son's 60th birthday. Turns out Patrick used to live in the same village as my uncle, on the French-Swiss border. He says he was there to organ-ise the transport of dangerous goods. 'A bit like Shearings then?' I say. Nan tells me to stop it and help Patrick with his cardigan.

---

[25] He was wrong.

A few hours later, in a pub garden in London, I text my nan to see if she made it home. She says there was some traffic, but nobody minded. I've had a few beers by this point, so reply: 'I love you Janet. I knew you were a lovely person, but after seeing it every day this week, I know it even more.' And then: 'ps. mow all the bloody lawn.'

Part 4

Killarney, Ireland

Part VI

13

I'm not used to the likes of you. On ye get

When I think of Ireland – and when I say Ireland I mean the whole thing, the island of Ireland – I think of stew and stories. I think of Wilde, Shaw and Father Ted. I think of the Easter Rising, the Potato Famine, and *Mrs Brown's Boys*. I think of Bobby Sands and Sally Rooney, the Giant's Causeway and Trinity College. I think of Roy Keane and Maud Gonne, Seamus Heaney and Paula Spencer. I think of Horatio Kitchener and his compelling finger, and Gerry Conlon of the Guildford Four. I think of emigration, emigration, emigration. I think of Celts and druids, Vikings and Normans, and a certain Patrick from somewhere near Stoke. I think of Davy Lyons and the Celtic Tiger, the breakfast roll and a Galway girl. I think of Ken Loach and Oli Cromwell, black Guinness and green grass. I think of the Troubles, Veronica Guerin, and my old mate Mick.

It's May. It's Manchester. It's two degrees. When David Snr gets on, he's poking fun at precise pickup times. He says he was told to be at the stop at 8.24am. He thinks it's hilarious, is telling everyone – ''ere, what do you think of this – 8.24 they told me, 8.24 and fifteen seconds …'

You can spot the jolly ones from a mile off. They walk in a jolly way. They've got their hands behind their back and their chins in the air. They greet the driver as if he were a lost son, a lost daughter. One jolly geezer has forgotten his brolly. Another's raincoat has got holes in it. For all their talk, the British aren't very good at weather.

I sneak a peek of a *Daily Mail* through the gap in the seats. Kylie Minogue is happier at 50. I can't read why – the print's too small. Less spinning around, I would have thought, less locomotion. Someone once said that (wo)man's unhappiness owes to his/her inability to sit quietly in a chair. Perhaps Kylie's learnt how to do it. Perhaps she's learnt how to sit down. The lady behind me hasn't though. She's fretting about the electric toothbrush. She thinks she forgot to pack it. The man with her says it's alright because he did it. 'Jack!' she says, slightly affronted. 'You're meant to be senile.'

At the Stretton interchange, the queue for tea and bacon rolls would be out the door if it didn't have the sense to bend. I go outside to wait in the sun. I'm glad I do because Jeff's out here and he's not one for small talk. Within ten minutes, I know his brother sailed to Dunkirk in a pleasure boat and his sister died of cancer at 49. She never smoked or drank and yet she was riddled with the stuff. 'I never got over it,' says Jeff. 'She was yellow! She told me not to come and see her, but I went anyway. She was a great sister. She bought me a pair of roller skates. I've still got 'em under me bed.'

Jeff worked for 50 years as a joiner, and didn't mind it one bit. 'We were all in the same boat. You finished school, you went to work. You did what you were told.' And who told you what to do, Jeff? 'My dad mainly. He wasn't a soft fella, and nor was he easily pleased. I played cricket and he'd come and watch and tell me where I was going wrong. I

I'M NOT USED TO THE LIKES OF YOU. ON YE GET

averaged 64 over my career, which is funny when you think that I was never doing anything right. I remember a final against Runcorn. I scored the winning runs. When I saw him after, I thought he was going to say something about me getting caught in the crease. He said he was proud of me.'

I keep Jeff talking. It's not hard. He says the world has changed and not for the better. He says the best government was Labour after the war. Says children used to be free, but now they're trapped in technology. On the bright side, Jeff got a bit of money in his uncle's will and spent it on cruises. He's happy to admit he's been around the block, but says that things have slowed down since his wife's ticker started playing up. He tells me they got married late (they were 23) and saved 750 quid over the next two years and bought a house.[26] He tells me not to look at him like that, says if I want a house, I just need to stop buying avocados and save my money. He says my generation think frugal is something that goes on toast. He says they go to Southport every Friday, without fail. They have two meals, lunch and dinner, then come home. 'It's our day,' says Jeff. What about the rest of the week? I ask. 'Ooh, we're busy.' He says he's only loved one person his whole life. He'd do anything for her. *Anything*, he says. And where is your wife, Jeff? 'She's in the queue.'

The call comes for Killarney. I upset the driver because there's no label on my luggage.

'Is that all you've got? A wee backpack?'

---

[26] Equivalent to £20,000 in 2020.

'It is.'

He smiles. 'I'm not used to the likes of you. On ye get.'

The coach is full. Our driver, Frank, says he's Scottish and he's got the personality to prove it, and that if we cannae understand him, then we're welcome to request a transcript from head office. We set off along the North Welsh coast to Anglesey. I give a nod to Llandudno and its various rabbit holes. That was March, and this is May: the other end of spring. We arrive at Holyhead, whence the ferries go. I get a text from Nan. 'I can imagine you now.'

Security wants a word. Frank tells us not to look guilty. 'I know some of ye have committed crimes against millennials, but try not to let it show on ye faces.' Security sticks its head in and says, 'Hiya, Frank.' And Frank says, 'I'm not telling ye, it's nothing to do with ye.' They both laugh and we drive onto a boat called Ulysses. We get off the coach and find our way to areas, decks and lounges. A lady called Chris trips on the stairs. Just a stumble. Her friend Carole and I help her up. Chris looks at me and then at Carole and says: 'I might do that again later.'

I spend the first half of the crossing up on deck. The early rain has cleared and it's bright. We're not the first to cross this sea on a jolly. The Celts did it a few thousand years ago, then the Vikings, then the Normans and Welsh and English and so on. Plenty have popped over, and not one of them welcome, I would have thought. The very first people of Ireland wouldn't have crossed this sea. They moved to the country during the Neolithic period, when Ireland and Britain and Europe were of a piece. Then rising seas intervened, and now Ireland and Britain are chips off the old block. So it goes.

I sit with Chris and Carole and a man who's not on holiday. The ladies just had lunch. Chris says she likes mango chutney, but not with curry, while Carole says she likes peas, but not mushy ones. The man, when it's his turn, says it's not normal me being on such a holiday. I say it used to be normal to lobotomise republicans, so perhaps normal's not what it's cracked up to be. He's not persuaded, and continues to stare at me as if I were a six-foot oyster, then says, almost in conclusion, that I remind him of his daughter.

'Oh yeah?'

'Yeah. You're an idiot.'

Then the man falls asleep – from mental exhaustion.

Chris shows me a picture of her grandson, who's into tofu and crashed two cars. Then she shows me a picture of her granddaughter, who's eighteen and wants to be a vet. And then Carole shows me a picture of her black grandchildren. 'Well, creamy,' she says. 'Like creamy coffee. They're not black, but I'm meant to say they are. They're gorgeous anyway. I love 'em. Their dad's South African. He's gorgeous as well.' Then she leans in and asks, *sotto voce*, 'Is it racist me saying such things?' I tell her it's racist only if she thinks all creamy people, black people, white people, Cornish people – whatever people – are bad or worse or inferior for being creamy, black, white or Cornish etc. 'Oh they can be bad all right,' she says. 'But it's got nothing to do with them being creamy.'

Chris tells me that she and Carole share grandchildren. At first I wonder if this is some kind of division of labour, some kind of babysitting initiative, but it turns out one's son is married to the other's daughter. Chris says it's a nice thing for friends to share. Another thing they share is a village near Leek in Derbyshire, and another still is widowhood. Their husbands both died four years ago – one of colon cancer and the other of pulmonary fibrosis. Chris says she was tempted to bury hers in his overalls, seeing as he was never out of them. Carole says she scattered hers in Rhodes because he liked it there. 'I went to a medium not long after and she told me that John says thanks. Then she asked if I had a message for John. I said yeah, tell him to wear sun cream.' I ask if life's been hard since their husbands died. They share a look. I take it to mean: not as hard as you might think.

I ask about their village, their area, how it's changed over the years. Carole says that Levison Wood used to live in the village but doesn't anymore, if that's what I mean. And they've lost the Duke of Wellington to Tesco, which sounds about as unlikely a turn of events as is possible. Yeah, it's all changed, they say, it's all different now. It used to be raspberry and vinegar for coughs, and if you broke your nose you were told to rub a dock leaf on it. The kids have changed as well. Chris says her granddaughter comes over and just sits there on the couch messaging her boyfriend. 'Massaging her boyfriend?' says Carole. 'No, *messaging*,' says Chris.

'Can't you confiscate her phone?' I say.

'You can't,' says Carole. 'They'd walk out. They'd go on strike. They'd get social services on to you.'

'You've got to let them alone,' says Chris, 'and go with the flow. It's the modern way.'

'But don't you think they're missing out?'

'I do,' says Chris. 'And more to the point, I've met the boyfriend and don't see what all the fuss is about.'

We disembark at Dublin and head south-west. An hour later, we enter County Limerick, famous for a type of poem. Frank encourages us to compose our own and send them forward for his inspection. I do as I'm told.

> *There was a wee fella called Frank*
> *Who couldn't decide who to thank*
> *For the luggage that he*
> *Was presented by me*
> *Because the label was unhelpfully blank.*

Then Frank gets all educational on us. He says the island of Ireland is like a saucer, with a flat central plain surrounded by low hills and mountains. He says the island is at once divided into 32 counties – 26 in the south, and six in the north – and four provinces – Ulster, Leinster, Connacht and Munster. Ulster is often used as a synonym for the north, explains Frank, but in point of fact Ulster contains nine counties, three of which are in the south. Killarney, if we were wondering, is in the county of Kerry and the province of Munster. South Munster means Desmond and – 'bear with me', says Frank – it was the Earl of Desmond that led some famous rebellions at the end of the 16th century, against whosoever there was to rebel against – most likely the English. The population's growing these days, says Frank, but that wasn't the case for a long time. It was 8 million in 1841 and about half that 140 years later. One hell of a famine and an awful lot of emigration help explain the slump. Then, Frank lifts the mood – or alters it at least – by saying: 'As we approach Killarney, folks, I can tell you that Meghan and Harry have had a baby boy.' Ah, that's nice, they say. Isn't that good, they coo. 'They've called it Gary.' Silence.

We're staying at the Eviston House Hotel on New Street. My room's on the second floor and has got everything I require – namely, a mattress and a kettle for tea. I flick through the channels but there's nothing much on, only repeats of *EastEnders* and the news. I opt for the former. It's an episode with only Dot Cotton in it. As far I'm aware, Dot's lived in Albert Square since the Crimean War. Here she is now, at the kitchen table with a hot chocolate, recording a message on a tape recorder for her husband, Jim, who's either in hospital or dead, it's difficult to say. I've stumbled upon this, but not many people my age and below will have done. They've too much control over what they're doing. When I was younger, you had less control of your intake, less autonomy. I might have been desperate for *Gladiators* or *Blind Date*, but TV didn't care, I had to put up with *One Foot in the Grave* first, and then *Keeping Up Appearances*, and then *Two Fat Ladies*. As a result, I know who Dot Cotton is, who Captain Mainwaring is, who Victor Meldrew is. I didn't pursue the knowledge, it simply landed on me, like cultural shrapnel. It seems to me that the

latest crop of youngsters won't experience anything by accident – not on a screen anyway. Because they're able to curate
their cultural diet, it's likely they'll only ingest stuff they relate
to, and avoid anything they don't. Whereas my generation
copped a load of old whether we wanted to or not, today's
youth will be shielded from their elders, and the resultant
dislocation will be to the detriment of intergenerational relations. Our cultural diets determine our understanding of the
world; they influence and delineate our fields of interest and
affection. If we only watch one thing, we won't recognise
others. I won't labour the point: everyone could do with a
bit of accidental Dot.

I go downstairs to the bar – which is more like a pub,
really – to see what the crack is. Frank's here. I tell him he
could probably write a book, what with all the trips he's
done. He says he's seen more people than hot dinners, which
doesn't sound right to me, but never mind. He says he used
to do the Moscow trip, and one thing he learnt was that if
you parked in the wrong place in Russia in the 90s, you soon
knew about it. When I ask him for a highlight, he tells me
about the time one of the guests didn't come down for her
breakfast.

'Was she not keen on it?'

'No, she was dead!'

We're joined by Marty, who's also on our tour. By his own
admission, Marty's a gay Scouser with learning difficulties.
He's also a Catholic postman, and wearing a bumbag and a
gilet. I don't think anyone has ever made such an instantly
favourable impression on me. Marty orders himself a gin

and orange, then admits to not really knowing the difference between Catholicism and Protestantism, and asks us if we could shed any light on the matter. Frank says he'd rather not get into it, if it's all the same to Marty. Marty sees where Frank's coming from, and so changes the topic. He asks Frank if he's in a relationship. Franks says he is and it's mostly great, but admits that sometimes life can be easier when you've only yourself to worry about. Marty says being gay's a bit like that; some of it's great but a lot of the time he just can't be arsed. Marty doesn't mind telling us he wouldn't mind having the odd day off being gay, perhaps even the odd week.

'Have you thought about it, Ben?'

'Thought about what, Marty?'

'Being in a relationship?'

'I think about it a lot, Marty.'

'I'd do it part-time if I were you. Who wants a drink? It's my round.'

I walk down Main Street to the Killarney Grand. It's packed. You couldn't avoid a conversation if you wanted to. I start one with Connell, who's about my age and in an advanced state of non-sobriety. Connell reckons two things: that there's a girl under his skin and that Irish people are welcoming apart from the ones from Clare, who only welcome people from Clare. Then he asks what sort of holiday I'm on, and I tell him.

'What the feck are you doing that for?'

'I can't say exactly.'

I'M NOT USED TO THE LIKES OF YOU. ON YE GET

'For the crack, is it?'

'Oh, I don't think they're into drugs.'

'Not drugs you—'

'I'm joking.'

'Eejit. Will yeh have another pint?'

'Yeah.'

'Gas.'

'Connell?'

'Wha'?'

'Can I ask a question?'

'Course yeh can.'

'Do you know who Dot Cotton is?'

14

It's Judy bloody Garland

I walk down the aisle of the coach with my head bowed. I'm hungover. I'm wearing sunglasses. I'm not even sure where we're meant to be going. 'It's Judy bloody Garland,' someone says. On our way out of town, Frank points to a few nice buildings and says that if Killarney's a good-looking place, then it's no thanks to Oliver Cromwell.[27]

The Ring of Kerry is a 110-mile circuit that takes in all the county's hotspots. One such hotspot involves a goat. I'll let Frank explain. 'Every August, the people of Killorglin take a wild goat—' and make it a Lance Corporal? '—and parade it around town before getting a schoolgirl to crown it. The goat is then put up on a pedestal in the town square

---

[27] Prior to Cromwell's 'conquest' of Ireland in the middle of the 17th century, England already had considerable sway in the country – it was a so-called client state, which is one hell of a euphemism. The English seem to have treated Ireland like some kind of experimental allotment, 'planting' Protestants around the country as though they were a root vegetable. The reason Cromwell came over in 1649 was to make sure his allotments weren't being got at by Royalists and Catholics. His campaign began with a prolonged siege of Drogheda, just north of Dublin. Then it was down to Wexford. Then Kilkenny. Then Clonmel. Then Waterford. And so on. Within a few years, Cromwell's New Model Army had taken the entire island, and in the process killed roughly 500,000 Irish Catholics – about a third of the population. If the Irish sometimes appear to have a chip on their shoulder, chances are it's because the English put it there.

for a few days before being dethroned and returned to the wild, where it no doubt tells all its mates what it's been up to. You can imagine their reaction. "What *are* ye oan aboot, Billy?"' The annual coronation is in honour of a goat who came rushing into the town to warn of the imminent arrival of Oliver Cromwell and his Roundheads. That Cromwell had been and gone by the time of the goat's arrival, and that most of Killorglin was already in bits, are details the locals prefer not to dwell on.

The Bog Village Museum is perhaps the least auspicious sounding museum (or village) on the planet. In accordance with its promotional signage, the museum gives an insight into how people lived in Ireland in bygone centuries. (Suffice to say they didn't have Wi-Fi.) In recent years, the museum has diversified its appeal by serving Baileys coffee and toasted sandwiches in a neighbouring building. I order a 'cheese onion ham' only to be told they've only got 'ham cheese onion', like it says on the board. I say very well, I'll have one of those then, but don't ever accuse me of being inflexible.

I sit down with Carole and Chris. The first thing Chris does is offer me half her toasted sandwich.

'I've got one coming, Chris.'

'Well have this until it comes.'

'I'm fine, honestly.'

'Suit yourself.'

'But thank you.'

'We missed you this morning. Did you stop out late?'

'Later than I might have done.'

'Well don't make a habit of it because you missed a good morning. We were pulled along in a cart by a pony. The driver was indecipherable. It was very entertaining.'

We continue to the Dingle Peninsula, which is the westernmost point of Ireland, and therefore of Europe. In days gone by, it was mostly rebellious Catholics that could be found loitering in the waters here (James II, Wolfe Tone). These days, it's a dolphin called Fungi, who was first seen in Dingle Bay way back in 1983. When you consider that most dolphins live to about fifteen, it's reasonable to describe Fungi as a fogie. And yet despite his advanced age, Fungi the dolphin is yet to display any right-fin inclinations. Frank, being Frank, is quite cynical about the whole thing. 'The locals inflate a dolphin then charge tourists €15 an hour to see the wee bastard.'

Just beyond the village of Waterville, Frank directs our attention to a sort of craggy island just visible off the coast – Skellig Michael. Turns out there's a monastery on the island, and it turns out that Frank can't help but think that when it comes to spreading the word, sometimes religious folk don't make life easy for themselves. Frank goes on to tell us that the *Star Wars* films were partly shot on yonder crag, which means that these days about ten boats a day are taking tourists across so they can see what they've already seen. We're told – though Frank might be pulling our leg – that if you look carefully during *Return of the Jedi*, you can see a monk in the background taking a leak.

Then Frank orders us off at a viewpoint, and he's right to. It's an almost fictional setting. You wouldn't say the land was abounding in anything. It's spring and yet nothing much is springing. It all looks rather trim and nibbled. A modest line of hills bisects the scene. If the hill line were a sound-wave, the frequency would be low: its dives are shallow, its climbs are slight. Not much of the scenery is associable – can be associated with other things, stuff or ideas. There are some dwellings, and some electricity cables, and of course I recognise the sky; but little else refers to, or harks back, or brings to mind – not with any crisp explicitness – which is what makes the scene peaceful, I suppose. Having said that, the drystone walls that divide the land speak of plunder and seizure; of subjects and spoils; of the planting and plotting of Protestants. There's less of that these days of course, but still these walls talk, and not everything they say is fit for a postcard. I take a picture of Chris taking a picture. Her pink jacket stands out against the grass and the gorse. She has her phone raised like a candle, and her hair's the same shade as the sky. Her trousers and shoes look new and purposeful. She's ready for golf, for the catwalk, for the hills. 'It's wonderful we can see such things,' she says. Ah shut up, Chris. You're after my heart.

At dinner, I sit with a couple – Sandra and John – and Marty.

'You alright, Marty?'

'Yeah I'm good, thanks, Ben.'

'What did you think of the Ring of Kerry then?'

'I thought it was very good, Ben, but I wouldn't want to do the post round there.'

Sandra and John are from Stoke. I admit I've never been to Stoke, and John admits I needn't let that bother me. Sandra says the town centre is really quiet these days, which isn't only bad for the town, but also the people, and especially the older people. Sandra's worried they don't get out, that they don't pop to the shops, not like they did. If they pop to the shops, they see people, and people see them – they become attached and involved, in small but important ways. It might just be a pork chop and a few carrots, but in effect it's more than that. Amazon or whoever isn't going to keep an eye on you, show an interest, remember your husband. Towns are an endangered species, she says; it's not right.

Sandra and John do their best to buck the trend. They get out every day, if only for a coffee. They've been getting out every day for a fair while: it's their 50th anniversary next year. They met at work, where John was a driver and Sandra was in the office. Sandra was with a bloke from Birmingham at the time but decided it was in everyone's interest for her to be open-minded and give John a go one night after work. She never saw the guy from Birmingham again. I ask if they'll do anything for their anniversary. 'Probably go out for a coffee,' says Sandra – 'though I might upgrade to a latte.' John says there'll be no such upgrade, not if he's got anything to do with it. Sandra laughs but Marty offers John a quid to pay for the upgrade, says life's too short. There's a nice awkwardness to dinner.

I'm still very hungover. It's a struggle to sit up straight, to eat, to engage. Usually when one's feeling acutely hungover, one self-isolates. One might eat a tin of custard and watch

Pointless. One doesn't tend to arrange for an intimate dinner in County Kerry with relative strangers. I excuse my imperfect self before pudding. Sandra is sympathetic, and even worried I'm coming down with something. 'You do what you want,' says Marty, 'you're on holiday.' I don't deserve their company. Not this evening.

Frank's in his usual spot at the bar. We half watch Liverpool against Barcelona. Frank supports Hearts – Heart of Midlothian – but never says so if Scottish punters ask because what they're really asking is whether he's Protestant or Catholic, and he'll be damned if he's getting into any of that malarkey. Frank doesn't take sides these days; he sits on the fence and the fence is a rainbow. He learnt the hard way that ideology doesn't pay. 'I once played a song on the coach called "The Fields of Athenry" and lost half my tips. I vowed not to do that again.'[28] Despite Frank's stated impartiality, he doesn't half celebrate when Barcelona score for a second time. He cheers as if he were a Catalan. I look at him for an explanation.

'I cannae stand Liverpool.'

'I thought you were colour blind?'

'Aye, but some colours are brighter than others.'

---

[28] 'The Fields of Athenry' was a big hit in 1979. The song tells of an Irish Catholic who stole some corn during the famine of the 1840s ('so the young might see the morn') and was deported to Australia. It is anti-English, and in particular anti-Charles Trevelyan, who was Home Secretary at the time of the famine, and therefore calling a lot of the shots. Presented with reports that hundreds of thousands of Irish were perishing, Trevelyan said that God was punishing them for their wickedness. Not the sort of thing that usually gets to number one, but there you go.

I ask what Frank's come to expect regarding tips. He says you just do your job and hope for the best. Unless they're from Yorkshire, in which case you don't hope at all. He shares his favourite tipping story. 'There was this one fella, a Londoner, hobbling about all week, slow as a snail, in agony he was. And yet when it came to the final disembarkation, when I normally go round collecting the tips, this old geezer was off the coach before I even had the handbrake up.' Frank reckons there might be a lesson to be had from the episode, i.e. that it isn't age that acts as a barrier to performance, but incentive.

More than people who don't tip, what really gets under Frank's skin is when people don't *listen*. Frank doesn't mean to suggest that when it comes to oratory he's up there with Churchill, but nonetheless, if he's saying something, then it doesn't tend to be for the sake of his health. 'One time, I was giving a wee history of such-and-such place, and these two girls directly behind me were going on about what they had made for their husbands' dinners. Not just the night before, but *ever*, all dinners ever. I slapped the microphone and said: "Are we alright, ladies and gentlemen?" (I don't like to pick on anyone.) "Not everybody wants to hear about Limerick – so much is admitted – but *nobody* wants to hear about what yous made your husbands for dinner in 1986." Oddly enough, they left a big tip.'

We step outside for a smoke and Frank says a few more things, which is a bit of a habit of his. I guess it's an occupational hazard. When you've got a microphone in front of your nose most of your life, things just sort of slip out. He says now that the Liverpool left-back is having a shocker, that farmers look the same no matter where they're from, and that he can't stand eating a three-course meal alone with people watching him saying, 'Ooh there's the driver, what's he having?' He says the barman doesn't charge him for his beer, and in return Frank doesn't charge the barman for listening to his shite most evenings. He says that what you've got to remember about the working class of his generation is that they all bought houses on the cheap and have good pensions and have probably been frugal all their lives, and so when it comes to wealth, they're probably in the top 10 per cent of the population, something that isn't generally reflected in the tips Frank gets. He says he couldn't believe it when he saw my little backpack, and then – the two somehow being related in Frank's mind (perhaps he's thinking of a snail) – asks if I own a house.

'Nope.'

'Are ye paying into a pension?'

'Nope.'

'Do ye stand to inherit much?'

'A Ford Mondeo. Lupus.'

'And you're a freelance something?'

'Yep.'

'And you're not married to Princess Eugenie or Paris Hilton or anyone like that?'

'Nope.'

'In which case you better strap in, pal, because you're pretty much f*cked.'[29]

---

[29] It is for such advice that one travels.

I have a pint at a pub up the road called Reidy's. It's a lovely place. There's a banjo in the courtyard (and a man with it like), and various nooks and unexpected rooms. The banjo makes me think of my dad, but only for a bit. I'm too hungover to be sentimental. I give Megan a call. 'How ye?' I say, but then I realise it's her voicemail. I sit down and look through my pictures – a toasted sandwich, Marty with an ice cream, Chris and Carole on the coach, talking softly, sensibly, sweetly. Then I put the phone down abruptly and slide it away from me. Ah, bejaysus.

I take a walk in the rain: Ye Auld Sweet Shop, The Grand, your man Jesus on a traffic island. I hit a ring road, then go inward on St Anthony's Passage, which delivers me to Main Street, and from Main I find New. Nothing new about me though. Same old trick. It slips down my throat and then sits under my skin, pinching my verve, nipping my nerve, squashing my mojo. A pursuit of happiness, one pint at a time. Nonsense.

> *There was a man called Ben*
> *Who in search of ying, yang and zen*
> *Drank six pints of beer*
> *Most days of the year*
> *Then repeated the process again.*

Outside the hotel, I light up a cigarette. I look at the image of infertility on the packet, and fantasise about it being my last. As I smoke, I watch the takeaway across the road and think about brushing my teeth. 'Whoever carries into the afternoon the law of the morning must pay with damage to his soul.' That was Carl Jung. I'm not fully persuaded by the sentiment – it's a bit severe – but I think there's something in it. We've got to act our age, to go with the flow, to evolve. I'm caught with one leg in the playpen of youth, while the other's desperate to stride ahead. I'm going to pull my groin at this rate.

Then I see Michael Fassbender. He's crossing the road, hood up, eating a doughnut. It's definitely him. *Shame, Fish Tank, Hunger* – I've stared at that face long enough to be sure. I don't begrudge him the doughnut, not after what he did playing Bobby Sands in *Hunger*, which involved losing weight to within an inch of his life in order to give credence to his portrayal of a hunger striker. I'd like to ask Michael about another physically impressive performance of his. At the start of his career he starred in a Guinness advert. In it, he swims from Galway to New York to apologise to his brother. I'd like to know what he was sorry for.

15

You can't take a picture of them. They're not us

The breakfast sausages are grand and Gordon and Rowan agree. Though she's only having a half because she's poorly and has to monitor such things. She says they used to fly all over the place, but these days they tend to stick to their own doorstep or thereabouts, which is no skin off their noses since it's not a bad doorstep, not when you give it a proper look. Gordon says it's human nature to ignore what's under your nose. Then he corrects himself and says that, these days, the opposite is true because it tends to be a smartphone. Rowan says that smartphones are clever at what they do but very addictive. She remembers watching a girl at the football (Nottingham Forest) take at least 25 pictures of herself and then spend the rest of the match fiddling with them. I say that perhaps such behaviour is not unreasonable given that Nottingham Forest haven't given a captivating performance since 1992. They both take this dig on the chin and then Rowan adds: 'It's not just a young person thing though. My sister's as bad. She'll take a picture of a plate of chips in Wetherspoons, and then fiddle with that for ages.'

'What's she fiddling with chips for?' I say.

'Because even the chips have to be aspirational,' says Gordon.

They're retired. Gordon took a year off to care for Rowan then didn't go back. He reckons he's got time to enjoy things now, time to try things. The garden is an example, says Rowan. She doesn't think Gordon said a thing about gardening his whole life, and now he won't shut up about it.

'Sometimes he comes to bed with his gloves on.'

'You can't be serious,' I say.

'I won't actually get into bed with them on,' says Gordon. 'But I've been known to brush my teeth in them.'

I ask what Gordon's approach is in the garden.

'Approach?'

'I mean, how do you go about it?'

'I just whip it out and bang it in.'

'I see. And what do you bang in exactly?'

'Kale, sweetcorn, beetroot, parsnip, lettuce, cauliflower.'

'Quite a bit then.'

'I do asparagus, but asparagus takes three years. If you don't wait three years for your asparagus, it will be the last thing you don't do.'[30]

'Isn't asparagus an aphrodisiac?'

'Well I've not noticed owt,' says Rowan.

Rowan says that, compared to Gordon, her fingers aren't very green at all, not least because she only gets one week off hospital every four, which is when they try to get away. She says 'poorly' is her euphemism of choice, which she likes to modify with 'quite' and 'very', as the situation demands.

---

[30] Turns out Gordon was exaggerating. It's *better* if you leave it three years. It won't be the last thing you don't do if you don't.

'When I started being "very" quite often, that's when Gordon got a mobile phone.'

'I'm quite good at it now,' he says.

'Well you've had a fair bit of practice, haven't you, love?'

They're chatty these two. I hear of Rowan's nephew who's studying at Salford, and I hear of Gordon's brother who cycled the Ring of Kerry in his boxer shorts. I hear that Boots the chemist is the major employer in Nottingham, and that the Goose Fair still goes on and I should come along one year. I hear how to grow parsnips and chard and how they've never been to Manchester. I hear that Trump will get off the hook, that Merkel's a strong woman, that Fungi the dolphin has more chance of getting elected than Jeremy Corbyn. And then I hear Gordon standing and dusting himself off and saying: 'Right then, love. Now we've set the world right, let's go out and have a look at the blighter.'

Given that it was effectively a blind date, and could have gone one of a hundred ways, I'd say that this morning's breakfast was one of the best I've ever had. The conversation was enjoyably circuitous. I suppose a conversation is more likely to have such shape (or lack thereof) when the interlocutors are strange to one another, when there's no way of knowing what junctions you'll arrive at, conversationally speaking. You don't expect to turn off for asparagus, or take a left for respiratory disease, or go straight across for the Nottingham Goose Fair. I like that.

I go up for another piece of white pudding and another slice of toasted soda bread. Waiting on the latter, I observe to

YOU CAN'T TAKE A PICTURE OF THEM. THEY'RE NOT US

the other person waiting that they seem to have been doing so for some time. She says she put it in ten minutes ago, but it hasn't come out yet. As she says this, my piece of toast shoots out. 'Ah,' she says, 'here it is.' Bloody boomers.

The first time I boarded this coach, I was met with silence. Now Sandra says 'Do you want a mint? We're all having mints', and Marty says 'Did you sleep well, Ben? I slept well, Ben', and Carole says 'Did you stop out last night then, Ben?' It hasn't taken much for the general atmosphere to change, for us all to become more fraternal and familiar – just a bit of proximity and time and shared adversity (some of Frank's jokes for example). But there's another side of the coin, of course. There's a flipside to our new togetherness. I've already started to hear some of my lot speaking ill of those on the other coach, Edward's lot. There's a rumour they're somehow getting the best of the eggs and longer lie-ins. Give it another few days and we'll be saying they've been stealing cutlery and photocopying their drinks vouchers. If it doesn't take much to bond, it also doesn't take much to set oneself apart, to grow a little bias. As if sensing my train of thought, Frank says: 'Right folks, let's get moving before Edward nabs the best parking spot.'

We're off to a stately home – Muckross House – but on the way we're going to call at one or two spots, the first of those being Killarney's cathedral. From the coach, the church's limestone exterior looks pure and uniform, but up close, you can see that each block is a hundred colours. There's a tree in the grounds of the church that was planted for the local children who died during the Potato Famine. We're invited to go and touch it, and maybe spend a few minutes thinking about what it stands for. I accept the invitation, and end up thinking about Michael Fassbender as Bobby Sands again, dying of hunger over the course of 66 days, or about twenty minutes in the film.

Inside the church, of all the many things that are meant to please the eye, it's a poem pinned to a notice board that gets my attention. It's called 'Slow Me Down, Lord' and does such a good job of selling slowing down that you want to get on with it in a hurry. It makes you impatient to learn 'the art of taking minute vacations, of slowing down to look at a flower, to chat with a friend, to pat a dog, to read a few lines from a good book'. Marty doesn't need to be told. He's got the right idea. He's leaning back on a pew with his hands behind his head and his eyes closed, smiling like it was a month of Sundays. His reverie is broken by Frank. 'It's time to go,' he says. 'Get your skates on because I'm double-parked.'

Our next stop is just up the road. It's a piece of open ground that offers a view of Killarney and its lakes and mountains. Despite the fine view, what I want to photograph is one of the other coach parties posing for a group picture. I get them from an angle; from the side almost. Of course none of the group are looking at me, so in my picture they all look a bit demented and surreal. It's still a group shot, and it's still got the lakes and the mountains in the background, but it's not a picture any of them would hang on a wall at home, or touch up and share. It defies one of the unwritten conventions of group portraiture – that the subjects be looking at the camera. Or if not looking at the camera, at least be aware of it. Sandra from Stoke comes up behind me and says: 'You can't take a picture of them. They're not us.'

When Queen Victoria stayed at Muckross House in 1861, she gave six years notice of her visit – plenty of time for the house to be royally improved – and arrived with her own bed and a hundred mates. Apparently, the owner at the time almost went bankrupt sorting the place out for her. I have a peep through one of the back windows and decide that the rooms do a good job of giving a sense of how not many people lived in the 19th century. (The house was finished just a couple of years before the Potato Famine, for heaven's sake.) I hate to put a downer on things, but houses like this, however charming, are one side of a coin whose flipside is poverty and oppression. It's hard to have one without the other. The rhododendrons in the garden are nice, however, no matter which way you look at them.

I get back to the coach before anyone else. Frank's here having a smoke. It's as if I've disturbed him while he was mulling a few things over, because before long, he's telling me about the 2018 referendum in Ireland regarding the constitutional ban on abortions. The result was in favour of the ban being lifted – despite the best efforts of the church. 'The priests tried their best,' says Frank. 'They laid it on pretty thick. They put on buses to get people from the rural areas to the polling stations, and no doubt the drivers had a wee word along the way. Och, it's never been different, the countryside's always been conservative. It's the same in Scotland. They're in their little green bubbles, getting fed up, falling behind the times, whereas in a city, you've got no choice but to mix, to adapt. A year in Glasgow and it becomes harder to think in black and white, because you've seen all sorts, and you've needed all sorts, and you've needed all sorts *from* all sorts, if that makes sense. The edges get taken off ye. Aye, there'll be the odd bit of trouble, but that's just run-of-the-mill, that's just life. Out in the countryside, it's easier to – och, they're just not for changing, that's all. And the church doesnae help. It shouldnae have the influence it does. Nobody should be raised to think x or y on pain of going to hell, on pain of shaming the family. They should be raised to think for their selves, not told what to do. But it's nae easy. I told my daughter the other day: "Stop f*cking swearing, will ye!" In my defence I've been hearing a lot of her lately. She quit the uni not long ago and is back at home now, working in a pub. I worry the work won't stretch her, not in the way that uni might have done. I told her she won't be getting nothing off me. I told her Frank isn't working so she can watch Jeremy Kyle in her pyjamas. What did you think of the house by the way? You know I got locked in once? I was doing one of their guided tours and fell asleep in the drawing room.'

Dinner's decent: Caesar salad, leg of Kerry lamb, lemon meringue pie. I sit with Rowan and Gordon plus another couple from Canada who met in New Guinea and now live in Wolverhampton (as you do). Brexit comes up during pudding, in relation to one of the hotel staff, who's Lithuanian. The Canadians reckon people are scared of what they don't know; Gordon reckons people would be scared of themselves if they knew what they were made of; Rowan reckons they just wanted a bit more control; and I reckon that a fool who knows he's a fool is that much wiser, which is my way of saying I've stopped thinking about it. Then Mrs New Guinea asks for the buttered carrots and Mr New Guinea says that an argument against democracy is five minutes conversation with any voter, and an argument against referenda is the very existence of people.

'And what do you fancy in place of democracy?' I say.

'Gerontocracy.'

'Rule by the—'

'Rule by the old. Have you heard of Plato?'

'Did he play for Coventry?'

'He said it's for the old to rule and the young to submit.'

'I'm guessing he wasn't sixteen when he said it.'

'Presumably not.'

'And what would you have the young submit to exactly?'

'The most terrific pensions you have seen in your life,' he says.

I wouldn't mind something like gerontocracy. I certainly wouldn't mind some sort of Supremely Sage Council of Elders that had a say on policy and national well-being and what-not. It wouldn't be based in London but would tour the country, dispensing advice, telling yarns, getting a handle on things. You could say the House of Lords plays a similar role

– that of an enlightened guardian, a check and a balance – but then you could say Plato played for Coventry. By what criteria would councillors be elected? It couldn't just be age, for age is no guarantee of good sense or kindness. I suppose you'd have to pass some kind of sagacity exam, or wisdom trial. I wouldn't be surprised if it turned out the only people eligible were the Two Fat Ladies.

Frank's at the bar, in his usual spot.

'How ye Frank?'

'Say that again?'

'How ye?'

'Are you meant to sound Irish?'

'Is that offensive?'

'Not to the Irish because you sound Spanish.'

'Do I feck.'

'Stop it.'

'It was a grand dinner, so it was.'

'Stop it.'

'Your man from New Guinea is after ruling the world.'

'Are you wanting a lift home?'

There's football. Spurs are in Amsterdam. I feel bad for watching. I could be out taking the temperature of the town or mixing with the others. But then I reason that the town's probably seen quite enough of me, and that the others don't want me gassing to them when they're trying to listen to the live music, asking about the 60s, about the basic state pension, about the young ones these days. Intergenerational relations are fine up to a point – roughly 7pm – whereafter you just want the football and a … bottle of non-alcoholic beer. Besides, Frank's old enough. He counts.

Because it's a lousy first half, and because he doesn't know how to do otherwise, Frank tells me a few things. He tells me that in 1921, after two years of fighting, the Irish War of Independence came to a halt when the British agreed to negotiate. The key men on the Irish side were Eamon De Valera and Michael Collins. The latter was sent by the former to London to get the whole country back, despite the former knowing the latter didn't stand a chance in hell, not least because it was blindingly obvious that the Protestants in the north were not prepared to come along for the ride. When Collins came back from London with independence for only 26 counties, he pleaded for people to see that Ireland now had the freedom to achieve freedom. 'But he was marked a traitor and a coward,' says Frank, 'and was killed by his mate in Cork while De Valera was fishing in Long Island.' A civil war followed, between those who felt 26 was enough (pro-treaty), and those who felt it wasn't (anti-treaty). Over its two years, the civil war claimed more lives than the war of independence that preceded it. 'And now, because of Brexit,' says Frank, 'the whole shebang is being dragged up again. It took a long time to get this lot reading from roughly the same page. It took a lot of dead people. The war of independence, the civil war, then the Troubles when it all flared up again – for *30 years*, man. It hasn't gone away, and it wouldn't take much for it all to properly kick off again. Och, but that's just an opinion. Are ye sure ye don't want a pint?'

Frank decides to call it a night. We've to be up early, after all. We're off to Dublin, where we'll stay the night before catching the ferry the next morning. I stick around to watch Spurs come back from two down to win. A woman is gutted.

'Are you Dutch?' I say.

'I'm from Gateshead.'

'Then why are you pissed off?'

'I can't stand Spurs.'

'Why?'

'There's a man on my street who likes 'em.'

'And?'

'And I don't like 'im.'

Ah for feck's sake.

Frank's spot at the bar is taken by a bloke from New York. His name's Shaun and his great-grandfather left him a house in Dingle. Shaun brings the family every year: his two sons go golfing and he goes drinking. When he says drinking he laughs and hits me on the arm with the base of his hand in a friendly way that really hurts. He says his wife is normally drinking with him but she's back home minding the grandchildren. I ask if he misses her. He says 'Not yet!' and laughs and hits me again in the same spot and I think: if this is what Americans do when they go after their roots, then I wish they didn't have any.

But Shaun's a sweet guy, there's no two ways about it. And he seems to like me. I'm not saying anything especially *neat* but he nonetheless seems to be finding me a hoot. Perhaps this is what happens when your wife stays at home to mind the grandchildren. He says he's been happy just about every day of his life since he retired. He asks if I've heard of the people who say they enjoyed their jobs so much they never worked a day in their lives. I have? Well those people clearly didn't know how to *live*, not as far as Shaun is concerned. Do I want his advice? Avoid getting paid for something. He says he worked on the railway for 50 years and can assure me every single day of it sucked. Now he's retired and has a decent pension and spends the money on whatever the hell he wants, and spends the time on much the same thing. He loves his family, but he loves being a stranger as well, sitting at a bar, shooting the breeze – making new buddies. (Of course, when he says *buddies* he …) His sons are both surgeons. The wife of one of them died of a brain haemorrhage six months ago, just weeks after giving birth to their third child. I say: f*ck. He says: ain't that the truth. He shows me a video of his granddaughter playing baseball. He laughs and hits me for the final time when the girl trips up heading for first base.

'Now ain't that something?'

16

These days, even babies don't know they're born

It's 6am. There's a knock on the door. I answer it. The man says nothing. I say nothing. (The onus is surely on him?) After what feels like a minute but is probably only a few seconds, he asks for my luggage. 'I don't have any,' I say in my pants. 'Okay, goodnight,' he says in his trousers. I dare say not many of my days will start like this.

When I get on the coach, Frank's making an announcement. He says that judging by the weight of the cases, he presumes we've all nicked the TVs. I'm still half asleep.

'You're quiet,' says Sandra.

'Was it a big night?' says John.

'He says it weren't, but you never know,' says Gordon.

'Give the lad a break,' says Rowan.

'He's a dreamer,' says Carole, 'a thinker. Aren't you love? You've got thoughts and dreams.'

'I have, Carole,' I say, 'and I bet you've got a couple of each yourself.'

'I do,' she says. 'I'm getting a new kitchen this summer.'

And then we're off. To Dublin. Yonder turbines wave us goodbye, while dark cattle snooze in bottle green fields, below heavy, muscular clouds. Chris is chipper this morning. No heaviness or snoozing for her. She's got rose-tinted genes this one. I've been listening to her since we left Killarney. She won't stop annotating the world. I'm surprised Carole has any eardrums left. 'Ooh what a lovely day. Ooh what lovely houses. Ooh what a lovely breakfast that was. Ooh what muscular cows below bottle green clouds.' Carole is generally an uncontrollable enthusiast herself, but she's being put to shame today. It's as if someone's put a vial of concentrated dopamine in Chris's beans, and now she's full of them. She'd be a lousy critic. Everything would be lovely.[31]

We stop for a wander at Tralee, the main town of County Kerry. The Rose of Tralee beauty pageant takes place every August in the car park on our right, says Frank, should any-one fancy their chances. Though he doesn't think any of us is likely to win; not considering it's been going on since 1959 and the same person has won every year. Initially you had to be from the town to enter, explains Frank, but it soon became apparent that that wasn't going to work, so they extended the catchment area to Kerry, but it soon became apparent that that wasn't going to work either, so now the only criteria is that you're a bit Irish and still alive.

We park up next to the county museum. I'm surprised to see Marty looking as sharp as he does. He was putting the drinks back last night. He said people back home call him Party Marty and he was going to show us why. He even had a special Party Marty T-shirt on. He must have seen away a dozen gin and oranges, all the while describing the trickiest

---

[31] Note to self. Get Chris to write a review of this book for the *Derby Telegraph*.

postal routes on the Wirral and making sure everyone in the bar was alright. I was worried for the man. I certainly didn't think he'd be in great shape this morning. To be honest, I didn't think he'd be in any shape. But here he is, as bubbly as usual. What the hell did they feed kids in the 50s? They're made of different stuff, I swear, and it can't all be bread and dripping. 'I'm immune to hangovers, Ben. I've been wanting one for years. To see what all the fuss is about. It's my metabolism, you see, Ben. Plus all the orange I have with the gin.'

I walk into town along Denny Street, which is a wide, Georgian-seeming avenue that could be in Dublin or Liverpool. You're never far from a monument in Ireland, and here's one now, quietly remembering various rebellions against various instances of Anglo indecency. There've been so many such instances that they've had to be consolidated and put on the same pedestal.

I reach a shopping street called The Mall. John from Stoke's sat outside a bookshop on a bench in the sun. He says he's waiting on Sandra, who's in the shopping centre. John was in there for a bit and says it was dead. He reckons that in 50 years, the very idea of a shop will be a thing of the past. He reckons kids will hear mention of a shop and look up and ask, 'A shop? Say what, Grandpa?' I'd put John on my Supremely Sage Council of Elders, for what it's worth. I'd put most of this coachload on it to tell the truth – if only on a trial basis.

Carole and Chris wouldn't need a trial. They'd be the first names on the team sheet. I spot the pair on Denny

Street heading back towards the coach. When I catch up with them they're talking about Christmas shopping. Turns out Chris likes to get hers done by the end of summer, while Carole likes to buy for two Christmases every other autumn. Carole knows that her method carries certain risks: sometimes things have gone out of fashion by the time they are presented; and sometimes things are no longer appropriate or politically correct – for example, she once got her niece a gluten-free cookbook, but fifteen months later, the niece was tolerant again. Another thing Carole has to say about her Christmas shopping is that her expenditure remains roughly the same no matter how many grandchildren she has, because with each one that comes along, the spend per head goes down accordingly. She says this way of doing things has caused some problems in the past, in short because each year the heads want more and not less. Which is ridiculous of course. When Carole was young, she got a packet of handkerchiefs and couldn't believe her luck, while Chris remembers getting a carrot and being over the moon. Carole says that one of her grandchildren is two and already has *everything*. 'These days, even babies don't know they're born,' she says, which is certainly something to consider. And they're not better for having more, no way. Kids don't know how to *imagine* anymore. They don't know how to be bored.

'Who doesn't?' says Frank, who's leaning on the nose of his coach, smoking.

'Kids,' says Carole.

'Well I could certainly teach 'em,' says Frank.

As we ride the N21 north-east, I ask what Carole's up to next week. She says she's busy, babysitting mostly. She doesn't mind though; she likes having the grandchildren. Her husband used to say that they ought to have had the grand-children before the children. Children are a lot of work, says Carole. Plus there aren't any gaps, no pauses for thought, no intervals like at the theatre when you can have a wee and some ice cream. But now, life's one big interval, and having kids around is nicer, easier. She reckons the kids like it as well. She reckons children should spend as much time as possible with their grandparents. The love is different. It's calmer.

'Are you wanting children, Ben?' says Carole.

'Maybe down the road a bit.'

'Have you a partner then?'

'I do. Megan.'

'Not the royal one?'

'That's her.'

'You know they've called it Archie? Not Gary like Frank said. Have you got a picture of Megan?' I show her a picture. 'Ooh she's lovely. Isn't she Chris? Isn't she lovely?' Chris has a look but – quite uncharacteristically – doesn't seem that fussed. 'How did you meet then?' says Carole.

I offer my rehearsed lines, that it was Halloween, that it was a party, that I had a pumpkin on my head and so on.

'Did you hear that Chris?'

'No, I didn't.'

'Our Benjamin had a pumpkin on his head.'

'When?'

'When he met Megan.'

'Did he?'

'He did.'

'Well how did she recognise him?'

'She didn't.'

'Oh.'

'But that didn't stop her.'

'Is she a vegan then?'

'No she's not a— is she a vegan, Ben? No she's not a vegan, Chris, of course she's not.'

We stop in Adare for something to eat. Frank says there's also a few local attractions we can look at, but I've consumed enough for one week. There's no more space in the filing cabinet. All room's taken up with dolphins and poems and bits of life advice – avoid getting paid, have grandchildren first, strap in because you're pretty much f*cked and so on.

I walk up the main street until I find a little café, where I have some pasta and make a start on Graham Norton's new novel, which I bought in the bookshop in Tralee. The café's pretty quiet so the girl working there's able to tell me more about herself than might otherwise be possible. She says she's never heard of Graham Norton; that she has a pet rat called Chester; and that although she sometimes gets bored in Adare, she'd sooner be bored somewhere small than bothered somewhere big. At that moment, Chris and Carole walk past and wave through the window. Then a minute later, Marty does the same. The girl asks what's going on.

'How do you mean?'

'Well how do yeh know everyone round here?'

'You want the truth?'

'Go on.'

'I'm famous.'

'Bollix y'are? Are yeh?'

'Afraid so.'

'So who are yeh?'

'Graham Norton.'

'Feck off.'

'It's true.'

'So you're reading your own book? That's gas.'

I walk back to the coach with Marty. He's had a soup and a sandwich and a sit down in the church. It was a Protestant one, but he reckons no one will mind. 'They were lucky to have you, Marty,' I say.

Frank puts a CD on to see us through to Dublin. It's an Irish fella telling stories about two other Irish fellas, Murphy and Casey. I'll paraphrase a section, to give you an idea. 'Murphy says, Murphy says to Casey, "What do you think of the euthanasia, Casey?" And Casey says to Murphy, Casey says to Murphy, "They're as bad as the youth in Ireland, Murphy." And Murphy's son, Murphy's son asks if he can get an encyclopaedia for the school, and Murphy says, Murphy says, "You can feckin' well walk like the others!" And then Murphy, and then Murphy gets done for doing 80 miles per hour. He says to the police office, says to your man, "It's impossible. I've only been driving twenty minutes."' And so on. The coach loves it.

I'm happy. I could dress up the sentiment but that's what it comes down to. It's the same feeling – or almost the same feeling – as the one I had sitting next to Nan, waiting for the coffee to cool down. There's a bit of sun, and there's a bit of laughter, and I'm not at all impatient to be somewhere else. We're going along nicely, across Ireland, through the afternoon. Chris leans across Carole and shows me a picture of her dog.

'She misses me,' says Chris. 'She'll kiss me all over when I get back. She kisses Carole too.'

'Kisses me?' says Carole. 'She blooming well licks me makeup off!'

My hotel room is on the edge of Dublin, and three times the size it needs to be, which means I can unpack the TV I nicked without it getting in the way. I watch the motorway from the window. The scene is reassuring somehow – all the motion, all the toing and froing. It implies purpose and co-operation. And it's quite pretty, to be honest, seen from this room, from this evening. The lines are nice, and the colours. I suppose lines and colours are what pictures come down to. Though that's not to say that's what they amount to – something's added, is always added, by an invisible hand. A red van has pulled over on the hard shoulder. It's a younger couple. They seem to be having trouble with the satnav.

At dinner, I'm next to Ann and opposite Clive. Turns out Clive has no discs between his vertebrae and is in constant pain and no surgeon will go near him. That's what Ann says, and Clive does nothing to suggest she's lying. They married a year ago, and met six months before that. Their respective partners died of blood clots in 2015. Clive got cancer soon after their wedding, then both his knees went and had to be changed, and now his back's knackered. Ann says it's been the best of times, the worst of times, but Clive disagrees. 'It's been the best two years of my life,' he says. 'And I've a tattoo that says as much.' Ann isn't a big fan of the tattoo because Clive plans to update it annually, so changes the subject to her grandson who works for a gourmet sausage roll company that supplies the Queen. The grandson also got married a year ago and for a present, Ann did a painting of a sausage roll in a wedding dress. Ann always wanted to paint but didn't until her first husband died. She prefers watercolours because they spread nicely, and you can really catch a sky, a sea, a flower – if you've a mind to of course. It's calming – the painting that is – because you don't think of anything else, which is good if your husband has just … She regrets waiting. Waiting to paint. She regrets thinking she couldn't. Then I hear about her knitting and how she did a shawl for Clive, but to be honest, I'm struggling to keep up with Ann's yarn, and Clive can tell. He knows his wife has a habit of going on and he likes it. It makes him smile, despite his back. He says that perhaps Ann wants to make a start on her pudding. Ann gets the hint. And then doesn't, because now she's telling me that she and Clive aren't really coach tour people, but that Clive can't drive anymore so they thought they'd give it a go; and that when she's not painting or knitting or talking, she's volunteering at a care home; and that her friend Ethel is 101 and would beat me at Scrabble with her eyes closed. She finishes her pudding and gives Clive a look – a loving apology, an admission:

THESE DAYS, EVEN BABIES DON'T KNOW THEY'RE BORN

I know, I know. Then she turns to me and says, 'And what about you, Benjamin?'

⁓

It's a new dawn when I get on the coach. Clive asks if I got into Dublin after dinner last night.

'I did.'

'Get up to much?'

'I met a friend.'

'He?'

'She.'

'I'll ask no further questions.'

'You shouldn't have a mind like that, Clive,' I say. 'Not with a back like yours.'

It's a short drive to the ferry, then there's a bit of sitting about before we can get on the thing. Some get off to stretch legs, to fetch coffees. Carole doesn't. Carole turns to me and touches me on the arm and says she didn't have time for a shower this morning because she was meant to get a call from reception to wake her up, but before she went to bed – force of habit – she'd unplugged the phone.

'Why do you unplug the phone?'

'In case someone calls in the night.'

'Does that often happen?'

'No, because I unplug the phone.'

Chris had time for a shower – a long one she says. She was in there for three songs on the radio. Chris was up at five. Always is. Like clockwork. No need for an alarm. She's got her own system. Before she goes to sleep she bangs her head on the headboard five times. That does the job. It makes her wake up at five.

'Who taught you that?' I say.

'I taught meself!'

'And it always works?'

'Every time.'

'Well I hope you don't ever plan to get up at twelve, Chris, else you'll have a sore head.'

'It would never happen. I only ever do five. I've too much to get on with.'

Later, boarding the ferry, Carole shows me a picture of her John. And then she shows me some more pictures of her John, and as she does so she says quietly (and more to herself than to me) that John is Yani in Greek, Eoin in Gaelic, Juan in Spanish, and even Yahya in Arabic. 'If I'd known back then,' she says, 'I could have called him all sorts.'

Back at the Stretton interchange, we get off for the last time. I try to give Frank a tip, but he won't accept it. I try to put it in his top pocket but he slaps my hand away. 'Get away with ye!' Good old Frank.

Inside the lounge, I wait for the Manchester coach, while others wait for Preston, Stoke, Derby, Leeds. I ask Chris and Carole if they want a tea. The queue's not as long as it could be, but nonetheless, they might not fancy standing in it. They do want a tea, and try to push a fiver on me, but I won't have it. I deliver the teas and then sit a few rows behind them, close enough to hear Chris say, a few minutes later, 'I'm glad I didn't pay for this tea, Carole. It's rubbish.'

THESE DAYS, EVEN BABIES DON'T KNOW THEY'RE BORN

Part 5

Lake Como, Italy

17

Life's not about living to 96. It's about living to 84

When I get back to Manchester, I stay there, because I'm due on another coach tomorrow morning at 5.50am. To Lake Como. A deep body of water in the north of Italy lined with David Beckham and George Clooney. I check into the cheapest hotel I can find – the Britannia. It's above a disco. I spend the night subconsciously bopping; tossing and turning to nightmarish beats. In short, I don't get much sleep, which is a nuisance because I've got a 27-hour journey ahead of me, which is the sort of undertaking you need to be ready for, else it will feel like a test rather than an adventure. I know it's antisocial but I hope I get two seats to myself.

The lady sitting next to me is wearing a Union Jack travel pillow. I ask her about it. She sort of grimaces.

'I lost my husband a year ago.'

'Sugar. Sorry. But I don't follow.'

'It was his. And now I use it. I think he won it in a raffle.'

'And does it help?'

'Oh yes. I sleep like a log.'[32]

'And you're looking forward to the holiday?'

'I'm looking forward to everything. Even the tunnel.'

---

[32] A very noisy log, she might have added.

'The tunnel?'

She nods. 'Some hate the thought of all that water over them, but I'm alright because I quite like water.'

Then, something about the tunnel prompts a thought or memory, because Jill says, 'I need to get better with my long irons.' For the uninitiated, a long iron is a type of golf club which is meant to (but reliably does not) make the ball go a long way. 'I'm jealous of those that can hit a nice long iron,' says Jill. 'I used to be quite good with them. But then I stopped playing for seven years when I was looking after my husband. I just started again. It's nice, but a bit sad as well, because every time I play I think about why I can.'

Jill says those seven years left a mark on her – not a bad mark, she wouldn't say that, but a mark nonetheless. Her comment makes me think of *Wild Strawberries*, the Ingmar Bergman film, in which Professor Borg, who is a bit of a Scrooge, picks up some teenage hitchhikers on his way to Lund from Stockholm to collect a prize, a sort of lifetime achievement thing. The professor enjoys the company of his passengers more than he expected to. They soften him, enliven him, take him to new and old things, through dreams and visions and memories and talk. One result of all the dreaming and remembering is that he crashes the car. No it isn't. That's wrong. One result is that the professor comes to see that certain things are carried with us through our lives: deep affecting moments, character shaping events: a heartbreak, a betrayal, a loss, an act of neglect – or, in the case of Jill, a period of care. The film is good for plenty of reasons, but for me its chief virtue is its invitation to see that reflection is good, that taking stock is good, that intimacy is good, and that going on long, slow, capricious adventures is good, and better still if the travelling party is made up of provocative youngsters and provocative oldsters and provocative whoevers, for then the range of feeling and thought is broader, more colourful, more affecting. A note of caution though. At the end of the film, when the youngsters hop out of the car and say farewell and the professor smiles and waves and says that he would like to hear from them sometime, his remark goes unheard, because the young, too eager maybe, are already out of earshot.

Seventy metres under the seabed, Jill tells me she's on a diet. From what I can tell, the diet mostly consists of Greek dishes involving lamb, because that's all she mentions. She gets up one of the recipes on her phone. Reading the method out to me, she pretends there's an instruction to put the lid on and do nine holes. Jill's quite pleased with the phone. It was a present from her son. She shows me a picture of him (he looks like Phillip Schofield), and then pictures of things she generally approves of, like swordfish and Cyprus and the indoor market in Shrewsbury. Then, passing Saint-Quentin, she shows me a double-spread of her *Sun* and asks what I think of Nigel Farage. I say I don't think much of him, and she says she thinks he's funny. She flicks through the paper and annotates and remarks as and when. Added together, the annotations and remarks get us through a quarter of France, and combine to form a slightly bloated, slightly abstract haiku.

What do you think of Farage? I find him funny.
Jagger? Not another baby. Would you look at that. Would you look at her.
The Tottenham manager is ready to quit.

Danny, one of the two drivers, takes to the microphone. He says the good news is we're halfway through France, and the bad news is we're now on the most boring road in the world and will be for the next fourteen hours. I sigh at the news, but Jill smiles. Without doubt, the holiday's already started for Jill. I reckon it would have started for me as well, had it not been for getting no sleep last night, and the prospect of getting no more for another twenty-odd hours. When I tell Jill that I can't sleep sitting up on something moving, she says it's because I'm an Aquarius. Jill dabbles in astrology, you see, and won't go near a Pisces if she can help it. She's also a busy gardener, a keen pastry chef, and an occasional poet. One of her poems – about eating alone – was published in her church magazine. She's also into birdwatching, walking and foraging. Occasionally, she's able to combine the three: she'll be out walking and spot a finch or a kingfisher or a chough and some wild herbs or mushrooms or whatever. Foraging is in her genes, she reckons. There's an ammonite on display at Swansea University that was discovered by her maternal grandmother. Jill thinks she might have got her independent streak from her maternal grandmother. Either way, her friends think she's odd for doing things on her own – be it playing golf or going for a walk or going on holiday or going out for a cigarette. She misses smoking. If she's honest, she misses it more than she misses her – no, she won't finish that sentence. Suffice to say, she enjoyed smoking, and only gave it up recently and reluctantly, which is to say she still has the odd one or two now and again. Another of Jill's guilty pleasures – alongside smoking, jam sponge and teeing her ball up in the rough – is chocolate. Of course, she tries to watch her weight, but when there's so much of it, well, it's tempting to take your eye off it sometimes. Besides, life's not about living to 96, it's about living to 84, and so if Jill wants to have a cigarette and a square of chocolate on the tenth tee, and the occasional jam sponge, then she will. She quotes Oscar Wilde, who said that temptation resisted is poison to the soul. I point out that Oscar Wilde died at 46, and not from an excess of jogging.

Six hours later, with my right cheek pressed to the cold glass of the window and Jill's snoring in my left ear, I decide that I'd dearly love to be somewhere else and horizontal. I don't mind where – a trench, a morgue, the Korean Demilitarized Zone – just so long as I could stretch out. I'm not one to be precious or territorial, but to say that Jill's leaking across the threshold is to put it mildly. I can feel her pillow against my cheek. Not always, but now and again it's there, which means that Jill's facial features are about fifteen centimetres from my own. I'm not saying that's bad per se. I'm not being ageist. I'm just saying it's not normally how I get to sleep. I know my suffering is comparatively tiny but nonetheless, it's hard to bear graciously. A case in point: I want to poke Jill in the eye, just to give her a hint that leaning in the other direction might not be the worst idea in the world. Or pinch her nose. Or take one of my socks off and put it in her mouth, just briefly, for like a second, just long enough for her subconscious to associate this side with danger, and that side with safety. If I were at liberty, I would be in a bed and dead to the world. As it stands, I'm wedged between a cold window and Jill, increasingly uncomfortable, with sleep but a dream. They call this overnight service *Night-Rider*, which makes it sound sexy, risqué, desirable. *Night-Survivor* would be more like it.

We stop at a Swiss service station. It's dawn and there are mountains. I watch some of my lot enter, spot the prices, work out what that is in pounds, share a look that says 'Are they taking the piss?' and then discreetly reverse as if they were just browsing and didn't want anything anyway. Which is fair enough, because Switzerland is laughably expensive. But to hell with it, I need to buy some stuff, if only for something to do, so I get a black coffee and a chocolate bar and a pastry and some salted nuts, and it costs me more than the money I saved by taking the *Night-Rider* instead of the slower service which involves staying in a hotel overnight. There's a lesson in that I reckon, a bit of low-hanging wisdom, if only I could be arsed to reach up and claim it. Jill is awake when I get back on the coach. She looks five years younger. She looks amazing.

'You look awful,' she says. 'What have you got there?'

'Vital supplies, Jill. Did you sleep well?'

'Like a log.'

'Yeah, a f*cking noisy one,' I say, to myself, in my head, more than once. 'Pleased to hear it,' I say. 'Do you want half a Twix?'

I'm not doing this on the way back. That's what I decide. Halfway through my coffee. In fact, I might not even go back. Not after this odyssey. I feel like Ulysses on the home stretch, or one of Hannibal's elephants, or one of Keith's pigeons after flying back to Cumbria from sodding Cuba. Jill tells me to look at the snow. I make a noise. She says I could be a bit more enthusiastic. We enter Italy.

'Bit of housekeeping, folks,' says Danny. 'We're about an hour away now from Lake Como and your accommodation for the week, the lovely Britannia Hotel.'

The Britannia? Are you kidding me? Another one. If there's a bloody disco …

'There'll be an opportunity to have a good wander around the local area this morning, folks.'

You what?

'Officially, rooms are available from midday …'

Oh for the love of …

'But in our experience, that doesn't tend to be the case.'

Thank God. Thank the merciful heavens.

'It'll likely be closer to three, I would have thought.'

Shoot me.

18

They're talking of switching rooms because their neighbours were at it half the night

We've arrived in time for breakfast, which strikes me as an odd notion given that I haven't slept in months. The dining area is a grand, opulent space – Italianate is probably the word. If you get down here early, you can get a window table with a view of the lake. If you don't, you get a view of those with a view of the lake. I'm not bothered either way. A good view would go over my head right now. I've barely been able to see since the Italian border. I can hear well enough however, and in particular, I can hear well enough the table of Irish folk next to me. They're talking of switching rooms because their neighbours were at it half the night. Your man thinks it was actually next-door-but-one, but your woman won't credit the idea that a man could have done something to provoke such appreciation. 'Besides,' she says, 'the couple in that room are too old for all that. They both use walking frames, sure they do. They're past their sexpiration date, so they are.' But your man's not having any of it; he says there's no such thing. 'There certainly is and you should know there is,' says your woman, 'bearing in mind that we've not ourselves discussed doing it – *discussed* doing it, mark – since the Good Friday

Agreement.' And your man says, 'Well I had to get to the chipper, did I not?'

There's nothing for it. I go out for a sleepwalk. I go out the back of the hotel then follow a winding road up the hillside for a mile or so, to the village of Griante, where there's a *trattoria*, a town hall, and, up on a shelf of rock, a small church. The latter's bells toll as I approach, signalling the start of something, or the end of something else. I sit on a bench in front of the church and watch the youngest villagers – more forgetful than their elders – emerge from their houses and climb the hill in a hurry. I can see olive trees, and the lake, and the hills and mountains wearing wood coats and snow peaks. Closer, above the olive trees, dark green shutters rest against yellow and orange walls, and a tennis court is calm and still, uncalled for this Sunday.

I stand at the back of the church and listen to the shared prayer and song. Two of the Irish women from breakfast are here. The atmosphere is heavy and light at once. I don't feel moved as such, but nicely content and beside myself somehow. I catch or half catch the odd word: *confesso, spirito, pesto*. The last time I was in a church, I read a poem about slowing down. God knows there's no chance of me speeding up right now.

I enter the *trattoria*, the one just down from the church. I don't want to be presumptuous, but I'd say the few people in here aren't on the Shearings holiday. They look as local and established as the church up the road. I'm reminded instantly of an Ernest Hemingway story – any of them, all of them. His main man is on the run – that's me – and stops in here for some rabbit stew and risotto alla Milanese and a mug of grappa, before continuing to the frontline to blow up a bridge or catch a fish. I drink an Americano at a heavy wooden table, watching the men stirring sugar into their coffee. There's a copy of *La Provincia* on the table. A politician is up to his neck in something, and I don't think it's acclaim.

I meet Vinny in reception. He's got his room and he's happy with it – lake view, balcony, Bob's your uncle. I tell him where I've been – up to the village, to the church, to the pub – and he knows where I'm on about. He's been here a few times, you see, and some were better than others. A few years ago, he had a bit of a heart attack upstairs in his room, and Rita, his wife, had to rush up to the village to fetch a doctor. 'And what happened?' I say. 'She said it was a lovely walk,' he says.

Vinny asks if I've plans for the evening. I tell him I saw a place that's showing the football later. He says he'd tag along if he was allowed, but he's not. Vinny doesn't mind a bit of football. He used to captain Rochdale when they were in the second division, played against Bobby Moore, even left a mark on him. Vinny asks if I play, or if I used to. I tell him that I had no composure on the ball, that I preferred to panic instead and then accidentally kick someone in the shin. I give a demonstration of what I mean. I don't try to make it funny, but it makes Vinny laugh. He tells me he's now got short-term memory loss on account of heading the ball so many times. 'It was like heading a cannonball. And if you weren't seen to be doing it twenty times a match and with a smile on your face, you were hauled off for being a wuss.' He's on these pills now, to help with the memory loss, but he says quite seriously and not as a joke that he can never remember to take the bloody things. He has to rely on his wife Rita, who thankfully never headed a ball in her life. And here's Rita now. Vinny tells her to tell me how heavy the football was back then, but instead of doing that, Rita asks Vinny how he expects her to know. I ask about the book Rita's holding. 'It's about a woman who loses her husband on purpose and then hooks up with her ex in Paris,' she says. 'See what I have to put up with?' says Vinny. 'And she says watching *Match of the Day* gives me ideas.'

18.00. After sleeping for a few hours, I go down for dinner. There's no set seating plan, so I join Jill and a bloke called Graham from Sheffield. It's a buffet-style affair, so I help myself to pasta and salad and then pistachio ice cream. Graham says the fella he was sat next to on the coach is stopping at another hotel and won't be doing any of the excursions. Jill asks why and Graham explains that the fella came on the same holiday with his wife a few years back, but she died recently so he's doing it again as a sort of pilgrimage, though he reckons he can only cope with the nostalgia up to a point. 'There's a million ways to grieve,' says Jill. 'One's enough for me,' says Graham.

The conversation gets to Jill's work at the job centre in Telford. It gets there via Graham talking about Sheffield, then *The Full Monty*, then the demise of the steel industry and then unemployment. Jill says that when she started working at the job centre, they told her to look out for people with paint on their clothes, which was considered a sign that they were decorating on the side. Then Jill mentions someone who slashed their wrists in front of Jill's colleague when her money was stopped. Graham says that although there are plenty who will happily have their cake and eat it, there are plenty more who could do with a bit of support but won't go near a job centre because they think admitting you need help is admitting you've failed or something. 'I think I might get some more ice cream,' says Jill. 'My husband liked ice cream.'

After dinner we move downstairs, where there is a bar and a man playing the keyboard and singing. Graham and I find a table, while Jill goes up to the bar to get some drinks – gin for them, coffee for me. When she gets back with the drinks, she says the Italian barman spoke English 'like a posh Welsh schoolboy'. As I'm trying to hear in my mind's ear what Jill's going on about, Graham remembers an Italian boy he met on holiday in Naples some time ago who had the most horrible Lancastrian accent he'd ever heard. Turns out the Italian boy had never been to Lancashire, but his mother – also Italian – had learnt English in Blackburn and he'd got it off her. When Graham gives us an approximation of the boy's accent, Jill says it sounds neither Italian nor Lancastrian. Graham says alright then, give us your posh Welsh schoolboy. She does so and Graham has to admit that it's not bad. Then Graham says that I don't sound like I'm from Portsmouth, and he knows what he's talking about because his daughter

THEY'RE TALKING OF SWITCHING ROOMS

lived there until she died at the age of 53 from smoking too much. Then he mentions that he's got a 60-year-old son and for some reason I find the idea funny.

'What is it?' says Graham.

'Nothing, nothing.'

'Come on, spit it out.'

'Ah, just the idea of … no it's nothing.'

'Come on lad!'

'It's just. The idea of a 60-year-old son, that's all.'

'Well he didn't come out that way.'

'I know, I know.'

'The man's had a life. He's all grown up. I don't tell him to brush his teeth.'

'You're right. I'm sorry.'

'In fact he tells me to brush mine.'

Graham points to my soft drink and says that an all-inclusive holiday is a funny spot for a detox. And now that Graham thinks about it, nor was being a publican for 30 years much good for detoxing. 'People used to say, "Give me a pint of bitter Graham and one for yourself", and I never learnt the knack of saying no. We say it were the good old days but it weren't really that good. It was so smoky in my pub you couldn't see the person next to yer. My wife didn't smoke but she worked in the pub with me, so she might as well have done. She got lung cancer and died at 53, same age as my daughter.'

Jill shifts the subject from smoking and lung cancer to the paintings on the wall – and one in particular, a reproduction of a Picasso. Graham doesn't think much of Picasso. He's got nothing against him, but just doesn't fancy his pictures. Graham prefers Lowry because he had a look at ordinary people and did 'em in a way that appealed to them same people. I tell them that my girlfriend's a painter and Jill says, 'Is she? Go on then, give us a look.' I get up a painting on Jill's phone. It's called *Love Storm* and shows two young lovers embracing in a kitchen after an argument – quite a big one by the look of it. Graham has a look and says, 'Is my nose really that big?'

19

Now there's no whistling because he never comes home

I sleep like a log. An actual log. Not the type of log Jill sleeps like. Then I go down to the dining room, where I start with a bowl of prunes, a decision which causes a man wearing socks with sandals and a white vest under a leather jacket to observe, 'They'll teach you what your arsehole's for.' Of all the possible sentences to get my day up and running.

It's hard to be sure from twenty metres, but it looks like the man's eating prunes as well. He looks a bit like Silvio Berlusconi, the former Italian Prime Minister. His hair's slicked back and he's wearing a sizable gold necklace. That'll teach me what my arsehole's for … Tch. I'll teach you what my – no, no I won't. I think I'll leave it there. I think I'll fetch the honey.

I'm prevented from fetching the honey by Richie, a waiter, who insists on doing it for me and getting me a coffee while he's at it. I ask Richie in my best Italian what he thinks of the area. He says in English that his parents were killed and his brothers groomed and that he lived in a war zone until being granted refuge in Italy, with the result that he's got no complaints for the moment. Milk? *Latte?*

Today's excursion is a lap of the lake. We start by heading north, towards its apex. Doing so, Danny brings us up to speed regarding the region of Lombardy. He says there were Celts here before the Romans scared them away to Wales and Cornwall and Ireland; that polenta and rice are more popular than pasta and pizza; and that Mussolini was shot just over there – in a village called Dongo.[33]

Benito Mussolini rose to power after the First World War. He was assisted in doing so by an army of fascist enforcers known as Blackshirts, who, it's fair to say, weren't known for their discretion. Mussolini's message was a simple one – let's make Italy great again. It was also an effective one: it carried him to the highest reaches of the State, where he consolidated his supremacy by dismantling the mechanisms that could be used to oust or undermine him. At the start of the Second World War, Italy remained neutral, but when the tide turned against the Allies, Mussolini rowed in behind Hitler. It would prove to be the last thing he rowed in behind.

---

[33] After the fall of the Western Roman Empire in 465, this part of the world enjoyed a range of visitors, chief among them the Germanic Lombards, whose whole nation – yes, whole nation – migrated here from the Carpathian basin, which is somewhere near Hungary. Then, in the late 700s, a bloke called Charlemagne came to town, on a mission to get something called a Holy Roman Empire up and running, which, from what I can tell, was just a massive Catholic Germany whose leaders were modelled on Caesar and Augustus and all that mob. Then, the Spanish somehow stuck their nose in locally around the 17th century, and then the Austrians *really* stuck their nose in locally around the 18th century, which is where they left it (give or take a dash of Napoleon) until 1859, when Lombardy was annexed to the Kingdom of Italy as a result of the Second Italian War of Independence, which involved little Sardinia teaming up with France to boot out the unwanted Austrians. The biscuit guy – Garibaldi – was crucial in all this.

When Italy was taken by the Allies, Benny donned a pair of comfortable loafers and went on the run. He made it as far as Dongo, where he stopped for one coffee too many.

Because you can't photograph such things, such stories, such events, we take pictures of the lake instead, and each other, and the jetty, and the small pleasure boats. I take a picture of a lady from Eccles (at her behest), and then ask about the cake named after her hometown, which gets us on to baking and then cooking generally. She says her husband won't let her in the kitchen since he retired. She says he didn't even know the house had a kitchen until a few years ago. She says his chilli con carne is terrible. She says he does the rice in the kettle. She says she doesn't want to be emancipated if it tastes like that. But of course she's allowed into the kitchen when there's washing up to be done. She says it's a murder scene after every meal – even breakfast, when they only have fruit and cereal and perhaps a yoghurt. If she's frank, she preferred having him at work. At least he came home whistling every day. Now there's no whistling because he never comes home – how can he when he's always in the bleeding kitchen? I suggest he might be struggling with having less to do these days, less purpose. She says she knows he's got nothing to do, but she just wishes he'd do it somewhere else.

Back on the coach, and back on the move, I ask Jill if she was up late last night.

'Who told you?' she says.

'No one. But I take that as a yes.'

'I was in bed by one and up by seven.'

'And is your room alright?'

'Oh yes. Very nice. Very operatic.'

'And did you sleep okay?'

'I didn't actually.'

'Perhaps you should keep wearing your travel pillow.'

'I would, but it's got a puncture.'

'How did it get that?'

'I'm not sure, but I think it might have been your beard.'

'Really?'

'I reckon you might have been getting too close.'

You know how when you stare at a word for ages and it starts to lose its meaning and sense and seem absurd and *wrong*? Well that's happening now, regarding the natural environment. Everything around me has started to blur and unfold. I'm staring at this mountain and that lake and I'm thinking: *what the hell even is a mountain? What the hell even is a lake?* Before I've chance to start answering my own questions – a mountain is what happens when bits of the earth's crust run into each other and something has to give; a lake is a big puddle – Jill is saying, 'It's a buzzard! It's a buzzard!' and the moment of quiet contemplation is lost. I ask Jill what a buzzard is exactly. She says they're brownish and love catching voles. When I ask what a vole is exactly, Jill says, 'Are you taking the piss?'

We round the lake's topmost hairpin and head south to the village of Dervio, where we stop to have a look at an old church and the ruined castle beside it, whose surviving walls look brittle enough to be snapped off like bits of cracker.

Danny directs us to a *belvedere* (nice view in Italian), where everyone starts clambering on the medieval walls and pulling themselves up by the railings, like children on a climbing frame, the better to see the view. And they're right to, for the view's a belter. The water is a royal blue, and the vibrant green of the hills is only darkened here and there by the shadow of clouds, while the long, surrounding summit wears a thin kerchief of snow, which might be gone within days. Someone says, 'There's nowt like it near Wigan.'

We stop in Lecco for a bit of lunch. The town's at the bottom of the lake's right leg, if it is understood as an upturned Y. There's another upturned Y in front of me now: a young woman is straddling a young man who is sat on a lakeside bench. Her meaning in doing so – one assumes – is to let the young man know how delightful he is. They need a room this pair, two even. I reason that this must be their fourth or fifth date. Any fewer and they wouldn't have the temerity to take such liberties, any more and they wouldn't want to. You don't see elder couples behaving like this. Not least because their joints couldn't cope with some of the trigonometry.

I find Lecco's main street and then take a side one, hoping for somewhere small and quiet and in the sun. I find the place I'm looking for. I sit at one of its three outside tables and order sparkling water and the *menu del giorno*, which is salami and bread, then penne puttanesca, and then *ossobuco*, which is a piece of veal in potato sauce. The pasta is three types of salty – it's coming from the capers, the olives and the Parmesan, and in the final analysis, is coming too much. The best part of the meal is the bread and olive oil, and watching the locals come and go on their lunch breaks.

Ciao, Marty!

Ciao, Beppi!

Ciao, ciao!

Come sta il cane?

Perfetto, perfetto.

Come sta il donna?

Bella, bella.

Okay allora.

Allora.

Ciao, Marty!

Ciao, Beppi!

You might not get the tongue, but you get the picture. Italian small talk, street talk. At the table next to mine, the talk is less small, however: two ladies speak in whispers to protect me from their scandal. They don't want their sins – or the sins of whoever they're discussing – on my conscience. Paying the bill – *la quenta* – I see that if you fell from another planet you could land on worse spots than Lecco – among the balconies, the old stone streets and buildings, the lake, of course, and the *menu del giorno* and the bread and oil especially.[34]

Walking back to the coach, I spot an intergenerational encounter outside a café on Via Roma. Two people are sitting at a table, facing off. I see them in profile briefly, and then obliquely as I continue down the street towards the

---

[34] Turns out I asked for the bill in Spanish.

lake. I won't assume that one is grandmother and the other granddaughter, but I will assume that one is over 60 and one is under five. The point is: they are leaning into one another, almost touching noses, both grinning equally – at the occasion, at their good luck, at the prospect of what's to come. I can't be sure they're on good terms, but they're definitely making it look that way. It's enough to make you want grandchildren, or grandparents, or more grandparents, or grandparents again, and whatever that pastry is they're sharing.

On our way back to the hotel, we stop outside George Clooney's house. Jill is visibly and audibly excited – she even has a puff of her inhaler. And she's not alone in her excitement. The sight of Clooney's house has the entire coach spellbound, even the blokes. They're using their cameras to zoom in. Someone thinks the kitchen window's open. Someone can see a massive pepper grinder. Someone thinks they saw him through frosted glass – which means he was probably getting out of the shower. The very thought does something to Jill. I watch her inch closer to George's perimeter. I watch her look over her shoulder to make sure a few people are looking. And then I watch her remove her bra from under her blouse and fling it over the wall into George's garden. I ask her what she did that for. She shrugs her shoulders and says, 'Well, I've plenty of others.'

A mile or so down the road, with Jill's knockers bouncing around like there's no tomorrow, I ask if she's got a bit of a thing for George then. She says not really. She says if she's got a thing for anyone then it's David Dimbleby. She even went to the filming of *Question Time* when it was in Telford, and again when it was in Shrewsbury. She was tempted to ask David a question. I ask what she would have asked. 'I don't know,' she says. 'Maybe if he fancied nine holes sometime.' David, if you're reading – you'd have been a fool to say no.

I was alone at first. I got through a bowl of soup and half a bowl of pasta before Jill spotted me. She was sat with three others but said she couldn't let me eat alone, not in Italy. I ask if she can recite the poem she wrote about eating alone, the one that was published in the church magazine, but she can't. She can only remember the odd line. '*The stale dread / of the end of the bread.*' That's one she can remember.

'Are you going to that bar up the road tonight?' I say.
'Hm?
'For the singer you mentioned?'
'Oh yes. Six of us are going. Are you coming?'
'Nah – I'm still knackered.'
'You big baby. Have you ever been to Birmingham?'
She has a habit of doing this. Or rather: she's done this three times: asked a question I didn't see coming. 'I have,' I say. 'But not for years and years.'
'I love to go to Birmingham.'
'I've never heard anyone say that.'
'It's got the biggest Primark in Europe. It's so cheap.'
'Is that why you can afford to toss your underwear over garden walls?'

'And the Rag Market. That's very good. You can get six avocados for a pound there.'

'Jill, that's nonsense.'

'Why is it?'

'You can't get six avocados for a pound anywhere.'

'And the theatre in Birmingham's excellent.'

'How many times have you been to Birmingham, Jill?'

'I go once a month.'

'Have you friends there?'

'No.'

'Family?'

'No.'

'You just go because—'

'Because I like it.'

'Once a month?'

'Yeah.'

'You've heard of London, right?'

'OMG don't look behind you.'

'What is it?'

'About a hundred Italian fifteen year olds.'

'Really?'

'The average age just plummeted.'

'And so did the peace and quiet.'

'Oh, to be that young again!'

'What would you do?

'What?'

'If you were that young again, what would you do?'

'Him, probably.'

'Jill. I'm pretty sure you can't—'

'I'm joking. Him *and* him.'

'Jill.'

'That would equal 30. I just hope they're not on my corridor. Are you in a book club?'

See? 'No.'

'I'm in three. And I'm in a walking club, but I think I told you that. Did I tell you that?'

'You did.'

'We're reading a book set in Italy at the moment. There's a young man in it who rides a motorbike. He's always greasy.'

'Do you like reading then?'

'I do, but mainly I go to the book club to get out of the house. It's not that I don't like my house. I do. It's nice. It's just … a bit big now.'

'You say you had to care for—'

'Alzheimer's. And the less you know about that the better. People say I haven't grieved properly. They say I should stay at home and grieve properly. But I don't want to do that. I'm going to Austria in a couple of months. If I get that chocolate thing will you eat half?'

20

They took him to hospital in a gondola

Rita's sitting alone, and she doesn't mind if I join her. She says Vinny isn't coming down just yet. He's doing his physio. He's got no right knee, you see, because of the football.

'No knee at all?'

'There's a cap, but it's not really connected to much, so it just slides around.'

'And what does physio involve?'

'Sitting on the balcony reading the paper most of the time.'

'Was he good at football then?'

'Oh yes. He was captain. If you got tackled by Vinny, you stayed tackled by Vinny.'

'Is that right?'

'That's what he used to say. But he was soft with it. I remember he was really sad one Saturday night because he'd broken someone's ankle in six places.'

Rita went up to the church yesterday. She walked up there on her own. She's not religious, she just felt like it. She used to be religious but just sort of forgot, or kept forgetting rather – to go to church, to pray, to trace things back to God. And if you keep forgetting something – well, it might mean it's not ever so important to you. Rita considers herself an intelligent tomato, that's her way of looking at things, and so long as she goes back into the soil somehow, back into the system – so long as she's recycled – then she'll be happy – well, not happy because she'll be soil, she'll be dead, but I know what she means. Rita used to be a hairdresser and still does the odd bit now and again – the odd cut, the odd colour – but mostly she goes into a local school to listen to some of the kids read, the ones who don't have ideal domestic situations. She also goes in an hour before school starts to make toast three times a week, which sounds a bit questionable to me. 'Anyway,' she says, 'here comes Vinny. He must have smelt the bacon. Watch he doesn't tackle you.'

Jill ended up on the dance floor last night. That's what she tells me, on our way to Tirano, from where we'll take a train to St Moritz in Switzerland. But it wasn't her fault. It was her mum's fault. Her mum loved a boogie, and now Jill's got it in her genes.

'Did you say your mum was Welsh, Jill?'

'Oh, very Welsh!'

'And what did that involve then?

'Sorry?'

'Being very Welsh.'

'Oh. Well. Just not being English, really.'

We head north and then east towards the Swiss border. Again, the sky is clear; again, the motion picture is glossy and stark.

'My dad worked on the trains,' says Jill. 'He was a guard.'

'I hope he was a lenient one.'

'I doubt that very much. Not unless he had a character transplant on the way to work each morning. The most lenient thing he ever did to me was letting me tie my own laces. He was in Italy during the war, caught Yellow Fever in Venice. Not a bad spot to get it. They took him to hospital in a gondola. When you cook risotto do you use that special rice or just normal stuff?'

Jill knows a lot of words. That's what I'm hearing, what I'm noticing. Not just words like risotto and laces. She knows a lot of proper nouns. She knows the name of things. For example, she often points to passing flowers and nominates them: bougainvillea, giant daisies, jasmine, periwinkles, oleanders. She says she didn't used to know the names. Says it's only since her husband died, really, since she started getting out more. And golf helps. She's always in the bushes. She doesn't always find her ball, but she almost always finds some flowers she hasn't seen before. She'll get someone to come over and say what they are, and if they don't know, then she'll take a picture and find out later. Jill's explanation of how she knows the names now but didn't before makes me think of a poem by Clive James that I read in a newspaper when he died not long ago. The poem says something about flowers, about learning their names, about noticing things, about losing your ball but finding something else.[35]

I used to think Jill had two settings – talk and snore – but I'm seeing a third more and more – or hearing a third rather: silence, quiet, reflection. I've been hearing it more

---

[35] 'Once, I would not have noticed; nor have known / The name for Japanese anemones, / So pale, so frail. But now I catch the tone / Of leaves. No birds can touch down in the trees / Without my seeing them. I count the bees.'

since we swapped seats. She's by the window now, and I think there's more for her to reflect on out there, more to be quiet about. She turns away from the window presently and offers me a sweet. I take one and she says that her grandmother had a rotten sweet tooth, if I'll forgive the pun. She used to make something called lap cake. Jill used to help her make it in the kitchen. Not that she was much help, but at least it kept her out of the way of her grandfather. If Jill made too much noise – folding the currants, greasing the tin – her grandmother would tell her to keep it down because Grandad's picking his horses. He was always picking his horses, as far as Jill can remember, though she admits that when it comes to memories, kids cling on to certain things – the cake, the horses – at the expense of just about everything else. He always needed a drink when he was picking his horses, says Jill. You knew when he'd picked one or two because he'd be sucking Parma Violets – a type of confectionery. He was at his best when he was fishing. Those were Jill's favourite times with him. He used to make her wear dark clothes so the trout couldn't spot them. Then, if they caught something, they'd fry it up when they got back and have it with boiled potatoes and leeks if they were in season.

'How old were you when they died?'

'Who?'

'Well not the trout, Jill – your grandparents.'

'They both died on my eighteenth birthday.'

'Christ. That's a bit weird.'

'Not really. It was a car crash.'

Sometimes, you meet people who make you see that the people you thought talked a lot don't actually. I meet Lyn outside a café in Tirano, waiting for our corkscrew-train up into the mountains of Switzerland. Over the course of one small cappuccino, Lyn tells me the following: that I should forget Shearings and use a company called Travel Sphere instead because there are young people on those ones; that she has camped throughout Russia and compared to that experience, this is all fluff; that she's a university librarian; that she always has a deconstructed kettle on her person; that she likes reading – Toni Morrison, Jean Rhys – but to really let off steam, she watches quiz shows on TV; that if it's an education I'm after, I could do a lot worse than watching *Coronation Street* from start to finish (that's over 10,000 episodes), paying special attention to Maureen Lipman's character; that I should write that down – *Maureen Lipman*; and that I should teach English abroad, apart from where they already speak it. I might be wrong, but I don't think I say a word or make a noise during the transmission of all this information. When the call comes to make our way to the platform, and Lyn moves off and I'm left alone, I try to imagine how I might take all that she's said and compress it and trap it and ferment it and distil it – that is, make use of it – but I can't, simply can't, just cannot imagine converting all of the above into a takeaway kernel of anything. Some things can't be broken down. Some things can't be harnessed. Some things just disappear without a trace.

The first thing you notice about the carriages of the Bernina Express are the size of the windows. And the first thing I enjoy looking at through those windows are the horny cows at Brusio, and then the sweeping circular viaduct which winds us upward and onward into the green, springy hills. We pass a lake (ooh), a field of dandelions and buttercups (ah), and then a huge car park (oh). You can imagine the amount of pictures being taken, the amount of videos. One guy's filming the entire ascent through the back door: the falling valley, the receding towns, the diminishing signs of man. I have to look through his parted legs if I want to cop a look at what's behind us.

And I do want to cop a look. I do want an eyeful from all sides. And so, like most of those on board, I flit around to get the best angles, the best frames. Of course there's a risk of seeing nothing for wanting to see it all. A case in point: backdoor-man throws a wobbly when his battery runs out halfway through our ascent. He isn't cheered up or calmed down when someone suggests he just watch the footage twice. Graham's got the right idea. Graham doesn't stir. He calmly watches one side go by, occasionally sharing a thought – 'Cor, that's alright; I wouldn't mind one of those in my garden.'

It's the sheerness of the colour that I'd want in my garden. It's the severity of the palette that gets me. The light was meant to be good in St Ives, but up here it's like someone is flooding us with extra voltage from behind the scenes. It's the yellow of the flowers, and the green of the grass, and the blue of the sky. That's what it is. That's what gets me. I see now why so many colours take their name from nature. Orange, lilac, salmon, amber, aqua, lemon, silver, olive, fuchsia. Nature knows what it's up to. Nature does it best. It's telling that when a delay is announced, people cheer.

The pause gives me a chance to talk to my neighbour, Sharon. She's a social worker. She likes the job because she's good at it, and because she's good at it she gets the trickiest cases – normally children who were forced to grow up too quickly. As if to demonstrate her credentials, Sharon offers me half an orange. It's lunchtime all round by the sound of it. Or elevenses. It looks like Jill smuggled most of the breakfast buffet out this morning. She's even brought cutlery. She reckons she's got a teaspoon in her cleavage. I'm happy to take her word for it.

A long tunnel keeps us in the dark. It's a welcome respite from beauty. You can only handle so much before you need to turn your back and rub your eyes. At the end of the tunnel is winter: the landscape is otherworldly and totally covered in snow. Sharon asks if I mind all the old people, and I think: *mind* is a funny verb, isn't it? It can so easily be positive or negative. To have in mind, to watch out for, to find bothersome. I say, 'Yes and no, Sharon,' and then leave it at that. She doesn't ask me to elaborate because her attention has been taken – and mine with it – by someone skiing uphill with the help of a bright orange kite. The skier is antlike next to the mountains, amid the snow. They're going to beat us to the finish line by the look of it – St Moritz is just around the corner.

You could not describe St Moritz as bustling. Perhaps in the winter it is, when people come to ski and snowboard, but right now it's got the feel of a film set that has wrapped for the day.

Not so much *après-ski* as *après-vie*. That's not to say the town is without virtues. The municipal car parks offer splendid views. The public toilets are beyond reproach. And if you've got ten quid and want it off your hands pretty quickly, all you have to do is go into any of the bars around here and order a black coffee. When I thank the waitress for taking the money off my hands in French and she replies, '*Nein, nein. Hier ist es deutsch,*' it is the first time I've been told off in German for speaking French.

I make my coffee last almost an hour. I'm joined halfway through by Dan, who's on the Shearings holiday with his grandparents. We're pretty much contemporaries, and yet struggle to find much to talk about. Perhaps we've got too much in common. At any rate, when he tells me that he works in a pub in Harrogate, all I can manage is to agree. After the coffee, Dan and I go our separate ways, which is a mistake on my part because I'm soon lost and late for the coach. When I finally get back to the coach a cool twenty minutes late, you can be sure there are a few remarks directed my way. Mr Prunes thought I might have checked-in to the public toilets (he'd seen me photographing them), while Sharon wonders what on earth I did with the extra time. If anyone had been worried about my disappearance, they do a good job of keeping the fact to themselves. Though Jill does say that she was saving me her last macaroon, but then gave up and let someone called Sidney have it – 'Not that he needed the sugar boost. He drinks a litre of lemonade a day.'

Jill reserved a table for six. You're not meant to, but she saw some Germans reserving a table for five and was inspired by their example. Or, as she puts it, 'Anything they can do, I can do better.' I reckon the sixth person – who hasn't shown up yet – was simply invented to allow a morale-boosting victory. I'm surprised she hasn't come down wearing her travel pillow.

Ossobuco is on the menu and they're impressed when I'm able to say that *osso* means bone and *buco* means hole and it's to all intents and purposes a veal chop. I opt for pasta and pizza and then *fiore de panna* ice cream. Graham is quite impressed with the veal, and with the food generally, but reckons they do better stuff at the pub his daughter runs in Sheffield – The Fat Cat. Sharon asks if it's just the one daughter Graham's got. He says sometimes he wishes it was, but no, he's got four. Or had four rather – he's always doing that, getting the has and the had wrong. She was good, was Andrea. She worked for Virgin, in the head office. She met Richard Branson once. He came in with flip-flops on and told them to keep it up. Graham says that his mother said more than once (because it was true more than once) that when something horrible happens, you have to move on. Even if you don't think you can. 'You don't expect to bury your child,' he says. 'But you do it. And then it's tomorrow.'

He brushes up well, does Graham. That's Jill's opinion, which she shares with me as he's getting his pudding.

'He certainly dresses better than I do, Jill.'

'He does, doesn't he?'

'I wouldn't mind his trainers.'

'They're Skechers.'

'Are they?'

'Shame about his cough. He used to be a bingo caller, you know?'

'Is that right?'

'He couldn't do that anymore. Do you think he's a Pisces?'

Graham returns and says he's got a book I might like; says he'll run up and get it and meet me downstairs in the bar. Jill says she'll see Graham in the morning then because she's going out on the town with Sharon.

'Wish us luck,' she says.

'I wish the blooming town luck,' says Graham.

I watch him waiting for the lift. In his Skechers. In his nice clothes. Coughing into his clenched fist. If the bloke's got a bad bone in his body, then I can't pick it. That's a nice impression to have made on someone, I think.

21

If you want to know the secret to a long, happy marriage, it's 1) stay alive and 2) have separate bedtimes

I take the book Graham lent me down to breakfast. It contains the paintings of George Cunningham, who was (I hope) unusual in his refusal to show anyone his paintings nor look at the paintings of anyone else, lest their judgement (in the former case) or excellence (in the latter) proved a deterrent. George's lack of confidence had a significant root: an art teacher who told him as a young man that he couldn't paint for toffee and would amount to nothing. After hearing these words, Cunningham didn't paint again until he was laid off at the age of 50. If only for his painting *Cemetery Road*, I'm glad that George got the chop and was compelled to repurpose. The depicted road is lively despite its name. It shows people and animals and trams and vans in a colourful, ordinary commotion. It also shows a pub, The Royal Oak. The landlord's in the doorway, smoking a fag. I could be wrong – it's not the biggest reproduction, and nor is it as sharp as it could be (the book was published some years ago) – but I think the landlord's wearing Skechers. The book says George was a man who could see beauty in a quartet playing dominoes in a pub. He could see it in many other things besides.

When I board the coach for today's excursion, Mr Prunes says: 'We've had a meeting and have decided that if you're ever late again, we're going to have a quick vote as to whether to leave you or not and I don't fancy your chances.' Jill has moved, so I've got two seats to myself. Perhaps it's a pre-emptive strike. Perhaps she's heard I'm flying home and has called time on our travelling partnership before I could. Or maybe she just finds me boring compared to the others. Oh, hang on. Who's this? It's the old bra-flinger herself. Jill hasn't moved. She's merely late. 'Sorry,' she says to the coach, 'I was stockpiling.' She plonks herself down next to me. She looks nice in her floral dress and lemon headband. 'I got you a kiwi,' she whispers, and I think: fine, just don't tell me where you're storing it.

We drive to the town of Como for the outdoor market. The market runs alongside the old city wall. I stroll between the stalls with Graham and Sidney. It's good to finally get up close to the latter, since I've heard a lot about him. I've heard that he drinks ten litres of lemonade a day and sleeps half an hour a night and single-handedly built Somerset. He's certainly dressed for action. He's wearing a fanny pack over the shoulder, cycling shorts, a handlebar moustache and aviator sunglasses. Purposeful attire indeed.

Sidney's purpose isn't to shop, and nor is Graham's. They do a couple of lengths for the hell of it, and demon-strate a polite amount of interest in the socks and handbags, but they're not shoppers at heart, and they've both already got more souvenirs than they know what to do with. When the chance arises, I'm not surprised that they sit down at a café for some refreshment. 'Ooh, that's more like it,' says Graham. 'We'll do our shopping from here,' says Sidney. A lady comes to take our order. She says *ciao* to the three of us. Sidney says, 'No, no – not tea thanks, love. Three cappuccinos if you would.'

Stirring sugar into his coffee, Sidney says he lost his wife a year ago, and that this is the first holiday he's taken alone for 60 years. Still stirring sugar into his coffee, he says his wife would have loved this market. She used to love buying all sorts of crap they didn't need. She bought a carpet in India that cost a thousand pounds to get home. They already had carpet in every room, so Sidney had to lay it in the car. She brought back about five kilos of the Berlin Wall, which Sidney ended up making a rock garden of. And jewellery. Oh, she couldn't get enough of the stuff. If she had one issue with God, it was that he didn't give her enough ears. And clothes. Sidney's got 300 T-shirts and 90 pairs of jeans, which is a lot for someone who lives in a bungalow. When Sidney dies, it's going to be the biggest endowment to a charity shop in the history of man. But she was a good girl, the best. She looked after Sidney all his life, and then he returned the favour for the last bit of hers. Not a fair exchange when he thinks about it, which he often does these days. He's got a cleaner who comes twice a week now. Sidney felt bad taking her on, like he was betraying his wife, but then he reasoned that his wife would rather another woman was going round with the vacuum than have Sidney live in squalor. I suggest that another option was Sidney doing the cleaning himself, but he reckons that was out of the question, that he simply doesn't have the time, that he's got too much on his plate to worry about what's on the floor. He's down the town hall a lot – that's the thing. Might as well pay council tax he's there so often. They do bingo on Mondays, coffee morning on Tuesday afternoons (don't ask), a variety show on Thursdays, and bridge with a fish supper on Fridays. And at the weekend, Sid takes the 'oldens' out. One time, he took a load of 'oldens' to the IMAX cinema, but they could have been in Tesco for all they knew. No, he shouldn't be so dismissive. Some of them really liked it, you could tell, and maybe the others were just pretending not to give a shit. Yeah, that's a better way to look at it, thinks Sidney.

You'd be tempted to think Sidney was one of a kind, but he insists that most of his siblings are practically carbon-copies of him. When Sidney says he's one of fourteen, Graham asks, 'One of fourteen what?' Sidney's oldest brother would have been 100 and something by now. He died on the golf course, picking his ball out of the hole. He'd just got a double bogey, the poor sod. Sidney's mum had 74 grandchildren and over a hundred great-grandchildren. Sounds like Sidney's family don't mind an early night, and it sounds like their fondness has rubbed off on Sidney, who says that babies are what it's all about, that babies are the future, that I should have as many of the buggers as I can manage, because having none or just one is just wrong if you can help it, just plain daft. I say to Sidney that it can't be all doughnuts and discos having lots of kids though, that there must be some drawbacks, some challenges. Sidney concedes that at the start it will hit you for six (especially if you've had eight), and that even now it can be a juggling act fitting in his dependents between the bingo and the bridge and his daily routines, but dependents are good for you, they keep you honest, keep you on your toes, keep you in touch, keep you *needed*, and if they don't do any of that, it means they don't love yer, and if they don't love yer, it means you probably didn't love *them*. Sidney finishes his coffee and asks the lady if he can have a cup of the *ciao* now please, then says he'd live to 300 given the option, and wants 120 years minimum. He says every day is precious and yet to look at some people – him over there, for example – you'd think the whole thing was a chore.

'Yeah, but some people have reasons to be uncheerful, Sidney,' I say.

'Like what?'

'Ill health. Stress.'

'Rubbish. As far as I'm concerned, the only reason to be uncheerful is if you're dead.'

'Is that right?'

'Yeah. It is. I did a bungee jump off Clifton Suspension Bridge when I was 74 and had one hip. I learnt how to water-ski during chemotherapy. I was in the nightclubs until I was 65. I used to get the grandchildren to say I was their older brother. Then when I tried to use my bus pass as ID one night, they stopped letting me in. They thought I had uncommon interests.'

It's fair to say that Sidney keeps busy. And it's fair to say that he's not shy about the fact. He gets up at 5am every morning – (and no he doesn't bang his head to set an alarm) – and does an eleven-mile walk up to his mate's farm for some milk straight from the cow. Then after lunch each day, he'll do some star jumps and some squats in the front garden so everyone can see. Then in the evenings, he'll exercise his brain by going to visit some of the grandchildren and trying to figure out what it is they see in some of the crap they watch on telly. He doesn't mind admitting that most of his grandchildren make him scratch his head. And not just the grandchildren, the children as well. Take his son for example. He sent a wedding list through the other day. Now what's that all about? When Sidney got married, they were lucky to get a set of tea towels. Now here's his son asking for a fridge-freezer, a coffee machine and a trip to flipping Mexico. He thinks he's on the sodding *Generation Game*! They've got it too easy, that's the problem. Their appetite's all wrong. And they'll never learn, no matter how much Sidney tries to teach them. They're like a cult. They're brainwashed. Case in point: Sidney was walking to the shops with his grandson and his grandson walked straight into a lamppost. And they've too many options these days, that's another thing. Sid didn't know what a biscuit was until the late 90s, and now they've a billion to choose from. But you've gotta love 'em, says Sid. You've gotta love 'em.

Sidney goes in to pay for the coffees and his tea. When he gets back, he doesn't wait for us to thank him before telling us not to worry about it. 'After all,' he says, 'you can't take it with you. In Switzerland my salad was €44 and the others looked at me like I was crazy and I said, "Yeah? What? I'm on holiday!" Besides, my bungalow's worth 300 grand and I bought it for sixteen quid.'

Walking back to the coach, Sidney slows down a touch, even stops for a while to rest against a tree. He says he's probably due a lemonade, and that the *ciao* can sometimes go to his head. He says his wife loved her tea. He says she was discharged from hospital so she could die at home but didn't tell a soul, only mentioned it once she was in bed with a cup of tea. 'I think I'm going to say goodbye now, Sid.' That's what she said. Sid says it's funny, really, because this week's been harder than he thought, not least because pasta was her favourite food, and red her favourite colour. He wonders if I've noticed how much pasta there is in Italy, and how many red flowers. He says they're all over the place. There are even some plastic ones on his bedside table.

'How long were you together?' I ask.

'We're still together.'

'Sorry, I didn't—'

'Fifty-nine years.'

'So a long time.'

'Yeah, a long time. And if you want to know the secret to a long, happy marriage, it's 1) stay alive and 2) have separate bedtimes. She'd go out somewhere and say, "Right, see you later, Sid!" and I'd go out and say, "Right, see you later, love!" She was always out that woman. We both were. But I'll tell you what. When she got in, I didn't half love her, and when I got in she didn't half love me.'

We start walking again. We're definitely going to be late. They'd vote to leave me but would they vote to leave Sidney?

Come to think of it, they probably would. I ask if Sid would consider loving again.

'Another woman you mean?'

'Well, yeah.'

'I wouldn't risk it. What if she were boring and did microwave dinners?'

I'm later for dinner than normal. Vinny and Rita and Graham are just finishing up. I enjoy a bowl of soup in their company. Graham and I brace ourselves when Vinny knocks red wine over Rita, but she's not bothered and nor is Vinny. 'I often do it,' says Vinny, by way of an explanation. I tell Graham I liked that book he gave me, and the pictures in it, and the fact that Cunningham got there in the end and saw beauty in unlikely corners and so on, but he's not interested in art this evening, he wants to talk about old football injuries with Vinny. The pair are currently remembering a particularly tough centre-forward who played for Port Vale. They're in agreement that if you came off the same pitch as him with all your teeth, then you'd had a good game.

'Jill says you're flying home,' says Rita.

'He's never,' says Graham. 'Are yer?'

'I'm thinking about it.'

'Why?'

'Because … I struggled on the way here.'

'How struggled?'

'With … all of it.'

'If you struggled with that I shouldn't mind knowing what you find unbearable. I expect you think that ravioli's unbearable. I expect you're going to struggle with your ice cream, will yer?'

'Leave off him, Graham,' says Rita.

'I'm only messing, but I'm not. Bloody jellyfish his generation. They're nice and all that, I'm not saying they're not, but they're about as tough as – I've seen more backbone in a Jacob's cracker. And what's Jill going to think?'

'How do you mean?'

'Well it's a bit offensive, int it?'

'It's nothing personal.'

'How can it not be personal? You sit next to the woman. She'll think she's done something wrong.'

'No she won't.'

'She will. She's a sensitive woman. She told me as much this—'

Graham stops talking abruptly. He does so, I think, because he's just realised that one consequence of my jellyfishiness is that there'll be an empty seat next to Jill, for 27 hours, overnight, which is just the opening he's been—

'Nah, fair play to yer,' says Graham. 'The lad's got to do what he's got to do. That's one thing that's good about his generation – they know their limits, they look after themselves. Fair play to yer. When yer flying then?'

'Friday morning.'

'Good lad. Smart that is. Got to hand it to him – looks after himself. My granddaughter's the same. She's into self-preservation. Always reading books about it. That's why she's a vegan.'

Graham raises his glass to me, wishes me a safe journey, and before he can offer to help me pack, I go up for my pudding.

22

And then some paramedics arrive

I return Graham's book at breakfast. He says it's a good job I remembered because it's not his. One of the blokes at the hospital where Graham's a volunteer gave it to him.

'What do you volunteer for?'

'Because I enjoy it.'

'No I mean, what do they do to you?'

'Nothing. We just sit and have a chat.'

'Wait, what – with the patients?'

'That's right.'

'Ah, okay. I'm with you.'

'You thought I was going in to chat with the doctors?'

'No, I thought you were volunteering to be tested on and used as – never mind. That's good. They must like that. Do they like that?'

'Some more than others, I'm sure. Because most of 'em are younger than me, they probably reckon I'm rubbing their noses in it. One bloke who I sat next to and offered a biscuit to told me to eff off. Just like that. I said fair enough but I'm 'avin your biscuit you miserable git. Are you going to Milan?'

'Milan?'

'A few of them have just left.'

'Who's going?'

'Jill and Sidney and that lot.'

'I expect Sid's walking, is he?'

'He's going to propel them with the sound of his own voice. I could have murdered him last night.'

'What happened?'

'He just wouldn't take no for an answer.'

'What did he want you to do?'

'Slow dance with him.'

'Christ.'

'To Whitney Houston.'

'Ooh.'

'Anyway, if you nip out, you might catch them. They're at the bus stop. Here, take this with you.'

I take the orange with me, but it's no good, I've missed the bus. I have no way of contacting any of them, so there's no point pursuing. Instead, I get the ferry across to Bellagio, which is the small town at the tip of the peninsula that makes Lake Como do the splits. Sharon the social worker's had the same idea. I spot her as we're getting off the ferry. We join forces and go for a stroll. This isn't exactly original on our part – there's not much else to do; Bellagio's no booming metropolis. But it's certainly a good-looking place. You've got the lake on both sides, and the pink and yellow and orange buildings, and the cobbled staircases that run from one side of the peninsula to the other. We climb one of these stair-cases now – Salita Serbelloni – which is narrow and medieval and lined with bakeries and shoe shops. When we linger at the top to enjoy the view, I tell Sharon that I had a good old chat with Sidney yesterday, which was great, because he's great, but that one of its consequences was that I felt a bit reflective and despondent, because sometimes spending time with people who are jubilant and gung-ho and exceptional can make you feel a bit crap by comparison. Sharon agrees that Sidney's certainly a character, and has many virtues, but she also says that people who are the life and soul of the party are often fighting some very private battles. Through her work, Sharon's seen a fair few people whose outward and inward selves are like chalk and cheese, so I should bear that in mind before I start drinking lemonade and doing star-jumps and breeding like a rabbit, believing the outcome will be unmitigated enthusiasm and gratitude *à la* Sidney. I tell Sharon she should be a social worker.

We walk down Via Garibaldi and then around Piazza della Chiesa. We sit under the bell tower of the San Giacomo Basilica. I ask a bit more about Sharon's work. She explains that she retired a few years ago but still does stints out of town. She'll be parachuted in (figure of speech) to assist local councils with their social care efforts. Her husband doesn't mind her being away for weeks, sometimes months at a time. He knows the work is all-consuming, that you can't do half a job. He'll give Sharon a call on Friday afternoon and say, 'So are you coming home this weekend?' The space is good for them, says Sharon; it lets their relationship breathe. You see the ones joined at the hip and wonder who applied the glue or staples. 'It never looks comfortable, does it?' says Sharon.

We walk back up Via Garibaldi, and back down Salita Serbelloni, and as we go, Sharon's saying she's going to take her sons to Ascot this year, for the horse racing, for a proper day out; and that on this type of holiday, she finds it easier to socialise with the loners like Sid and Graham and Jill and me because the wives don't like it when she talks to the husbands, because they think she's a threat, that she's going to run off with their hubbies to Sardinia; and that she doesn't really like Italian food if she's honest. The talking and walking and browsing is a piece of cake with Sharon – *un poco di panettone*. It's a nice piece of cake as well. I feel like I'm in a low-budget – or *no-budget* – version of that film *Before Sunrise*, wherein the main pair stroll around Paris or Vienna just chewing the fat. They end up marrying in the sequel, and then having a family and splitting up in the one after that. I don't think that will happen in this version for several reasons, not least Sharon's husband. And Megan of course. She'd certainly have something to say (and something to paint) if over the next ten years I got married, had three children, and then divorced in Greece off the back of a conversational stroll around Bellagio on a Shearings holiday.

We stop for coffee. Sharon adds sweetener to her latte, stirs, sips, adds a bit more, then asks me if I know what grief is. I say no. She says that might be my problem. She says I'll cheer up after I've had a bit of grief in my life. As a diagnosis, it's oddly similar to the one given by Deborah in Llandudno, who said I needed a tragedy and then offered to push my nan down the stairs. I ask how one can gain perspective and gratitude and so on in advance of the grief. She says one can't. I go in to pay the bill, but Sharon's beaten me to it.

Jill and that lot didn't make it to Milan. They got to the train station at Como and then learnt that the train drivers were on strike. Jill says that Sidney – and this won't surprise me – was on the loo at Como station when the automated door opened. Sid puts it another way.

'I was on the English throne and what happened? I'm on display to the concourse!'

'What did you do?'

'What did I do?'

'Yeah.'

'Well, what do you think I did? I covered my nipples and pressed the frigging button!'

Jill says they took the setback in their stride. In some respects, it was a dodged bullet as far as Jill's concerned. She was under the impression that Milan was a quaint little town. Instead, they went up to the church in Griante. They just sat there, really. Jill lit a candle for her husband and Sid lit a candle for his wife. It was good, says Jill. Yeah, it was, says Sid.

Dinner is mushroom soup and turkey with baked fennel. I sit alone and read as I eat and I don't mind how that looks. It's an interesting finale: a son kills his mother so his wife might escape. I hope Graham Norton's not writing about what he knows.

I skip dessert and take a coffee to the lounge instead. Before long, I start to hear the entertainment coming to life downstairs in the bar. The Rolling Stones, '(I Can't Get No) Satisfaction'; '(I've Had) The Time of My Life' from *Dirty Dancing*. I imagine Sidney clapping and spinning and thrusting and grinning and admonishing anyone who won't do the same. I imagine Jill and Sharon, strangers last Friday, throwing each other around the dance floor. I imagine Graham – the gentle giant to Sidney's restless pixie – sat in his preferred spot, smiling at one of his own quips, delivered in that cherishable Yorkshire accent of his. Or if not smiling at one of his own quips, smiling at the sight of Sid doing the 'lawnmower', or Jill pouting and pretending to have a pair of castanets. Vinny, if he's down there, will be taking it easy because of his knee, though he's probably up on his balcony spilling red wine on Rita. Gabriel and Joan will be at their favourite table, working through the cocktail list, and young Dan will be sat with his grandparents, chatting and mingling, enjoying their final night away. I imagine the bar staff putting a brave face on it, doing what they can to enjoy the various British ways of asking for booze. I have to imagine all these things because I'm not going down there, not tonight. Sometimes it's nice being on the fringe, getting a taste from the edge. Sometimes it's just nice to imagine and start a new book. Besides, I can't clap and dance like they can; I don't have the same cause, the same character, the same animating principle – not yet anyway, not tonight. So for now, I'll let them be.

Then the music stops abruptly. And then some paramedics arrive. I go down and Jill says that a woman fell over, that she was jiving with this bloke like there was no tomorrow and then bosh, she smashed her head against the floor and was on her arse. 'He was spinning her like a top, Ben!' says Sidney. 'I said to Jill, "I don't like the look of that. That's reckless is that." And where is he now? He's buggered off, the twerp.' The lady's fall has brought the night to a close.

They say she's going to have a big bump and won't be going out for a kebab, but will otherwise be fine. I say my goodbyes in case I don't run into this lot in the morning. Jill gives me a kiss. Graham pretends to. Sharon's in the loo. Of course, Sidney has the last word.

'You won't see me in the morning, Ben.'

'No?'

'I'm off out early.'

'Yeah?'

'Going to get up at dawn, walk up to that church.'

'Sounds good, Sidney.'

'You've heard of the early bird, right?'

'I have.'

'The one who catches the worm?'

'Uh-huh.'

'Well that's me, mate. And you know why?'

'Because—'

'Because I frigging love worms.'

❧

I'm alone in a preferred corner, which gives a wide angle, and the right amount of light. It's quiet – just the rattle and bustle of the dumb waiter, of cooks changing trays. I can see Sidney in a new T-shirt, holding court with a group I don't know, showing off his worms, doing a re-enactment of what happened to the woman last night. There's no Sharon or Graham or Jill. No Vinny or Rita. They're probably packing. The coach leaves in about an hour. I should like to hear from them again, but I've not said as much. No details have been swapped, no numbers taken, no promises made to stay in touch. This travelling coincidence was enough, it can end with a few honest farewells – I suppose that's the feeling. I wait at the bus stop happily, all things considered.

Part 6

Pitlochry, Scotland

23

She says that thanking God gets easier and harder every day

At the Normanton interchange, there's a lady of maybe 90 sitting on a bench, puffing away on a fag. I imagine telling her to pack it in. Then I imagine her response. 'What, so I don't die at 70?' Her face is brilliant. Its years are shown like the rings of a tree. The American writer Grace Paley called it – 'it' being the loosening and folding of skin as we age – the 'rotten handwriting of time', which is one way to look at it. There are other ways of course. I've heard that in Japan, when a broken vase is pieced back together the cracks are emphasised with gilt, and finally the broken thing is considered more beautiful than the unbroken thing. It's certainly an optimistic take on damage, though doubtless there are times when the Japanese are straightforwardly pissed off they dropped something.

I sit on a bench opposite bay thirteen and talk with a couple off to Eastbourne. They're a colourful pair. He's got a canary jacket on, and she's in lime green trousers. They're not backwards in coming forwards either. Within a couple of minutes I know that he was conscripted to be a cook in Germany after the Second World War. He says the gig was part of his national service, and that it was a funny time to be out there because the war may have been over, but the Germans were still scared, still shaken, still shell-shocked.

Their world had been turned upside down and given a shake. 'You could blow 'em over, the poor buggers. Or kick 'em over, which is what the sergeant major generally opted for.'

They'd both bring national service back if they could. I ask if they're sure they're still up to it. He grins and she says, 'No not for us, silly, for school leavers. They'd learn some discipline that way. God knows they could do with some. Trouble is you can't clip them round the ear these days, can you? I remember pinching some rhubarb from an allotment and hiding it under my bed for weeks because I was terrified what the police and my parents would do if I presented with it in the kitchen.' I ask if this was recently and he grins and she says, 'Point is, I knew there'd be consequences and I feared them. These days, they don't fear a thing. They're wild. Not all of them of course. Our grandsons are lovely. If a bit spoilt. You should see what they get on their birthdays. It's not good for them – no way. They've got everything and yet reckon they've got nothing. We had no choice and it was good for you. It was stew or you went hungry. And it weren't much different when it came to marriage. You weren't fussy. You couldn't afford to be. He was an apprentice butcher on four pounds a week. It was that or nothing.'

He didn't stay an apprentice butcher. He saw an opening in copper tubing and climbed into it, then became a driving instructor. He says it was a lovely job in the 80s, on the back lanes, out in the countryside. She would sit in the back with a magazine, smoking out the window, touching his right arm down the side of the seat. When he'd done all his learners they'd stop somewhere and find a field or drive to the airport and watch the planes. He's been retired twenty years and he doesn't mind it one bit. She minds it a bit because he gets under her feet, but still, they get along, better than ever, even. They keep busy in the greenhouse, growing tomatoes and flowers, and the radio's always on. And there's the family, she says. Oh yeah, there's the family, he says. And there's events, she says. Oh yeah, the events, he says. This year alone they've had a birth, a death, a wedding, a christening, an engagement and a divorce. (And that was all the same couple!) Above all, they appreciate just being around still. Not everyone is, you know. His brother isn't, that's for sure. He collapsed on the bus with a ruptured aneurysm. 'And what's more,' she says, 'it was the wrong bloody bus.'

The thinking used to be that if you got threescore and ten (70), you were lucky, but you could keep a Vauxhall Cresta going with some of the tablets they've got these days. To say nothing of new parts – well, you can get the lot. And if they can't get you a new part they'll do their best to fix up the old one. He had a displaced stomach last year. They only went and stapled it in place, as if it was a piece of carpet. It's good, they say, people living longer – they mean, why shouldn't they? They've paid their taxes, fought their wars, brought up their families, done a fair bit of work. Why shouldn't they get a bit of breathing space at the end of it? A bit of time in the greenhouse with the radio on in the kitchen? Of course some of the government would rather they just dropped off their perches at three-score and ten and saved them some money, but they'll be old in time, and we'll see what they're saying then.

Having said all that about modern medicine, the treatment he swears by is two pints down the pub at lunchtime, and a drop of whisky in his tea. After all, whisky means the water of life in Gaelic and he only has five or six cups a day, unless someone comes over or there's a national emergency, in which case he stops counting. And her medicine? She says that him being down the pub is her medicine, that and their caravan. When she says caravan, she notices that their top halves are in sunlight and their bottom halves aren't. 'Look how bright your jacket is,' she says. 'Yeah,' he says, 'No bugger will miss me in this. I'm high-vis.'

The call comes for Pitlochry. When I get on the coach, someone asks if I can shove their bag overhead. Then another lassie asks if she can borrow me to open that and stow this. I do as I'm told and realise that it's the first time it hasn't felt at all awkward or peculiar getting onboard with my elders. It feels normal.

Malcolm's our driver, and from Newcastle by the sound of it. When he says 'Reet, ladies and gentlemen. How's it gan?' most of the coach says nothing because they think he's just clearing his throat, but the two or three who understand Geordie reply, 'Geet champion, yee propa radge gadgie yee, Malcolm wor laddie.'

Flicker and Mary aren't Geordies. They're sat in the row behind me and across the aisle, so they're not exactly the easiest pair to access but I manage. Flicker says she lives in Derby but comes from South Africa and leaves it at that, whereas Mary says she lives in Derby but comes from Scotland and doesn't. She says that she was born in Dundee but moved to Coventry when she was sixteen. She says she got a job in an office, as a secretary. She didn't much like the work but she got a husband out of it. He was a junior manager and she married him when he got a promotion. She says you had to think on your feet in those days, because there wasn't the money there is now. She says she enjoyed 55 years of happy marriage and thanks God for every one of them. She says that thanking God gets easier and harder every day. Easier because the things she's thankful for seem to have got bigger somehow, more obvious, and harder because she's got a bit of arthritis in her hands. When we pull into Washington services, Mary says, 'Excellent. I've needed a wee since Easter.'

Pauline gets on at Washington. She asks me to shift over because her mates are in the seats across the aisle and she doesn't want me in the way. I do as instructed and by way of thanks, she tells me that her son has a Shih Tzu called Benji; that she remembers when the Angel of the North only had one wing; and that yonder factory is where there'll be making the new British passports. When Malcolm makes a joke about people from the south of the River Tyne, Pauline asks if he's been going on like this the whole time. I tell her that, to be fair, he's only just found his voice. 'Well, ah hope he loses it again,' she says.

I ask Pauline what Newcastle was like back in the day. She says it was poor, simple as that. She says if you weren't building ships you were down the mines. She says you were thought posh if you weren't working your fingers to the bone.

Things have changed though. Pauline's got richer every year of her life, give or take the odd wobble. That's why there's things like salmon teriyaki in the fridge, and why she can go on holidays. She goes with her auntie and her auntie's husband – those two over there. She looks across to them now – they're both snoozing – and then beyond them to the vastness of Northumberland. She looks at the openness and emptiness and then looks at me and says, 'You wouldn't think we were full, would you?' Then she looks at my shorts like she's never seen a pair before, and says,

'I suppose it's hot where you're from, is it?'

'Twenty-eight yesterday.'

'What, Fahrenheit?

The land turns Scottish. You'd need canny vision to notice, which is why there's a sign and a flag. We stop for lunch just across the border. I have haggis on a jacket, and a can of irn-bru. I sit with Flicker and Mary. The former looks at my lunch as though it were a collection of sins. She knows she's doing it as well, because she says she's always telling her grandchildren not to say they don't like something until they've tried it, and now here she is raising her eyebrows at my lunch, having never tried a mouthful of either. 'Don't do it, Flicker,' says Mary. 'I've had both and as the Lord is our shepherd, let me be yours – stick to your cheese sandwich.'

Mary's got a nice habit of saying what she wants. She does it now. She says the death of her son-in-law about a year ago has been harder to deal with than the death of her husband. Chiefly because of the suffering of her daughter and grandchildren. He was a senior bank manager and complained of headaches for years but carried on regardless. He said he had no choice. In fact, what he had was a brain tumour. The doctor said he'd better make some memories while he still could. They went down to Cornwall. Mary was illegally squeezed in the back with him and the two kids. She'll never forget it. It was wonderful in spite of everything. Mary has a tear in her eye. Flicker touches her friend on the arm and then looks at me and says, 'Actually, would you mind pouring me a bit of your drink?'

Walking back to the coach, they ask if I do this often. I say it's my sixth one. They ask if I've enjoyed them. I tell them that I have, that they've done me some good. They ask in what way. I say that before I went to Scarborough, I was grumpy and complacent and scared of getting old, whereas now I'm still those things only a little bit less. 'Besides,' I say, 'I met a man that keeps his wife in the boot, and I took my nan to Wales and now I call her Janet.' Mary asks if I get on with my nan then. 'She can be a pest,' I say, 'but that's just her age.'

We're on the A68, heading north-west towards Edinburgh. Pauline enjoyed her lunch – just some sandwiches her son made this morning. Her son reckons Pauline's got it easy, reckons she's living the life of Riley, whoever he was. I ask how Pauline knows that Riley was a man, and she says that if he had it that good then he must have been. Anyway, Pauline's son goes to work and she goes to Menorca – that's what he likes to say. And it's true. She goes at least twice a year. She goes with her family (the ones who aren't working, anyway) and they always stay in the same villa. One time, Pauline's daughter came along with the grandkids, but Pauline just ended up babysitting so that won't be happening again. The grandkids are nine and thirteen. The latter has a French exam today now she comes to think of it. He's been stressed all weekend. Pauline told him not to worry because what doesn't kill you makes you stronger, but he said in response that her statement was objectively false. 'They just won't be told,' she says.

Steve Wright's on the radio. Malcolm must be a fan because he's turned it up a bit. I know the voice well. When I was about thirteen, I used to work in the homebrew shop my grandad managed. We had a radio out the back and in my memory, Steve Wright was the only person that was ever on it. It wasn't the busiest shop in the world so there was plenty of time when Grandad and I would just chew the fat while he did the books and I picked my nose for two quid an hour. We've got a good relationship now and it probably owes a lot to those long quiet days when we got to know each other without meaning to, with me bagging up hops and him checking we had enough yeast. Steve Wright must be well into his 60s by now. His voice hasn't aged a day.

19.00. The Pitlochry Hydro Hotel. I've been sat with the only other diner under 50. Craig's not on holiday though. He's in town to oversee the construction of a road in the forest. He supports Celtic because he's a Catholic, but that's not to say there aren't people who switch trenches. (That is,

Catholics who support Rangers, and Protestants who support Celtic.) He says you'll get the odd scrap after the football but it'll probably be Celtic fans fighting each other over a decision the referee made. He says Glasgow has transformed in his lifetime. He charts the city's progress over vegetable soup: Capital of Culture in 1990; a decent wedge of money from the European Union; Commonwealth Games in 2014. Then he gives me a quick lap of the country over Spanish chicken: Glasgow is music and gigs; Edinburgh – Auld Reekie – is the festival and the castle and Hogmanay; Dundee is the arts and gaming; Aberdeen is oil; Stirling is William Wallace and Robert the Bruce and Bannockburn; Inverness is … 'Actually, to be honest, I have nae a clue wha' Inverness is up tae.'

When he's done with Scotland, he points to the older diners with his spoon.

'Ah feel sorry for this lot ye know,' he says.

I give this some thought and then say, 'That's good of you, Craig, but don't forget that you're the one project managing a trunk road.'

24

She grew beetroot and potatoes all day and in return she wasn't shot

I study a map of the local area in bed. There are some intriguing places in Perthshire, that's for sure. Carpow is obviously where your car blows up. Powmill must be where they grind down the exploded cars and turn them into shortbread. Pool of Muckhart is where you go when you're sad because your car's now a biscuit. Killin is where you go if you've got a really bad back (because you were in the car when it blew up). Balbeggie suggests a droopy testicle; Findo Gassk is surely a mechanic; Innerwick is strength you didn't know you had; Moneydie is constantly in recession; Dollar isn't; Dull is the least interesting place on the planet; Loch Drunkie is where you go if you live in Dull; and finally, Loch na Ba is what you'd say if you were trying tae reason with a sheep. All things considered, perhaps the most suggestive region of the UK.[36]

---

[36] I later discovered that the village of Dull is in a relationship with Boring, Oregon. Some of the news headlines when Dull and Boring first hooked up are enjoyable. 'Boring group makes Dull decision: Partnership official with Scottish village'. (*The Oregonian*, August 2014.) 'Dull, Scotland, makes Boring, Oregon, more interesting'. (BBC News, August 2014.) 'Dull Residents In Scotland Hope For Boring Link To Town In The US'. (*Huffington Post*, May 2012.) You can see that the headline writers responsible for the above got into the spirit of things. The same can't be said for the person who wrote a BBC headline in

I sit with Flicker and Mary for breakfast. We talk about their church over kippers and porridge. In short, it's a busy wee place. There are several mums-and-tots sessions; there are women fellowship sessions; there's ongoing destitution relief activities; and there's light entertainment most days like speed dating and book clubs.

'Speed dating?'

'Oh aye, people pop in on their lunch breaks.'

'And I suppose if one thing led to another they could, you know …'

'Not in God's home, they couldn't. We wouldn't allow it. Would we, Flicker?'

'I think Ben meant get married, Mary.'

The idea behind all of the above is a simple one – to be there for the community. The idea isn't to convert or take confession. It's simply to open doors and arms and hearts and say – come on, let's have a cup of tea and a natter. It's about compassion, says Flicker. 'We all have our ups and downs, don't we? So it's good that there's something there when we're having the downs. It doesn't need to be much, but it needs to be something. I can tell you that if it wasn't for my church I would have jumped out of a window several times by now.' 'Aye, and not a ground floor one I bet,' says Mary.

June 2012. 'Boring in Oregon votes to pair with Dull in Perthshire'. From a country that has given the world Monty Python, this headline shows a contemptible lack of imagination and effort. Whoever wrote it should be submerged in the Pool of Muckhart and then taken to Powmill to be repurposed.

09.00. Pitlochry train station. I carry Monica's walker across the footbridge. She was standing at the bottom of the steps, giving the impression that getting up them with her hands full wasn't going to be a piece of cake. When we get to the other side, an announcement is made that our train to Aviemore will now arrive on platform one. Some take the news better than others. Monica says, 'That's bloody typical, that is.' And her friend Kitty says, 'Is it? When did it last happen to you then?' And Monica says, 'Well never, but still – it's typical isn't it.' I love how the mind works sometimes.

We head north-west towards Killiecrankie. The scenery is pleasant from the off – lots of heathery hills, lots of thistly braes, the odd Munro – but mostly, I chat with a couple of immigrants.

Basia was born in Nottingham to Polish parents. Her dad escaped Poland just after it had been invaded by the Germans in 1939, but was soon captured by the Soviets and sent to a Siberian prison. He was released a few years later when the Soviets switched teams, and ended up in England, where he joined the British Army. Basia's mum, meanwhile, had been deported to Magdeburg in Germany at the start of the war to be an agricultural labourer. She grew beetroot and potatoes all day and in return, she wasn't shot. In 1946, Basia's dad was posted to Magdeburg to serve as a peace-keeper. By this time, Basia's mum was no longer obligated to spend all day every day growing beetroot and potatoes, and was therefore at liberty to fall in love with Basia's dad when she met him on a tram. He heard her speaking Polish and then asked her if she came here often. About a year

SHE GREW BEETROOT AND POTATOES ALL DAY

later, they returned to Nottingham together and bashed out a family – Basia not the least of it.

Zoltan, Basia's husband, is Hungarian. He says he's lived in England for 63 years and of those years, the first 60 were the toughest. Zoltan reckons that, for some reason, people understand him more when he speaks English with a Welsh accent – which explains why he sounds like a tipsy, but perfectly intelligible, Tom Jones. He fled Hungary in 1956, during the uprising against the Russians. He got as far as Austria, where he bumped into a bloke from Barnsley who offered him a job in a coal mine.

'The bloke said, "Sign 'ere son and we'll be off tomorrow."'

'And did you?'

'Of course I did.'

'Did you know anything about Barnsley?'

'No, thank God, else I might not have come.'

By the time Zoltan got to Barnsley, he was surplus to requirements. The boss of the coal miners' union had decided that the imported Hungarians weren't in the best interest of the local miners. Zoltan didn't mind, not least because he'd already been paid. For about two months, he just played football down the park. Then he moved to Nottingham and got a job digging tunnels. He met Basia at the Polish Catholic Club, where she was a barmaid. Their first date was at the Goose Fair, the mention of which makes me think of Gordon and Rowan, and specifically the former brushing his teeth with his gardening gloves on. Odd – but nice – how things come together.

I've hardly glanced out the window. I've missed the grouse and the glens and the lochs and the Tay. I might have even missed East Kilbride. I don't mind though. Sometimes things heard are better than things seen. More often than not, a landscape will still be there tomorrow (and tomorrow and tomorrow) – there'll be another chance to have a look, that's the point. Conversations are different. They don't stick around. The constellation of unlikely elements that brings them about will expire and unform by the time you reach the next station. My conversation with Basia and Zoltan ends when the guard comes through to check tickets. She knows that the Shearings lot are on a group ticket but needs some persuading that I'm a part of it. 'He's one of us!' says Kitty.

At Aviemore, the group scatters in the station car park. I haven't got much shopping to do, so walk up the Grampian Road to a chip shop called Smiffy's. I have haddock and chips, and then a battered Mars bar.[37] A television above the counter gives awkward news about the state visit of President Trump. The news is awkward chiefly because the subtitles are getting the wrong end of the stick. Apparently, Trump just said: 'Arm hair to dismember the deaf.'

Mary spots me through the window wiping my chops. She comes in and tells me to visit the public toilet while I can. When I say nothing, just look at her a bit confused, she adds that it's meant to be 50p, but the gate's open. Then she says

---

[37] As the Lord is our shepherd, let me be yours: don't do it.

she's got something for me. She takes a small book out of her handbag and says, 'Flicker and I were discussing it, and we'd like to give you this.' It's a copy of the New Testament. 'That'll sort you out,' she says, tapping the side of her nose.

The two of us find a bench in the sun and wait there for Flicker to reappear. Apparently, she's in the bookshop. I bet she's in there trying to persuade the bookseller that a big pile of New Testaments would look good on top of Richard Dawkins' *The God Delusion*. Mary tells me the last couple of years have been a challenge. First she lost her husband and a breast, and then she lost her son-in-law. But she got through it because the Lord is like a chemist. I try to picture the Lord in Boots. Mary mistakes my thinking for spirituality.

'I can see it on your face,' she says.

'Can you?'

'You're searching for something.' She nods to my New Testament. 'And you might find it in there.'

'And if I don't?'

'Go to Sri Lanka.'

Flicker reappears and the pair head off to look at the ski lift (apparently the busiest in Britain). I'm not alone for long. About a minute later, Monica turns up – Monica who found the platform change typical. She sits down, looks at my New Testament, and then at me, and then at my New Testament, and then at me, and then at the Grampian Road, and says:

'What's that then?'

'That's the Grampian Road,' I say.

'No not that, that!'

'That's the New Testament.'

'Well I can see that but what are you doing with it?'

'Just having a flick through really. It was given to me by—'

'Love is patient, love is kind, it keeps no record of wrongs. You can throw that away now.'

'Nice.'

'Corinthians. Did you have lunch at the chippy?'

'I did.'

'Me too. What did you think?'

'Decent.'

'I thought it was crap.'

We're back on the coach, and Malcolm's back on the mic. He points towards Killiecrankie and says that in 1689 there was a battle over there between a Catholic called James and a Protestant called William; that the battle was part of a wider Jacobite Rising whose *casus belli* was the replacement of the above James for the above William; and that, although the '89 rising ended with the Glencoe Massacre in 1692, the final nail in the Jacobite coffin didn't come until the Battle of Culloden in 1746.

At least, I think that's what Malcolm said. I can't be sure because Pauline, bless her, has been telling me about a TV show called *Outlander* for the last God knows how long. To be fair to Pauline, she's on point: *Outlander* is about a nurse who is transported from 1946 to 1743 to assist with the Jacobite Rebellions and fall in love with a Highlander called Jamie. Pauline says she tried to get her granddaughter to watch the series, but she wasn't interested. Pauline's worried about her granddaughter. She says the amount of time she spends on her phone isn't healthy. She says it's dreadful seeing her in tears because only 50 people liked her selfie. As far as Pauline's concerned, all Pauline can do is keep telling her granddaughter that she's beautiful without any of the make-up, without any of the treatments, without any of the likes, and that at the end of the day, it's not what a person looks like that matters, but how much money they've got. No, she's joking, of course she is – it's how kind they are, it's how nice it is talking to them – that's what she tells her.[38]

Pauline's also worried about when her granddaughter graduates. A degree used to be a free pass to whatever job you wanted but not anymore. Pauline never went to university. Never even considered it. She'd never heard of the place until she started cleaning one when she was 27. She can't think of one person from Washington of roughly her age that went to university. She's not saying they're not bright though. No way. Most of her friends are proper bookworms. She says you can learn a lot from books. She says you can't always be sure what it is you've learnt, but it'll be something, alright. Books put ideas in your head – things to do, things to say, things to have a think about. Netflix is good as well though. Don't get her wrong. You can learn quite a bit off Netflix. Why, take *Outlander* for example. Pauline thought a

---

[38] Two summers ago, I went to the funeral of my friend's mum. At the end of the service, people were invited to come up to the front of the church and say a few words – a sort of open-mic eulogy. About a dozen people went up, and despite Jane Dobson having plenty of strings to her bow, all they wanted to remember was her kindness.

Jacobite Rebellion was a type of biscuit before *Outlander*. Not that the knowledge has been much use to her. It hasn't done the washing up or paid the bills. But still, there's no harm in it being there.

The same can't be said of our driver, she says. But she's only playing – he's growing on her. Malcolm's back on the mic now. He's got a true story for us. He says he was on the phone earlier to his pal, who's been going out with this really tasty bird, but had to dump her when he found various uniforms in her closet. Malcolm asked his pal what the problem was. And his pal replied, 'Well she obviously can't hold down a job, can she?'

I ask the lad in the sauna – one of the kitchen staff, I think – if he's ever had an achy face for about a month.

'No, but what you want is a mug of whisky and some weed,' he says.

'You reckon?'

'For sure. You'll forget you've got a face, man.'

I tell him that I've smoked weed once and never again; that I was about 21 and wanted to do a good job of the inhaling so took half a dozen big drags in quite a short period of time; that this was more than enough to make me want to take myself outside and walk around the block for the next six hours, convinced I was about to have a heart attack.

'So just stick to the whisky,' he says.

'You know what I think's causing it?'

'What?'

'My phone.'

'How come?'

'I got a smartphone a month ago and my face has been aching since.'

'Wait – a month ago?'

'Yeah.'

'What are you, a Mormon?'

'Actually I'm borrowing it from my sister. To take notes on.'

'Notes?'

'Yeah.'

'What notes?'

'Well, it depends.'

'No wonder your face is aching if you're taking notes. F*ck that.'

I join Tom in the jacuzzi. He's up to his neck in bubbles but is still willing to talk. Tom's the husband of Pauline's auntie. I tell him what Pauline told me about Newcastle back in the day – about the poverty, the lack of opportunities.

'Aye, it was the army or the pit for me.'

'And which did you go for?'

'The army.'

'Any scrapes?'

'Belfast and Borneo spring to mind.'

'What happened in Borneo?'

'More than was necessary. Let's put it that way.'

Tom asks me to excuse his voice. (It's a bit croaky and a bit quiet.) He's never drunk or smoked and yet he went and got flipping mouth cancer. He explains how they replaced most of his tongue with a bit of his leg. He pokes it out at me – the tongue, not the leg – and says: 'And three weeks later it started growing hair!'

'You are kidding, Tom.'

'I'm not. I've got a hairy tongue. But they got the cancer, so that's good. It's clever what they can do now.'

Tom says that serving in Malay was hard because the Indonesian dictator was playing up at the time; that he lived in barracks in London for a while, not far from Regent's Park; that he bought himself a moped and would nip around Camden and King's Cross like there was no tomorrow; that in Belfast they slept in portacabins for longer than he cares to remember; that after the army he became a postman, which meant that he went from marching to walking and from one uniform to another; that yeah, he liked that joke Malcolm made about all the uniforms in the cupboard; that he retired at 60 and lost his wife to lung cancer two days before their 50th anniversary.

The bubbles go off. Tom searches for the button but can't find it. Never mind, I say, it's easier to talk now. He says he joined a walking group and a choir – after his wife died, like. He says he sang at the Royal Albert Hall with 1,500 others, but they stuck him right in front of an organ so he could have been singing 'Hakuna Matata' for all the audience knew. He says there's a line in a poem. The poet's lost his wife and he says that her absence is his companion. Tom can see where he's coming from, he recognises the emotion, but he wanted more than absence. He says that Mandy – Pauline's auntie – helped him to heal. They met on a walk, up on the Pennines. She liked Tom's stories, and he liked hers. They moved in together with the blessing of their families. He's lucky, he says. Not just for Mandy but for everything, for this bubble bath, even. When he was a boy, he had to boil the kettle ten times on a coal fire to fill a tin bath every Friday. Tom was the youngest so would be the last one in, by which time it was like washing in the Ganges. I ask if he can think of any ways in which life has changed for the worse, but he can't, not for the life of him. He says maybe his body has changed for the worse, but that's alright, he can still do twenty press-ups, and Mandy does a mile in the pool three times a week, and besides, they're hardly after procreating. I ask if he can see anything on account of his glasses having steamed up. 'I'll be alright, Pauline,' he says. He finds the button.

I read the New Testament at dinner. I look up passages to do with pain while I wait for my mushrooms, but there's nothing practical about the relief of face pressure. I turn to Ecclesiastes during my hotpot, which is the book that's meant to be full of wisdom. From what I can tell, the message from Ecclesiastes is basically to be a hungry caterpillar – get stuck in, have a nap, spread your wings. While I get stuck into my crumble, I look up the passage that Mary has marked as her favourite. 'But Jael, Heber's wife, picked up a tent peg and a hammer and went quietly to him while he lay fast asleep, exhausted. She drove the peg through his temple into the ground, and he died.' Wtf, Mary?

The hotel's maintenance man is the evening's entertainment. His name is Mark and he's dressed as a clansman, a

Highlander. He's got a kilt, a shield and a broadsword, and he hasn't cut his hair since 2014 for the occasion. If you saw him in Tesco you'd call the police, let's put it that way.

Mark wants to show us how to make a kilt, or how to fold one rather. He picks a lady called Jenny to be his volunteer. Mark says he's going to dress Jenny in a tartan plaid kilt. Jenny doesn't fancy his chances. That's what her face says. Mark says first of all, he's going to get Jenny to lie on the floor. Jenny really doesn't fancy his chances. That's what her – ooh, hang on, I talk too soon, her face tells a lie: Jenny is on the floor. Mark tells Jenny to stop looking up his kilt. Jenny says he's not to worry as she's not got her glasses on. There's a comment from the audience: 'If it's as long as his sword, you won't need glasses!'

As Jenny gets turned into a Highlander on the floor, I get a whisky for my face and sit down with Mary. She says she saw me reading at dinner and was pleased. I ask her about the passage and she says she just did it for a laugh. She says her mum played the same joke on her once. She remembers it well because her mother wasn't usually one for mucking around. She was a tough woman; could scare the life out of you. But Mary loved her all the same – not that she can remember ever telling her as much. She wishes she'd told her, wishes she'd told her more than once, once a month even. Not that her mother ever told Mary. No chance. You just had to assume – or hope rather. 'But it was different then,' she says, 'it was more formal, even between mother and daughter. We didn't have the words they have now – or if we did have the words, we didn't have the same ease with them.'

SHE GREW BEETROOT AND POTATOES ALL DAY

Just as I'm about to say, with as much ease as I can muster, that if her mother had any sense she would have loved Mary immensely, Mary says, somewhat off topic, that her daughter withdrew sex until Jeremy did more around the house.

'Who's Jeremy?' I say.

'Well, he's not the gardener,' says Mary.

'Your son-in-law?'

'Yes!'

'And was it effective?'

'Sort of. He bought a dishwasher the next day.'

25

I can't just sit here and wait for the rain to stop

I watch the D-Day commemorations in bed. Operation Overlord. That was the name of the Normandy campaign. June 6, 1944. The idea was to get 150,000 men across to France and turn the tide. A 95-year-old veteran is wheeled into view. He can't have been much more than a boy when Churchill told him to fight on the beaches. Dan Walker of BBC Breakfast asks the veteran if he's pleased to see all the politicians here. 'Politicians?' says the vet. 'Why should I be pleased to see them?'

I sit with Flicker and Mary for breakfast. We natter through a fry up. Mary says she doesn't remember much about D-Day. Says she was still in Scotland at the time and probably hadn't even heard of France. She asks after my face. I say it still hurts. I say it feels like the inside of my head no longer fits. Mary says she doesn't think she's ever had a headache. She asks if Gaviscon would help. When I tell her probably not, Mary admits she's often off the mark when it comes to prescriptions. She once gave a sandwich to a lad sat on the floor outside a shop. 'He was waiting for his mum!' she says. It's difficult to know what people need, says Flicker, placing a paracetamol next to my coffee cup. I swallow the pill watching Monica convey her toast and tea on the seat of her walker. She's done that before.

There's no morning excursion so I plan to linger in the lounge and move along with my book. I'm reading Diana Athill's *Somewhere Towards the End*, which she wrote in her 80s. It's about her life, basically, and the prospect of its completion. She thinks that as we age, we get more pessimistic with life generally because our own details are worsening. A remedy for this insidious pessimism, she says, is the company of younger people, because they serve as reminders that one is part of something bigger.

Speaking of something bigger, here's Malcolm in his trunks, announcing to the lounge that he's going down to decant the swimming pool. And here's Kitty from Liverpool, calling me over to sit with her and Monica and Alice. I sit on the edge of the couch at first, on the armrest, but within five minutes I've moved down and across and am practically sat on Monica's lap. They're an entertaining trio. Of the three, Monica most fits Diana Athill's pessimistic description. Not only were the berries wrong and the platform change typical, she also doesn't hold much hope for the young, for Labour, for the afternoon's weather. She's lovely with it though; she carries the negativity well, but it's there nonetheless. Kitty is the opposite. She's an optimist and a rampant one; she barely stops talking and seems impossible to upset. Alice is the quietest of the three. I'm told she misses her husband.

Monica asks me to help her send a text message. I tell her I'm probably the wrong man for the job, but she reckons

I'm bound to be better than her. She dictates to me. 'Woken up this morning by a clansman who came to fix the telly.' When I'm still struggling with the predictive text five minutes later, Monica finally agrees and gets Alice to do it. Once Monica's message has been sent, talk turns to the text message Kitty just got from her granddaughter Scarlett, who's studying History at Cambridge. Kitty makes a point of the whereabouts.

'She did go to private school though,' says Monica.

'So what?' says Kitty.

'Well, that's how it works. It's money that gets you there.'

'It's talent that gets you there,' says Kitty. 'She's a bright girl.'

'She's bright because her parents bought her a better education.'

'And what's wrong with that?'

'It perpetuates privilege is what.'

'Does it heck.'

Kitty wouldn't have minded being bought an education. She wouldn't have minded being bought anything. Her parents died when she was young. She was brought up by her uncle and aunt. She says her uncle was a lovely man, but very much a man of his time, which is to say he expected a dinner each evening and spent weekends at the pub. He was working class but voted Conservative all his life. Kitty also votes Conservative but not because her uncle did – at least she doesn't think that's the reason. Monica is Labour through and through but voted for the Lib Dems last time. She says she thinks the Labour leader is dangerous, but not because that's what the papers say – at least she doesn't think that's the reason. Kitty says what we need is Thatcher back. Monica says what we need is Attlee back. Alice says she doesn't bother with politics and hasn't for a long time. She lived in Spain for 30 years and it all went over her head out there. She moved back to England when her husband died, to be near her daughter. Alice admits she's finding the transition hard, and not only because of the weather. And you can tell she's finding it hard. You can tell that something's up. Monica and Kitty might bicker and tussle, but they do so lightly and with energy and humour. Their minds aren't elsewhere – they're on the matter at hand, whether it's private education or political leaders. Comparatively, Alice has been somewhere else since the moment I saw her. Alice says she's grateful for her neighbours though, meaning Monica and Kitty. They've been good to her, she says. She looks at them now, bickering about whether bus passes should be means tested, and then at me and says softly, and with a smile, 'I bet you've twice a headache now, Ben.'

Somebody puts the D-Day commemorations on the telly. It turns heads. Monica remembers the noise of the planes and the bombs and seeing Plymouth red with fire. She says one time, their cat refused to go into the air raid shelter with them, and when they came out an hour later, the house was in bits and the cat was in the oven, safe and sound. Monica has never doubted the intelligence of animals since.

Then Monica says that her dad was on the Prince of Wales battleship when it was sunk by the Japanese off the coast of British Malaya. Monica was six at the time. It was 1941, 10 December, lunchtime. It's the only history question Monica can answer without thinking. The news on the radio said the ship had been sunk and all on board had been lost. Monica remembers the telegram boy. She remembers his hat. The family were gathered around the wireless when he knocked on the door. Monica was sent to open it because they thought it was a neighbour. He'd swam away. Her father had. In the South China Sea. Away from the sinking Prince of Wales. He didn't want to be taken prisoner by the Japanese. He didn't think that would be a hell of a laugh. He was picked up by an Australian boat a day later and eventually made his way home. Monica and her son went to Portsmouth a few years ago to have a look at another of the ships her dad had served on – the M33. Monica found her dad's initials scratched into the frame of a bunk bed. Monica had a tear in her eye then, and she's got another one now. When they got off the ship, a woman said to Monica, 'Can I give you a hug?' Monica really appreciated that hug. Of course she got a hug off her son but it's nice when people you don't know sense how you're feeling. She asks if I know what she means.

I walk in the rain with my hood up and a book in my pocket. My purpose isn't noble. I toss a piece of orange peel in a stream and watch it run away, which is probably unethical. The rain is a gloss on the local stone and flowers. I turn right on Strathview Terrace and then right on Golf Course Road. I pass a pond and then continue uphill. Still the rain falls.

The clubhouse roof is obvious against the wet green fairways. It's the colour of strawberry, that's why. I borrow an 8-iron and hit 40 balls into a field. It's nice to think about getting my hips out of the way, keeping my head still, transferring my weight. The thoughts are so unimportant, they're helpful. They don't have fathers who fought in wars. They don't have opinions. They haven't had cancer. It's nice to hit towards the distant sheep and a lonely white-washed house. When I return the 8-iron, the professional says I need to think less about my technique and more about my target.

I have lunch in the clubhouse: a bowl of 'stovies', which is beef, potato, onion, cabbage, gravy and mustard. It's basically whatever's left from a Sunday roast – whatever's left in the stove. It's decent. The extra time has done it some good. I eat it watching tourists tee off in borrowed blue coats. I read some more of Athill. She's saying that the thing about death is its abruptness. That's what scares her about it, scares us about it. 'The difference between being and non-being is both so abrupt and so vast that it remains shocking even though it happens to every living thing that is, was, or will ever be.' That's it, isn't it? It's that complete and utter abruptness, that unthinkable difference between on and off. Someone just managed to hit their ball backwards. Their mate's on the floor laughing. I can't just sit here and wait for the rain to stop.

I won some chocolates in a raffle last night. I didn't mention it at the time because the raffle wasn't the most scintillating hour of my life, and if I accounted for every minute of this holiday then my publisher would be sued for criminal extent. The raffle was in aid of a local Alzheimer's hospice, and the clansman did his best to keep it lively. But this lot couldn't have been less interested if they tried. I suppose their thinking was that if they're going to throw money at a hospice, it might as well be a hospice in their own backyard – a sort of investment, or timeshare. Anyway, there was a raffle, and I won some chocolates. I collect them from my room now and take them down to the lounge. Pauline takes two honeycomb logs which is a bit annoying. Tom takes something soft on account of his mouth cancer. Mandy's okay, but the Hungarian receptionist – Adrienne? – isn't: she has two. Zoltan doesn't mind if he does, and nor does Basia. Monica and Alice insist they're fine, that they don't want one, before taking about three each over the next half hour.

'Where's Kitty then?' I say.

'She's gone to have a look at the salmon ladder,' says Monica. 'I said to her, "What's interesting about a salmon ladder?" And she said, "I haven't seen one before. That's what's interesting." I told her with that attitude, she'll never get a rest. She's 85 but goes around like a two year old. Have you seen her outfit today? Red boots, green trousers and a yellow top – she's a flipping traffic light.'

'Has she always been so lively?'

'No,' says Monica. 'Certainly not.' She looks at Alice, who knows what's coming. 'She took flight after Keith died. He was bossy and impatient and – well, we barely saw Kitty.

I hate to say it – and she certainly wouldn't – but she's better off without him. It's like she's finally … I don't know, being herself. Which is lovely. Of course it is. But it's also tiring. She wanted to do sambuca shots at lunchtime. She got cross when I said I wouldn't and it turned into an argument. We can argue, Kitty and I.'

'I've noticed,' I say.

'Have you?'

'Well, yeah.'

'Thing is, I don't know where she gets her ideas from. Out of a cracker most of the time. We were watching the D-Day stuff, weren't we, Alice, and Kitty said there were too many foreigners. And I said what, in the world? And she said no, in the UK. And I said if it wasn't for foreigners, we wouldn't have won that bloody war, Kitty. Of course she said that if it wasn't for foreigners there wouldn't have been a bloody war, Monica, but she was missing the point. She's just a textbook Conservative, that's all, and a Scouse one at that. You don't get many Conservatives in Liverpool so she's accustomed to fighting her corner. But it's the wrong corner. It doesn't suit her. She'd do anything for anyone – and I mean anyone – and yet to hear her sometimes you'd think she was heartless. She's one of those people whose deeds are better than their words. She says there's too many here and yet she's been treating the waitress from Italy like a granddaughter. She needs to stop reading the *Daily Mail*. I've a mind to intercept the paperboy. My son – Martin – bought me this crossword book when he found out I was getting the *Daily Mail* one off Kitty. He's thoughtful, is Martin. He thinks of others – refugees, the disabled, Welsh people. And yet sometimes he forgets to feed his own cat. Weird. Anyway, he's always been good with me. I thought of him when you said you'd carry my walker across the bridge. You didn't make me feel like a burden. You made me feel important. He does that. Martin does that.'

'Is he still with that Malaysian girl?' asks Alice.

'He is. Sweet as anything, she is. She bought me a lovely present when they went on holiday recently, so I've got her some biscuits.'

'The ones you won in the raffle?' says Alice.

'Exactly. I tried one and they're very good.'

'Do you reckon they'll get married?' says Alice.

'I don't think so. He's not the marrying type. He's too all over the place. He fitted a bathroom for his sister last weekend, and he's taking a week off work to help his brother build a man-cave. I sometimes think you can tell more about a person from how they are with their family than how they are with their wives or husbands. It's easy to love your wife, to love your partner. It's not easy to love all your family. I mean actively love them. Oh, I don't know. All I'm saying is he's up every weekend to see me and he's all the kids' favourite uncle. He uses his love in a different way. That's what it is. He spreads it. Of course it does his girlfriend's head in. She wasn't happy when she heard about the man-cave. There's one chocolate left, Ben. Will you have it?'

'No, I'm alright.'

'No go on.'

'Save it for Kitty.'

'Sod that,' says Monica, popping it in her mouth.

I have dinner at the Old Mill down the road (a trio of salmon – poached, smoked and pickled) and then go back to the hotel for the entertainment. Tonight, it's a guy called Ronnie Ross, who's going to sing a few songs, tell a few stories. They'll be of a Scottish ilk, I fancy, given that Ronnie is wearing nothing but a kilt and an accordion.

I sit next to Jenny, the lady who looked up Mark's kilt last night. She's from near Leeds and her husband has been dead seventeen years. (Some people reveal their widowhood quickly, as if to explain or excuse their being alone. They needn't.) She's into horse racing mostly. Always has been. When she was about thirteen, she got a paper round so she could start saving up for a horse. After about three years, she was able to buy a small one with a leg missing called MacDuff. Then she saved up again and bought another one, and so on until she had a whole stable of them. Now she's only got a small share in a three year old (horse, I presume). She follows it around the country, wherever it's racing. She asks if I mind if we stop talking and listen to this song.

I don't. Not at all. It's a nice song. And Ronnie's belting it out. It's called 'Enjoy Yourself' by the sound of it. Its central message isn't ambiguous: time's getting on so have a laugh. This lot are getting the message alright. One bloke's got his arms in the air; another's doing a pretend drum solo that's completely at odds with the music; and plenty of others are clapping and swaying. You can tell Ronnie's done this before.

Whereas Mark had the audience under his kilt, Ronnie's got them in the palm of his hand. One gentleman has had enough. He's bored of tapping his foot and mouthing the words, so against the advice of his wife, he gets to his feet and starts dancing around the sofas and even right in front of Ronnie for a bit. When the song finishes, he does a little curtsy and takes a little bow. I get it on video. I'm not sure what I'll do with the footage. Maybe I'll watch it every time the internet is slow, or the traffic is heavy, or I'm upset because Portsmouth lost – that is, when I'm joyless without good reason.

Ronnie shifts gears. He drops an octave. He does 'The Ghosts of Culloden', which is a mournful ballad about a battle Scotland lost, and then 'Flower of Scotland', which is a mournful ballad about a battle they didn't. The gear shift causes a few to call it a night. They pass me on their way out. Basia asks where I got to at dinner. Pauline asks if I'm doing the excursion tomorrow. Kitty asks if I like her shoes. I don't mean to publicise my popularity, but rather the friendliness of my companions. I don't think I've been in a more friendly room (per capita) my whole life, apart from maybe once in Budapest.

Ronnie says let's finish with a classic, ladies and gents, let's finish with a favourite. The favourite is 'We'll Meet Again', the old war song. It was Vera Lynn who made it famous but it was Sheridan Smith who did it on the telly this morning, in front of the veterans. '*We'll meet again …*' It moved me. Her performance, I mean. The words. I watched it with Tom and Monica and Zoltan. '… *don't know where, don't know when* …' The song suits Ronnie. Suits his *timbre*, if that's the word. Although, I dare say it would suit anyone right now. '*But I know we'll meet again* …' They're all singing along now. *We're* all singing along now. And there's a few who mean the words all right. '… *one sunny day*'. When it's done, they shout for more. When it's done *we* shout for more.

26

There was that lark in the end

I wake up in bits. I've always struggled to do it in one go. But I don't mind. For me, the hour between the time one intends to get up and the time one does get up is the best in the world. I'll tell you who is up – the lark perched on the roof of the staff quarters across the courtyard. It's awake and doesn't care who knows about it. I'd love to know what it's got in mind. Its glee is unreal.

The curtains are the same as Scarborough. I noticed the lack of difference as I pulled them in stages as the kettle boiled – a little game to see if the widening frame threw up surprises. There was that lark in the end.

There are many things I'm getting used to regarding these holidays – the slow, absorbent journeys; the drivers' gags; the sight and sound of my elders – and other things I'm still at odds with. One is walking into the dining room on my own. It still causes a spot of discomfort and anxiety. Daft, really, because nobody cares, but still – there's a reason Jill wrote that poem about dining alone. You have to be a particular type to walk into a dining room like you own the hotel and everyone owes you a favour; to walk in with your back straight and your chin up and give everyone a virtual high-five in your head. When Monica approaches and says I should wear shorts more often, I think of Mick from Leicester.

I have a bowl of fruit and yoghurt and then a plate of hot stuff – black pudding, mushrooms, fried eggs and bacon. I try and savour it all. The atmosphere, the noise, the simple fact of being on holiday, of being away. But it never works when you try and do it. I suppose the trick is to savour things all the time and then just stop realising you're doing it. The couple next to me get up for seconds but take so long reloading that when they get back to their table it has been reset, which confuses the hell out of them. They both look at me as if I did it. I tell them what happened. He says: 'They'd jump in my grave.'

I have sugar in my tea for a change. Plopping in the cube, I think of Prince Philip in St Ives. What was it he said about tea and his wife?[39] In any case, I take the tea through to the lounge, where there's a group of four or five working on a puzzle. One of them started it on Tuesday afternoon, and now there's a select committee that does what it can as and when. They seem to enjoy it – the looking, the joining, the solving. It's social in a quiet, steady way: every hundred pieces brings them a bit closer. They're trying to piece together an idyllic scene. They're unlikely to finish, but I suppose that's not the point.

I'm on the coach and Pauline says she didn't sleep well owing to a lack of steps. I invite, with my expression, her to explain.

---

[39] He said: 'My wife was an incessant tea-maker. Whenever she doubted whether she'd done the right thing in marrying me, she'd make a pot of tea.'

She says she averages 7,000 a day, but yesterday didn't get anywhere near that – probably because she was in the jacuzzi a fair bit, and you can't get very far in one of them. She says she's done 1.5 million in the last six months.

'Christ, where've you been?'

'Just walking round the shops really. It helps that I'm fussy.'

'How do you count them?'

'On me phone. I have to keep it on me at all times. Which is easier said than done. I've dropped it in the shower more than once. I'm quite strict about it because I get money off me insurance.'

Malcolm's chatting with those in the first few rows. He's not being asked about Scotland or Perthshire or where the heck we're off to, but rather his home life – what he does with his days off (nowt), what he likes to eat (owt), what his wife thinks of him being away so much (she thinks it's class, mon). People like to know such things. Normal stuff. They want to know how he likes his tea and what he's got in his garden and what he watches on telly. Not everyone though. Not everyone has a taste for the domestic. Pauline's not interested. She's reading a sci-fi novel set on Uranus. I ask her what's going on. 'It's set in a future where everyone's programmed to live until they're 150, but people keep committing suicide at 115.'

Our first stop of the day is Dunkeld, a big village of low, whitewashed buildings situated around a few main streets – High and Brae and Atholl and Bridge – and a market-place called The Cross. The buildings were put up after the previous lot were put down during the Battle of Dunkeld, whereat the forces of William gained revenge for their defeat to the forces of James at Killiecrankie. One of the houses says that a Prime Minister of Canada was born on site, while the hotel next door boasts that Queen Victoria once had lunch here, which is far from an endorsement of the current chef.

We're decanted near the cathedral. It's a grey, moss-spotted erection, and twice as old as any of the Willies or Jimmies that fought at the Battle of Dunkeld. Its great age explains why it's getting some work done. I stare at the scaffolding and enjoy the mess of fabrics, the clash of meanings. I welcome all reminders that when it comes to religion, and when it comes to churches, there was no immaculate conception.

The best thing inside the church is also a fabrication – a tapestry of the last supper. Jesus and his fellow diners are evidently enjoying the occasion. They appear ebullient, almost manic. Perhaps they all knew this was it, that time was up. Such knowledge can transform one's appetite. Either way, beneath the tapestry are two chairs. The back of one says Joy. The back of the other says Gentleness. Nice things to lean on. Basia sits in the latter.

'It reminds me of Christmas in Poland,' I say.

'Really? Why?'

'All the people, all the action.'

'No, I mean how do you have the memory?'

'I lived there for a year.'

'Really?'

'Yeah, and on Christmas Eve – you know the custom of laying an extra setting at the table in case a stranger turns up?'

'I do, yes. We do it in fact.'

'And has anyone ever turned up?'

'No.'

'Well I did.'

'Did what?'

'Turned up.'

'Shut up.'

'I just knocked on a random door and said, "You know the lonely stranger? Well here he is."'

'And?'

'And I didn't like the carp.'

'So they let you in?'

'Let me in? It was a struggle to get out, Basia.'

The churchyard is popular. And quite right too. It's in a lovely spot next to the River Tay, among the undated trees and flowers. I watch a lady absent-mindedly lean against a headstone while nattering about her grandchildren, before realising and apologising to Douglas Murray (1712–67).

Mary wanders over and says casually that she just got a text from her daughter saying they're going to blast his kidney stones. Either she thinks I'm someone else (unlikely) or I've forgotten something she told me (less unlikely). Then she looks at my shoes and says I might want to clean them later with a toothbrush.

I excuse myself to take a picture of a lady between trees with the river behind. She's got her hands on her hips and a walking stick hanging from her pocket. She senses what I'm doing and apologises and shuffles off. I tell her the picture's better with her in it, but she thinks I'm joking.

I go to the butcher's on Bridge Street hoping for something tasty and local. The butcher is Scottish Indian, or so he says. He also says the chicken curry pie is nice, but I might not want it because it's not properly Scottish. I suggest that anything made by a Scot in Scotland is Scottish, thinking he might find the idea attractive, but the butcher's not persuaded. He picks up the pie in question and says it's about as Scottish as … He looks to his colleague. 'Wha's not Scottish?' he says.

In the end he gives me a Scotch Pie for nothing, which I eat just up the road on Telford Bridge. I'm happy with it. I like the chewy pastry and the well-seasoned meaty interior. And I like that I've stumbled upon Telford again. He's popped up a few times, has Tommy. He's repeated on me and I don't mind a bit. I liked his crossing in Wales and I like his go-between here, and Jill was from Telford of course. Telford isn't the only thing to have recurred now that I think about it. War has. Loss has. Pride has. Love has. Love has a lot in fact, one way or another. It's been the main thing, I'd say, all things considered, which I'm not going to moan about. Love and bingo.

I sit in the wrong seat. I don't realise until the lady who apologised for being in my picture is stood over me thinking, 'So now who's the one in the way?'

'Ah. Sugar. Whoops. Am I in your seat?'

'You're fine, love. I'll sit behind.'

'You sure?'

'Yeah. It will be a change of scenery.'

We head south towards Dundee, away from the Highlands. The sky is a fair share of blue and white. Trees are remarkable for being few, and sheep are creamy hints in the distance. Looking at it all, I realise my face is hurting less. It feels like my brain is shrinking, which is nice.

Our final stop is Blairgowrie, whose nickname is Berry Toon, which is much nicer, I think. The fruit pickers used to migrate here from Glasgow and treat the harvest like a holiday, but not anymore. Now others are getting a turn at the berries. Malcolm puts us down by the River Ericht and says we've got an hour. Someone asks what we're meant to do. Malcolm shrugs and says, 'The world's your oyster, pet,' but the woman isn't convinced. 'I don't like oysters,' she says.

The water's brown and not dragging its heels. This river used to support a dozen textile mills, which harnessed its flow to get one thing from another. They've all gone now. All those mills. They've stopped weaving, stopped spinning, stopped turning out yarns. Most are apartments now, where people make tea and toast instead. I can see someone by the kettle now. It could be my nan or Imelda or Rita. They look at me looking at them, which is nice for about a second and then awkward.

I enjoy the water's dumb, ceaseless slide. I can see myself in it. I'm as swift and as small in the end, and so are you. And yet despite that swift smallness, our lives can feel slow and big, long and vital. The misunderstanding is good for us – it puts a spring in our step, it puffs us up. But it's also good to look at a river and be reminded that our time on stage is but an hour, that our candle is but brief. To know we're quick and only passing can settle us, can humble us, can open us to what is new and other and else. It can make us wider and deeper, without altering our course.

The salmon is king. That's what I read. It's born here and then swims to the mouth of the River Tay before taking a left and rounding the top of Scotland and making for America. The journey does the salmon some good. It changes its shape and nature. It makes it pink and plump and mature. Then, when the salmon decides it's close enough to the States thank you very much, it retraces its outward journey back to where it was spawned, back to Berry Toon, where it makes love and dies. The cycle gives me food for thought, especially the bit about going home to reproduce. It might explain why I've been feeling a bit uneasy being back home in Portsmouth. I know that, at some level, people are expecting me to bonk and then die.

I continue upstream to Cargill's Leap, so-called because once upon a time, a bloke surnamed Cargill leapt across the river here. He had good reason to. He was a heretical Presbyterian on the run from Bonnie Prince Charlie. An onlooker who observed the leap is thought to have remarked, 'Not bad for an Elder.'[40] Following his leap, Cargill managed

---

[40] Jokes aren't funny if you have to explain that influential Presbyterians are called Elders because in old Greek *presbyteros* means elder.

to evade capture for sixteen years before being surprised in a chicken shop preaching about predestination. One hopes that Cargill enjoyed his extra time.

I stand in a doorway on Allan Street. Opposite, two old boys in flat caps are eyeing up rental options in the window of Next Home. Down the road a bit, Zoltan and Basia are doing their jackets up outside a pub, while Flicker's just gone into a fishing shop, leaving Mary in a café across the street, chewing someone's ear off on the phone. A walker has been abandoned in front of Davidson's the chemist. Its bright frame looks good next to the red pillar box on the sunlit pavement. The scene suggests someone got carried away and posted themselves. Here comes the owner. He's got a big can of shaving foam in each pocket, which bodes well.

I return to Wellmeadow for the pick-up. It's a triangular green with a war memorial in the middle. Quite a few of my lot are sat on its steps, enjoying the sun. Tom's showing someone his tongue. One shelf of the memorial is covered with rhododendrons. Mary wanders over to my bench. I wonder if she's going to mention kidney stones again. In the event, she wants to show me a very different type of stone, one fashioned from the compressed stems of heather. She's bought a dozen of them but doesn't know who they're for yet. She's going to keep them in the kitchen at the church and just wait and see. She asks me to make a note of her church in Derby, and then checks to make sure I've got it right.

'If you turn up, I'll give you one of these stones,' she says.

'But what if they've all gone?'

'Then I'll get one back and give it to you.'

'Nice.'

'Did you have a good walk by the river?'

'I did. I read about salmon. What they get up to. It's quite miraculous really. They swim from Scotland to Nova Scotia practically, then come back to breed and die.'

'Aye, and that's why they're great with dill and new potatoes.'

On our way back to the hotel, I poke Pauline and point to a coach with 'Insight Vacations' written on its side. I say I wouldn't mind a bit of that, but Pauline says she's been with them before and it was rubbish. Heading north on the A9, betwixt lush this and verdant that and all the chlorophyll you could care for, Pauline nods towards all the greenness and says she wouldn't mind living around here if it wasn't for the rain.

My last supper is nothing like the tapestry in the church. I'm on my own for a start, and there's chicken wings and cheesecake. I watch Basia and Zoltan arrive and rearrange things so they're perpendicular, not opposite. I can see what they're after. They want to see each other *and* the world. Zoltan shakes hands with the Hungarian staff, shares a few words with them in his mother tongue. He can't help it. He can't resist. Sure, he can speak English brilliantly with a Welsh accent, and sure, he bore tunnels in Nottingham for 45 years, but when Zoltan dreams of heaven, the angels speak Hungarian. Mary and Flicker come in nattering. Mary gives one of her gemstones to Malcolm the driver, then goes out of her way to pass my table and say, 'Okay?'

Kitty is alone in the lounge. I sit next to her. She looks at the people doing the puzzle, and then at me, and says:

'You learn about people when you're away, don't you?'

'Yeah. Yeah, you do.'

'I had no idea Monica finds it so hard. Getting around, I mean. And I had no idea – well, I had some idea that Alice was suffering but not the way she is. Monica says you're a carer?'

'Was.'

'I did care work for ten years. But then one day, I couldn't get a man out of the bath, so I quit.'

'So he's still in there, is he?'

'I knew you were going to say that. I had to get the neighbour in.'

There's silence for a bit. Which is okay. We both look at the puzzle.

'I used to help a guy called Anthony,' I say.

'Help as in care for?'

'Yeah. He's one of my best friends now. He's got cerebral palsy, which means he hasn't—'

'I know what cerebral palsy is, love.'

'Sorry.'

'You're alright.'

'So one time, I was trying to get him out of the bath, by sort of getting my arms around him with one foot in the bath and then sort of lifting and – well he's a strong lad and he convulsed suddenly and my foot in the bath slipped and I ended up in there with him.'

'God, was he alright?'

'Alright? He laughed his tits off.'

She sighs, but in a nice way, a fond way, and then says, 'You'd better go, hadn't you?'

'I had.'

'What are you seeing?'

'*Blithe Spirit.*'

'I know that one.'

'Yeah?'

'Generally Noël Coward avoids Liverpool, but I know that one.'

'Want to come?'

'No, you're alright. I'm going to get a drink and help with that puzzle, I think. But thanks. You can tell me about it tomorrow.'

Wisdom is a slippery thing. Confucius felt it was doing to others as one would be done by. Buddha felt it was about not fixating on oneself. Socrates felt it was about being curious and doubtful. Whatever wisdom is or isn't, we probably get more of it as we go through life, whether we want to or not. As a result – and allowing for huge, laughable exceptions – wisdom is older than us. Which means it is some places more than others. We should visit those places when we can. That's what I think.

Don't get me wrong: I'm not prescribing pensioners. I'm not saying that age is only and at all times a virtue, and

I'm not making any great, indisputable claims for cross-generational encounters. What I am saying – and I'm pitching this to my peers, really – is that the next time you find yourself next to a person the right side of 80, on a bus or in a jacuzzi, consider asking them what they do for a living. If nothing else, it might give the pair of you something to do until the bubbles come back on.

The past few months have left a mark on me. There's no doubt about that. At times it has felt like I've been standing on the shoulders of giants and taking in the view. I can say without qualification that I've been touched by my elders (in the right way), and moved by their example. Only a small amount – of touching, of moving – but an amount nonetheless.

If I had to look closer at that amount, and at that movement, and perhaps take all its warnings and cautions and wise words and *bon mots*, and then convert the sum into a simple learning or slogan or souvenir, then that simple learning or slogan or souvenir would probably sound something like this: if you want to fling your bra into someone else's garden, then fling it.

The sun is out. It's golden hour. Photographers love the length of shadow. Walking to the theatre, I wonder if there will be something deep and hopeful and playful and joyous in *Blithe Spirit* that will echo the music of these travels; a final, fitting sound, on which to end, on which to start.

There's no such sound, and no such thing. The play concerns a writer called Charles, which is probably its first mistake. He's writing a book about the occult and invites a local medium to one of his dinner parties. The medium accepts the invite and accidently returns Charlie's first wife from beyond the grave, which doesn't go down well with the second. The whole thing's much ado about nothing really – which is fine by me, and fine by the rest of the audience by the sound of it.

The drama up and the curtain down, I turn for home. Crossing the River Tummel by an unsteady bridge, I stop in the middle. I didn't mean to. I look upstream to the theatre and the mountains. It's 11pm. Just after. There's a slim moon in a still blue sky, and I can see my breath. Beneath my feet is the calm drift of the river. If this were a film, I'd hear Neil Young from a car radio: *come a little bit closer, hear what I have to say.* And there would be a montage of cherished faces – Carole and Chris, Kieran and Imelda, Gary and Janet and Graham and Frank. But this isn't a film, this is mere life, which is fine by me because I don't mind mere life. I lean on the bridge and am struck by how much light there is so late in the day.

Acknowledgements

So many people, for so many things. It's been a pleasure to add up my debt. My elders for a start, and especially the ones I met on my travels. My nan, Janet, for coming along. My other grandparents – Anne, Annie, Shaun, Ted and Thomas – for your affection and example. Mum and Dad and Ian for only ever being kind. My siblings, for giving me people to look up to, and producing children I adore. Their better halves for assisting in the latter. Megan, for everything. Everyone at Shearings (who were laid off en masse in May 2020, and have my best wishes). Ellen Conlon, for being a brilliant editor and cutting 60 per cent of what I wrote with a smile on your face. Ed Wilson and Helene Butler and Liz Dennis at Johnson & Alcock. Icon Books, for the opportunity in the first place and then excellent support. Lizz Duffy and Kaye Mitchell, for helping me love words and ideas. Booksellers, for what you do. The Society of Authors, for an emergency grant. Uncles Mike and Jim and Matt and John and Peter. Aunties Jo and Pat and Linda and Christine and Shirley. All my nieces and nephews and cousins and second cousins, and all my family in America, Jenny Campion especially. Friends that have done much to inspire and support me over the years, and to make life enjoyable – Richie, Charlie, Jenny, Andy, Russ Hickman, Ken and Amy Daniels, Tom Rees (and bros), Tim Hague (and your mum and dad), Paul and Stacey, Merle, Henok, Cheesy and your siblings, Vicky and Fraser, Meg and Ben, James and Susanna, Nicki, Dinita, Gabriella,

Milly, Zahra, Kirty, Usha, Patrick Ney, Davy and Bea, Greg and Shaheen, Jonny Rodgers and Amy, Lucy Burns, Danny M, George W and family, Vardy, Shelly Williams, Gentle Bren, Sandy, Thea, Rachel, Diana, Chloe, Hannah, Becky, Wilma, Nicole, Danny C, Matty James and Dicky Brember and the rest of the Boxing Day mob, Inese Zepa, Nadia Jogee, Anna, Scotty and Rach, Sam, Chris Chappell and family, Santiago Lemoine (the best bookseller in Spain), Camilla Williamson (the best *thing* in Spain), Peter, Davy, Lucie Wright, Debra Birch, Monia, Tall Chris, Tall Jamie, Small Natalie, Lauren M, Annabel, Josie Ryan, Jo Barret, Jane Fletcher, Liv Elbirk, Mick and Nicola, Margherita, Macarena, Mirek, Gosia, Ewa, Asia, Ola, Laura, Andrzej, Paulina, Tessa, Dominic, Marietta, Tony, Ania, Czesiu, Anita, Kuba, Marta, Kasia, Wiktoria, Alicia Payne, Jenny Harvey, Jesse Klein, John Baldwin, Lorna Wilson, Anna Topczewska, Carolina S, Caroline Phillips, all of Megan's mates (Ellie, Albie, Annie, Izzy …), Clara Schramm, Leah Sassoon and family, Lauren Abend, Anthony Ford-Shubrook of course, Giulia, Xavi, the German, Frank, Salvatore, Cath (and the rest of your keep fit class), Tony, Brian H, Kim and Steph and Jo (+Penny), Ashley Allen and family, Fi, Moe, Julia Trummer, Matt Whelan, Naomi C, Lee P, Jo E, Karl, Jackson, Matt B, Nathan G, the Aspex crew, Sarah Tate and Richard Hill, Paul Tate, Carole Edgeworth, James G and Holly, Baxter, Dunc, Luke F and Tara, Nat and Paul Smith, Maxine Patterson, Diana Patient, Pat McCubbin, the Weilers, Jo West, Tom Sykes and Amanda Garrie and Richard P and Paul V and all those with a mind to write in fair old Pompey town, Claire Hix, Liz Hix, Chris Hix, Sophie Hicks, Tess Hickish, Sophie VC, Iga K, John and Dom Currie, Lucie BF, Mike W, Iona, Katie Carleton, Thos, Terry, Flora, Octavia H, Linda F, Sylvia W, Karolina, Kate M, Kate P, Katie Lundstrom, Katie Blackpool, Dominique Lucas and family, Mike Bonsall, Craig and Jade Sweenie, Hywel, Howard H, Mark Dredge, Kenny Hedges, MHG, Doug Thorp, all the Nortons in Victoria, Gizem, Joel Jackson, Nathan P, Nat R, Jay Cunnington, Elizabeth Newman, Liz Slade, everyone at CERN, Matt Ryan, Sylvia Hewlett, John Gleadall, Emily LW, Chris White, Pat B and Charlotte, Michelle Douglas, Dave and Becky Morrison, all my mum's lovely friends, all my dad's lovely friends, Agnes Stow, Ivana, Sara W, Lauren S, Chris Phillips, Johny Katz, Lucy Hutchinson, Chris Hunter, Chris CG, Shane Rich, Rachel Oldroyd, Ed Wight, Iris and Mor, Suchi and James, Anita Lewis, Tom M, Tom K, Tom H, Joel M, Connell from *Normal People* … I do hope to see you all in the same room one day. That would be one hell of a party. I would collapse with love and gratitude, and then dance and talk and laugh for weeks.

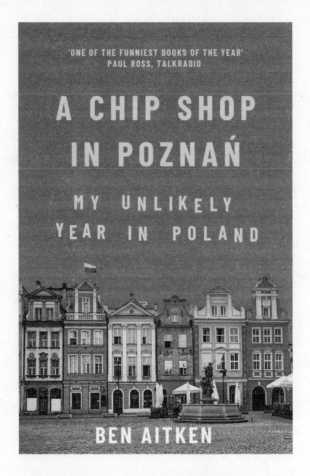

'One of the funniest books of the year'
– Paul Ross, talkRADIO

WARNING: CONTAINS AN UNLIKELY IMMIGRANT,
AN UNSUNG COUNTRY, A BUMPY ROMANCE, SEVERAL
SHATTERED PRECONCEPTIONS, TRACES OF INSIGHT,
A DOZEN NUNS AND A REFERENDUM.

9781785786266
£9.99